"I just finished Storyteller and want to tell you h[...]
I just could not put it down! It was thoroughly written, [...]
and very obvious that you have spent countless hours of thought and research in
preparation for this amazing book. Your book is akin to a medicine cabinet full
of sure-fire solutions for most of our society's ills."

Merlin Hampton
President of the Board, Christian Friends of Israel, America

"This is a fascinating and wide-ranging look at unique individuals whose lives have
significantly impacted the lives of others. The author has gathered together the
details surrounding each life that are sure to inspire and speak to each of us today."

Jim Kregel
President of Kregel Publications

"The stories written by Doug come as no surprise to me as they reflect many of
the same qualities I found in him. An evaluation of the years since my youth gives
cause to opine that never in my lifetime has the need been greater for stories revealing people of great character and integrity. The body of classic literature that was
long required has now been omitted, and subsequently, the character of many of
our leaders gives evidence of these errors of omission."

David E. Henard
Author of *Victory Stolen*
Associate Vice-President Eastern Illinois University (Retired)

"Amidst this collection of stories of heroes lies courage and commitment, the
silver threads which tie together people who want to make a difference. Bank
accounts have limits, but there is no limit to what a life can do when wholeheartedly dedicated to its purpose of existence. The book's crown jewel is that it encourages anyone looking for a hand to lead them off the sandy beach into the deeper
meaningful waters of life."

Ray and Sharon Sanders
Co-Founders, Christian Friends of Israel, Jerusalem

"Beautiful reads when you need a little uplift, but don't want a big book. I have
really enjoyed these when I sit down for a minute during the day."

Kindle E-book Review

"I've been creating interest and discussion with the grandchildren as we read the
book together. The Bible references and Christian character (implied and explicit)
give the work great depth. I was wowed by the research done. I'm recommending
your book to everyone who will hear!"

Reader E-mail

"I truly enjoyed your book! I did not want to put it down. The way you introduce
the book and the way you write is superb. You wrote just like you think and talk…
and it kept my attention. I want to order more copies as I have three grandchildren
and would like to send each a copy. Thanks for producing a book about real lives
and real people – you truly are a proverbial storyteller."

Reader E-mail

To Barbara, the "wife of my youth" (Proverbs 5:18b), closest companion for more than a half-century, and life partner in family, ministry, and adventure. By faith, she has accompanied me without complaint or hesitation, in both poverty and riches, from our start in Appleton, Wisconsin, through many states and countries to our current base in Vincennes, Indiana. As a bonus, she consistently overlooked my ADHD-related meltdowns, as well as patiently edited this book instead of sunning at the beach.

UNCOMMON CHARACTER

But God has chosen the foolish things of the world to put to shame the wise, and God has chosen the weak things of the world to put to shame the things which are mighty; and the base things of the world and the things which are despised God has chosen, and the things which are not, to bring to nothing the things that are.
(1 Corinthians 1:27-28)

UNCOMMON CHARACTER

Stories of Ordinary Men and Women
Who Have Done the Extraordinary

DOUGLAS FEAVEL

Printed in the United States of America

Aneko Press – *Our Readers Matter*™

www.anekopress.com

Aneko Press, Life Sentence Publishing, and our logos are trademarks of

Life Sentence Publishing, Inc.
203 E. Birch Street
P.O. Box 652
Abbotsford, WI 54405

RELIGION / Inspirational

Hardcover ISBN: 978-1-62245-448-8

Paperback ISBN: 978-1-62245-442-6

Ebook ISBN: 978-1-62245-447-1

10   9   8   7   6   5   4   3

Available where books are sold

Contents

Acknowledgments

I offer sincere and deserving honor to Jesus Christ, Abraham Lincoln, and Ronald Reagan; three accomplished storytellers whose lives display heroic character. Courtesy mentions are also extended to Mike Adkins, Dave Roever, Russell Stendal, Eva Kor, Charlie Plumb, and David Barton, my contemporary acquaintances in outreach work who tell their stories better than most, and in the telling, they always glorify God. My warm thanks to these for the depths of their inspiration and wisdom.

Prologue

By blending information with inspiration, stories bridge the past with the present; by sharing them, storytellers transform often dull, objective history into living, subjective heritage. Stories have inherent power to transform lives, and the most powerful stories are about transformed lives.

My lifelong appreciation for inspirational true stories was amplified when I retired from business and became engaged in several teaching roles. These educational experiences led along two parallel paths. One was as a volunteer instructor participating in multiple settings, including a state correctional institute, a county jail, several churches and recovery centers, and a year-round camp. The other path was as a substitute teacher accepting assignments for all grade levels, subjects, and area schools – both public and parochial (as well as closely observing the homeschooling of my grandchildren).

After a few weeks of challenging class sessions, I concluded that character was an under-represented, critical component of education because all other precepts could only be adhered to, and ultimately work, if character was at the core as the driving, cohesive force. I recognized the need to better understand the nature of character, as well as to find a complementary way to incorporate it into all teaching and training opportunities. The students in the volunteer venues desperately required do-overs in their failed lives. By contrast, the students in the substitute venues required help navigating outside of the artificial school environment where radical political correctness threatened to reach saturation.

I began to approach these objectives by drawing on three transformational stories from my past as a collective resource for rewarding, inspiring, and guiding the students, thus gainfully filling any remaining time in the lesson schedules. I immediately observed a heightened level of interest. No matter the age, background, or gender of the students, they all recognizably enjoyed hearing an inspirational story about positive human character – better still when the story was true, included a hero, and had ready application. There seemed to be no measurable exceptions within the student bodies, leading me to speculate that I had found something approaching universal acceptance. These positive reactions weren't due to the power of my undistinguished voice or modest physical presence, but rather resulted from the combination of empathy, inspiration, and eternal truth in which good stories are centered. I found an unattributed quote that encapsulated the noted responses as, "If you give a man a fact, he will learn; if you give him a truth, he will believe; if you give him a story, it will live in his heart forever." If, after gaining their attention, I was also able to capture their soul, then I could impart some indelible, take-away guidance, what I call *sticky-points*.

Additionally, I became more cognizant of a personal heritage that I hadn't previously realized in full. It was that the people I admired most, and who had the greatest influence on me, were prominent storytellers. Their ability to create and to share a worthy story contributed substantially to each becoming an individual of popular renown and monumental worldwide influence. The effect of the stories I shared was bi-directional, moving first the hearers and then, after witnessing the effect, the teller. I share my stories by heart, which is ordinarily taken to mean from memory, and while this is true for my telling, it's also intended to mean that my heart is invested in the stories as well. I began to more actively seek the seed ideas from which to develop additional stories. Once I had secured an adequate number of character stories, I integrated them into every subject, audience, course, and venue, including two proprietary courses I'd developed by necessity en route.

The ensuing trial-and-error phase of mixing storytelling into instructional material revealed two negative and two positive ubiquitous truths about human nature and how it's reflected in modern education. The negative ones were that far too many people settle on unwholesome role models as their personal heroes while they simultaneously lack discriminating mentors; and that positive character is on the decline and rarely formally practiced, taught, or upheld as a behavioral model. The positive truths were that people of all ages love true stories – even more if they're also entertaining; and that well-constructed stories have the power to guide and motivate where other approaches fail or are only moderately successful or enduring.

I humorously compared those early circumstances and objectives with

Scheherazade's in *One Thousand and One Nights*. She was the legendary fictional woman who told stories nightly to the king of Persia in order to retain her courtly position and prolong her life for one more day. More seriously, I related my sharing to the theme of *heroicstories.org*, which is "Restoring Faith in Humanity ... One Story at a Time." It's said that Abraham Lincoln very seldom created his own stories. That assumption is based on his quotation: "You speak of Lincoln stories. I don't think that is a correct phrase. I don't make the stories mine by telling them. I'm only a retail dealer." I confess that mine don't really belong to me either; I feel that they are bigger than me and that I'm only borrowing them in order to pass them along for others to enjoy and share.

The stories within this book seek to reveal uncommon character as it was put to the test by challenging circumstances and difficult choices. Specifically, they are the stories of individuals who were caught up in pivotal situations within their respective cultures, times, and geographies. I've emphasized the following elements: personal integrity, an international scope, universally valued criteria, the influences and interdependencies of change and choice, a broad historic time frame, and simple – yet inspiring – insights into ordinary, mostly unknown men and women whose deeds are worthy of our attention and emulation because they have left us a legacy of unselfishness, not one of domination or capitulation.

My primary mission was to document living character stories so their inherent instructional and inspirational value would be easily accessible to the reader. You will meet herein founders, teachers, rescuers, altruists, missionaries, attorneys, soldiers, scientists, writers, statesmen, martyrs, immigrants, businessmen, survivors, pioneers, and more – all heroes who have sacrificially earned the right to subtly counsel future generations on the nature of uncommon character. Some are still living, some have long passed; but all have made lasting, positive impressions on the world.

I've by no means fully developed the good character I unceasingly hope to have one day – the kind of character displayed by these men and women. Within a process I call *forever becoming*, I'm continually learning from them. These are people of decisive action – not philosophers, intellectuals, or academics. That's not to say these protagonists aren't capable of great intuition and thought, because they have shown they most certainly were so endowed. They are, above all, morally tested, with many having simultaneously undergone physical trials. I draw personal inspiration from the protagonists and their stories because they have been meaningful in my life; now I've chosen to share them with you more formally in a book. The reader will find each to be a worthy hero of uncommon character. This gripping collection of true stories regales their legacies of sound judgment and practical wisdom so that their stories have the potential to be of great benefit to present and future generations.

I wrote the initial portion of this book in Pacific Grove, California where John Steinbeck lived and wrote for an extended season. It was one of the most productive of the many writer's-escape locations I inhabited thereafter while finishing it. The book was completed in Ernest Hemingway's adopted hometown of Petoskey, Michigan. In Steinbeck's esteemed novella *Cannery Row* – written in and about Pacific Grove – he states, "And perhaps that might be the way to write this book – to open the page and to let the stories crawl in by themselves." My book is precisely the product proposed by Steinbeck, because the stories herein flow naturally out of my experiences, especially those while teaching. They are the outcome of my diligently gleaning the stories over a long period and then sharing them orally for a decade. Beyond rough outline form, this marks the first time they've been fully committed to writing, permitted to crawl in one by one, and then combine to form a book. I have tried to remain reasonably out of their way.

I believe *Uncommon Character* is unlike any other book in respect to its focus on unfamiliar heroes and little-known situations. Most of the heroes I've chosen are, by design, relatively obscure, thus providing a deep source of untapped resources relating to their rich lives, and thereby convincing me that there's need, demand, and opportunity for *Uncommon Character*. The selected protagonists may be flawed socially, physically, or even mentally; all the more reason for us to relate to them and to cheer their ultimate triumphs. Despite handicaps of any nature, they've all displayed admirable and exemplary responses when faced with difficult circumstances and entrenched opposition. Most have moved contrary to the drifting ideology of the public at large, choosing instead to hold fast to unchanging values. This juncture of internal strength and moral conviction, when coupled with compatible actions and results, is a virtue designated herein as uncommon character. The following quote from Billy Graham gives clarity to our understanding of this virtue: "When wealth is lost, nothing is lost; when health is lost, something is lost; when character is lost, all is lost."

As the stories I've prepared for you are recited and read, their past becomes part of your present, and just maybe some will slip into your future.

Irena Sendler

Separated by Good or Evil

For I will contend with him who contends with you. (Isaiah 49:25)

History teacher Norm Conard had a well-earned reputation for extracting excellence from students in his Creative Social Studies class. At the start of the 2000–2001 school year in south-central Kansas's small Uniontown Senior High, he challenged his incoming class to select an optional, long-term research project in observance of National History Day. Projects from his classroom had placed forty times in previous NHD competitions. At his urging, fifteen-year-old sophomore Elizabeth Chambers (who preferred to be called Liz) was the first student to accept the volunteer assignment. She was a troubled and somewhat rebellious teen, abandoned as a five-year-old child by her parents. This project became the start of her scholastic and social redemption. Mr. Conard said he hoped it would help her to understand the difference one person can make and that he knew she could become one of those special people.

Liz's search for a project theme led her to a small magazine clipping printed six years earlier in *U.S. News & World Report* and stored in a classroom file. The article briefly mentioned, among a list of many people, an unknown Polish woman by the name of Irena Sendlerowa, her maiden name Anglicized as Sendler (married name was Zgrzembski). As Liz investigated further, it soon became apparent that buried within the list was the seed of a grand story about a Holocaust rescuer, one lost and untold for more than half a century. One number associated with Irena in the article seemed too incredible to be true. Liz and Mr. Conard assumed it was a typo, so the first call Liz made was to the source agency in New York to confirm the data. Without hesitation, Liz was informed that it wasn't a typo; the number was accurate. If so, how could the world not know about this? How could Irena not be famous when her work surpassed that of so many acknowledged rescuers, such as the well-known Oskar Schindler? Liz had the beginnings of a personal mission, the likes of which Mr. Conard had encouraged her to pursue. She soon gained such affinity for the victims Irena had helped that her sleep was disturbed until her enthusiasm was better channeled into the project itself.

Mr. Conard enlisted a bright freshman, Megan Steward, to help Liz; not long thereafter classmates Gabrielle Bradbury, Sabrina Coons, and Janice Underwood also joined her. The students titled their overall work "The Irena Sendler Project." The most pleasant and surprising outcome of their research took place when the students sought to locate Irena's grave; it was then that they discovered she was alive and still living in her hometown of Warsaw, Poland. This was now more than dusty history; it became living legacy. The students utilized their findings to create a play based on Irena's WWII exploits. They titled it *Life in a Jar,* a name inspired by the method Irena had used to conceal vital, confidential documents.

The study group's play was submitted to the Kansas History Day competition in May of 2000, and it won first place. The statewide win earned them a trip later that year to the National History Day in Washington, D.C. They began performing their play in the local community with the admission revenues sent to Warsaw to assist Irena. By the time of her death, there'd been two hundred and fifty student performances of their play, beginning in Kansas, moving through the United States, then to Canada, and finally to Poland and the rest of Europe. The play is still performed, with 60 percent of the earned revenue donated to the Irena Sendler Life in a Jar Foundation. The foundation promotes Irena's legacy and encourages the education community to teach and to research the unsung heroes of history. After Irena became familiar with the play, she remarked: "You have changed Poland, you have changed the United States, you have even changed the world [by bringing this story to light]. [Because of your work] Poland has seen great changes in Holocaust education, in the perception of life during that time, and you have provided a grand hero for Poland and for the world. I love you very, very much. Your performance and work is continuing the effort I started over fifty years ago; you are my dearly beloved girls."

Before graduating from high school, Liz's core team collected over four thousand pages of original, primary research on Irena's life and on the children she worked with during the Holocaust and World War II. More than a hundred colleges and universities have used their material for classroom instruction. *National Public Radio*, *C-SPAN*, and the major networks all pursued the dual-interest story of Liz's study team and Irena Sendler's rescue work. Both stories contain universal themes: the former about a young girl's inspiring work in Kansas today, and the latter about a young girl's inspiring work in Poland yesterday. Both girls enlisted and led a small, trusted team of other young ladies to assist with their epic tasks. After several years of media attention focused on the students' project, Irena's life was fully brought to the world's attention – just as it had long deserved to be.

Initially, there was only one obscure website linked to Irena, but by 2008, there were three hundred thousand. Inspired by and based on the students' research, author Ana Mieszkowska wrote a book about Irena in 2005 titled *Irena Sendler: Mother of the Children of the Holocaust*. Since then, several children's books have been published about Irena's life. In May 2008, Hallmark Company announced production of a movie based on the book titled *The Courageous Heart of Irena Sendler*. The film premiered on national television in late April of the following year. Sometime thereafter, a documentary was also completed, titled *Irena Sendler: In the Name of Their Mothers*.

The Uniontown students – now mature and well into their marriages, families, and careers – continue to promote Irena's story and to research the related details. By the time of Irena's death, they'd completed six trips to Warsaw. On one of those visits, Irena wisely told the students: "You cannot separate people by their race or religion. You can only separate people by their good or evil. The good always triumphs over the evil." Irena told them what she really wanted out of the larger story was for "the Jewish community to know there was resistance and spirit among the Jews in the Warsaw Ghetto."

In 2007, when Irena was ninety-seven years old, the students' contributions were catalysts in her nomination for the Nobel Peace Prize. She came in second, narrowly losing to Al Gore's book and slideshow titled *An Inconvenient Truth*, the veracity of which has been debunked by over three hundred thousand scientists. Conversely, the more information we continue to firmly establish about Irena's life and legacy, the brighter her truth shines. Truth does not change and it grows stronger in the light, whereas lies can only exist in the dark.

Irena died on May 12, 2008, at the age of ninety-eight; it was, appropriately, the day of Liz's twenty-fifth birthday. The members of the project then began working with the Association of Children of the Holocaust in Warsaw to create a memorial statue in Irena's honor. It was unveiled on May 12, 2010, on Liz's twenty-seventh birthday and the second anniversary of Irena's death.

After the war, Holocaust survivors wanting to build new lives had no interest in dwelling on their painful pasts. The Jewish world's attention was rightly focused on establishing their families and careers, the new State of Israel, the Nazi trials, and the global threat of spreading communism. Irena Sendler and her story were further lost to the world because the Russian communists gained postwar control of Poland and forcefully united previously divided Poland and then merged it into the USSR block. They undertook their own forms of persecution against the surviving Jewish citizens and greatly mistrusted the patriotic Zegota, the non-Jewish underground resistance movement with which Irena was associated. The Former Soviet Republic has a well-deserved reputation for burying and/or revising any history not deemed supportive of their ideology or that exposed their infamous deeds. Irena's story, and her Christian faith, became victims of these global factors.

It was several decades before any of the rescuers began to be generally acknowledged. The related attention was initiated by the research conducted at Yad Vashem (translation: "remember the names"), the State of Israel's official Holocaust Memorial Museum in Jerusalem. It was they who had compiled the list that started Liz on her academic journey. The students' detailed research revealed this forgotten hero and the story that follows about her brave deeds during the Holocaust of World War II. Liz and her team rescued the rescuer.

What's in a name? Surprisingly, a lot more than is readily anticipated. If you were a Polish citizen of Jewish descent, it meant everything – life, love, liberty. The Nazi-led German army's occupation of Poland in 1939 was the longest, and very likely the most brutal, that any non-Germanic country suffered during the international conflict. The same is true regarding their mistreatment of the population, especially its Jews. The Nazis' confirmed objective was to eliminate all of Poland's native Slavic people: Jews, Gypsies, and handicapped first, and then the remainder. This madness included wiping out all vestiges of Polish national culture. (Poland's Jewish population was the largest in Europe, and subsequently, the Polish Jews suffered the greatest numerical loss of all subjugated countries.

Irena was born February 15, 1910, in Warsaw, the capital of Poland. She was an attractive young maiden of twenty-nine when the German military machine subdued her homeland and enslaved or murdered its population. She was already a capable medical nurse and social worker. Any citizen in need was potentially her client, and she extended no exclusions toward the Jews, even well after the Nazis prohibited assistance to them with the passage of their inhumane and intolerant Nuremberg decrees. Helping a Jew came at a cost: All members of an offender's household risked the death sentence if just one member's pro-Jewish actions were revealed. Władysław Bartoszewski of the Polish Resistance said, "No work, not printing underground papers, transporting weapons, planning sabotage against the Germans; none of it was as dangerous as hiding a Jew. You have a ticking time bomb in your home. If they find out, they will kill you, your family, and the person you are hiding." The occupying Germans were not the only threat to those who helped. Much of the population was already prejudiced against the Jews – the country had a long and ugly history of violent pogroms.

Irena joined the Polish underground resistance movement Zegota, and became the head of their children's department, operating under her secret nom de guerre, Jolanta. Her initial pro-Jewish effort was to forge new identification papers for Jewish families in order to assist them in obtaining passports to leave the country, or to hide their true identities if they chose to remain in Poland. Three thousand families were helped in this manner. After a year, these avenues were no longer available, as the Nazis forced the massive number of remaining Jews into ghettos that were filthier and more overcrowded than city slums. The Warsaw Ghetto contained the greatest concentration of Jews in the world, and now four hundred thousand were crowded into an area of one and one-third square miles.

Irena immediately sought commissioning from the Germans to check for signs of typhus, a deadly disease the Nazis feared would spread outside of the ghetto. The Nazis were unconcerned about preserving life within the ghetto; they just didn't want the contagion to exit the confines and place them at risk. It was the Nazi view that if a Pole like Irena died during the containment process, it was far better than risking a German life. Under the pretext of conducting regular inspections of the unsanitary conditions related to the frequent typhoid outbreaks, Irena voluntarily visited the ghetto at least once daily. On her visits, she brought in hidden food, medicines, and clothing as contraband gifts for the internees. Eventually, she enlisted a small team to assist her and help multiply her efforts. Eight-year-old Irena had become all too familiar with typhus, after her own physician-father died during an epidemic while caring for the infected Jewish populace of a village outside Warsaw. Now, regardless of her best efforts, she noted that five thousand ghetto residents were dying monthly from the disease and from starvation.

In August of 1942, Irena witnessed a large group of ghetto children being led out by armed Nazis. She was sickened, knowing their fate was likely to be death by Zyklon B poison gas. Irena reacted to the overwhelming number of deaths and murders by becoming righteously angry. She determined that she had to advance her rescue plans another dangerous step forward. Her focus became helping the Jewish children escape the ghetto so at least there would be Polish-Jewish posterity who might outlive the evil regime.

It was, of course, a very emotional and difficult task convincing parents to separate from their children and give them up to a Gentile, Catholic stranger. If her reasoned persuasions were successful in releasing babies, toddlers, and young children from their families, there remained the daunting task of finding sufficient non-Jewish people who were willing to take them into their homes and institutions. Many Polish citizens were pro-German collaborators who wouldn't hesitate notifying the Nazis in order to further secure their own tenuous lives. Little did they realize that after the Jews, they would be next; Hitler's mad plan was the annihilation of the entire Polish Gentile population. For other native families, even when sympathetic, the risk was considered too great.

Continuing to smuggle supplies into the ghetto, Irena developed several processes for smuggling out the children. She employed any creative, secretive means she could reasonably conceive. The older children were less challenging, because they could be led out through sewers and secret pas-sageways. Babies were more difficult. She disguised them as packages; or placed them in suitcases, tool chests, and backpacks; or hid them in ambu-lances, wheelbarrows, rugs, furniture, trash barrels, and even coffins. Irena would bring along her pet dog because she had trained it to bark incessantly whenever a uniformed Nazi was nearby. This created both an advance warn-ing and a distraction if she was ever stopped for questioning. While her dog was barking loudly at them, the Nazis could not easily hear any sounds from the babies hidden in her package, vessel, or vehicle. As an additional safety measure, infants were sedated so as to prevent them from excessively crying or thrashing about. Irena secretly spoke German, but she never let on; this tactic often proved advantageous during the smuggling operations.

All of the rescued Jewish children were given new identities and false documents, and then placed with willing Polish families, orphanages, and the convents, schools, or rectories of Catholic priests and nuns. Some of the children were subsequently moved to rural farms and others were sent to Israel or to neighboring countries. There developed a kind of underground railway facilitated by the organized resistance movement. Using thin cigarette papers, Irena created written documentation of the children's real family names, which were cross-referenced with their false names and with their adoptive family identities and locations. She then hid the papers in glass jars with tight lids and buried them under an apple tree – a tree so close to a Gestapo facility that it helped defray suspicion and discovery. This effort was risky but necessary in order to preserve the original identities and the locations, as well as the new identities and locations. Irena assured the par-ents and older children that, when the war was over, the borrowed children would be returned to their rightful families if at all possible. The lists were to be the means for fulfilling this promise.

In 1943, Irena was finally reported by a malicious informer. Without warning or trial, she was arrested by the Gestapo, locked in the notorious Pawiak prison, severely tortured, and eventually sentenced to death. Some years later, a holy card was found in her former jail cell. On it was written: "Jesus, I trust in you." The card was promptly returned to her, and Irena kept it until 1979, when she gave it to Pope John Paul II as a gift during a personal visit to his Vatican residence at St. Peter's Basilica in Rome, Italy. While in jail, there were repeated efforts by the Gestapo to force Irena to reveal the names and locations of the hidden children. She was beaten and had both arms and legs broken. Even under this extreme torture, she never disclosed any information about the children's new identities and never even confirmed the existence of the glass jar.

Her friends in the Zegota underground movement were able to save Irena's life mere moments before her scheduled execution. The German guards assigned to shoot her were approached, bribed, and told to report her dead. Thereafter, Irena's name was listed on the public bulletin boards among those executed. For the remainder of the war, she lived anonymously, in hiding. Once her wounds healed (although the healing was never total, as she always retained some permanent damage), Irena – with ongoing assistance from the underground – continued ministering to the Jewish children whom she had saved from the ghetto. Further direct work in the ghetto itself was no longer possible for her, and soon the ghetto was destroyed after a valiant but unsuccessful Jewish uprising.

Engaged in this manner for five years, before and after her capture, Irena was able, with the help of her own team of young girls, to save and sustain more than twenty-five hundred children by the close of the war in 1945. This was in addition to the three thousand family members assisted by the passport project. Immediately following the war's end, she unearthed the glass jar and attempted to return the children, as promised, to their families. Sadly, all of the parents and most of the unrescued older siblings had been murdered nearby at the hideous Treblinka death camp. The good news was that through the information contained in the jars, the children – who nearly all survived the war – were easily located. Although they were now orphans, the children learned their true family identities and related Jewish heritage.

A famous Talmudic proverb says, "Whoever saves a single soul, it is as if he had saved the whole world." Irena's life fulfilled that saying beyond anyone's expectation. Because of her work as a rescuer, she has been awarded the status of "Righteous Among the Nations" by Yad Vashem.

Many of the children Irena saved are still alive today. One lady, who was only six months old when Irena rescued her, remarkably became Irena's caregiver during her final years. Irena died in Warsaw, the same city where she was born and where she fearlessly worked throughout the Holocaust. Despite all Irena had done, this is what the humble hero said about herself: "I still hear the cries of the babies and their mothers ... I am not a hero, I could have done more; this regret will follow me to my death." Today, twenty-five hundred living testimonies (or ten thousand-plus, with the children and grandchildren of the next two generations) say otherwise. In modern Poland, she is referred to as the Angel of the Warsaw Ghetto.

Jesus – whom Irena openly served – commanded: *You shall love your neighbor as yourself.* (Matthew 22:37). Her life is a beautiful example of what it means to truly "love your neighbor" and to be "your brother's keeper" (Genesis 4:9). Jesus illustrated these precepts for all in the parable of the good Samaritan. Irena knew the parable and accepted what it meant, even at the risk of her own life. Irena said her parents instilled in her a caring principle so strong that if she were to see someone drowning, she was to attempt saving them even if she didn't know how to swim. She said, "Every child saved with my help is the justification for my existence on earth, and not a title to glory." Upon her death, Irena stood before God. She was able to respond without guilt if asked the questions God asked Cain: *Where is ... your brother? What have you done? The voice of your brother's blood cries out to Me from the ground* (Genesis 4:10).

For longer than half a century, Irena's engaging life story was lost to several generations. Had it not been for Liz's diligent efforts, its inspiration and appreciation could have remained lost to humanity forever. Irena's legend is growing exponentially, with her name and life readily displayed in films and books, and on statues and websites. It's appropriate to remember the contributions of Mr. Conard, Liz, and her friends that started the process in motion. The girls wanted to make a difference with their project and help to repair the world. They've met both objectives, and they're still on the job. Even though Irena has been gone for several years, her apple tree remains a growing and silent witness to the many lives delivered from unspeakable horrors.

And I will save your children. (Isaiah 49:25)

* * * *

Author's Note: As Irena witnessed, and as has often been true in the past, the Jewish people are currently experiencing persecution throughout the world, even in their ancient homeland of Israel. Today, there are still Christians like Irena Sendler who minister comfort to them, some doing so at the risk of their lives. There are organizations located in Jerusalem that provide support to the few who are on the frontlines helping, as well as general assistance to the multitudes who are suffering. Based on my direct participation, three that are worthy of mention are International Christian Embassy–Jerusalem (ICEJ), Christian Friends of Israel (CFI), and Bridges for Peace. On a broader geographic scale, there are organizations today that continue to minister in the manner of Irena Sendler, but to a larger constituency than just the Jewish people. Their outreach includes ministering to Jews and Christians throughout the world who are suffering persecution of any form. Five of these that are worthy of mention – based on my personal experience or observation – are Voice of the Martyrs (VOM), Open Doors, Spirit of Martyrdom (SOM), World Relief, and Samaritan's Purse.

Joseph Carey Merrick

Life As an Animal

Who am I, O Lᴏʀᴅ God? (1 Chronicle 17:16)

The measurement around my head is thirty-six inches, there is
a large substance of flesh at the back, the other part in a manner
of speaking is like hills and valleys, all lumped together, while my
face is such a sight that no one could describe it. My right hand
is almost the size and shape of an elephant's foreleg, measuring
twelve inches just around the wrist and five inches around my
fingers; the other hand and arm is no larger than that of a girl ten
years of age, although it is well proportioned. My feet and legs are
covered with thick lumpy, wrinkled, skin, also my body is like that
of an elephant, and almost the same color; in fact, no one could
believe until they saw it, that such a thing could even exist.

This detailed, physical self-description was provided by a young man
in his teens. It was transcribed directly from his brief two-page autobiography. Since the age of five, people called him elephant boy, and later
in life, elephant man. Prior to having it surgically removed, he had a trunk-
like flap of skin between his mouth and nose that was close to six inches
long; hence, more support for the nasty nickname. In the mid-nineteenth
century, medical operations were rare and performed without the aid of

antiseptics and anesthesia. Undergoing an operation was more likely to harm or kill through infection rather than to benefit the patient. This was the teen's only surgery; fortunately, it was a success.

He was born in 1860 in London, England; in America, our Civil War was just beginning. His given name was Joseph Carey Merrick. Though he was thought to be retarded because no one could understand his speech due to his facial deformities, he had a fine mind. His speech was unintelligible prior to the operation; it improved modestly, but sufficiently, afterward. Even though people ran away from him or drove him out believing him to be a dangerous monster, he possessed a beautiful, quiet spirit. If beauty is only skin deep, then so is ugly.

Joseph had a congenital disorder that caused tumors to form asymmetrically throughout his body, thus affecting his growth and development both externally and internally. His condition was accompanied by severe pain and disfigurement, a foul odor, and many limiting physical handicaps. Every year, the disease steadily worsened with a progressive overall deterioration. It ensured that Joseph's troubled life would also be unnaturally short. The attributes of the disease explain why his autobiography was a brief two pages, while most run in the hundreds. For Joseph to write anything with his deformed hand was difficult and painful, let alone to do so legibly and at length. Unable to communicate easily by speech or by writing, Joseph was left isolated and misunderstood.

What he had was a rare disease since identified as Proteus syndrome. It's named after the Greek god who could change his shape in order to escape from his enemies (also known as Wiedemann syndrome). Joseph's body was changing shape from what we commonly consider human-like to something shapeless, oversized, and somewhat reminiscent of an elephant. As sometimes suggested, Joseph did not have elephantiasis (aka elephantitis or lymphatic filariasis), and he did not have neurofibromatosis – two somewhat similar disfiguring diseases. Proteus syndrome is a very rare disease, and Joseph likely had the worst recorded case of it. No reader need fear catching it as it is congenital; you must be born with it. It's somewhat cancer-like in that it's characterized by the out-of-control, abnormal growth of bones, skin, muscles, blood vessels, and other tissues. Some who are afflicted have associated mental disorders; this was not so with Joseph.

No one in England, and in fact no one in the world – including medical experts – understood Proteus syndrome during his lifetime. Joseph's case was widely thought to be the result of an incident that occurred during his mother's pregnancy when the circus came to London. Today, we may occasionally have the opportunity to see a circus, but in a world full of Disneylands, Universal Studios, water parks, and Six Flags theme parks, the interest level in circuses is modest. In Joseph's world, however, circus excitement ran fever-high, and the preliminary parade was greatly anticipated.

No element of the parade was more appreciated than its final attraction, the elephants. As the crowd pushed to the front for a better view, Joseph's pregnant mother was knocked to the ground in front of a bull elephant. She was very nearly crushed, but survived unharmed. However, it was thought that her fear of the elephant entered her womb and caused the baby to take on elephant-like characteristics. Joseph accepted this as the cause. We know today that this was obviously not true, but it was the acknowledged attribution at that time; seemly confirmed as Joseph acquired a strange, elephant-like appearance, even more so with the passing of time.

During the first six years of his life, he was cared for by his loving mother despite his disabilities and abnormal appearance. After she passed away, while he was still at a tender age, Joseph was left in the not-as-good care of his father. For reasons unknown to us, his father acquiesced to demands from his stepmother to drive Joseph from the family home and move him into a workhouse. Workhouses were semi-public, semi-private institutions (often of a penal nature) where a person was forced, without any alternative, to perform hard manual labor from sunup till sundown, six days a week. The inmates went without compensation in terms of fiscal payment, but they did receive unelaborate bed and board (food). These workhouses no longer exist today, as they have been outlawed in our more enlightened culture.

For a season, Joseph's assignment was as a door-to-door street peddler, but he had no physical appeal, was challenged to exhaustion by the difficulty in walking, and was nearly impossible to understand in verbal communication. In a short time, Joseph was forced out of the workhouse and onto the street. This was not because he wasn't a diligent worker, but because his deteriorating physical condition didn't permit him to compete with the other more able-bodied residents. On the harsh, dirty, overcrowded, and unforgiving streets of Victorian London, he was at the mercy of the uneducated, fearful masses, and he quickly found there was no mercy. He was ridiculed, beaten, denied, harassed, and run out of neighborhood after neighborhood. He tried to disguise himself by wearing a huge, shapeless, bag-like, dark cloak with a hood over his head, cut with a few holes for breathing, hearing, and seeing. The covering failed to protect him, however, and he was still treated as less than human, and not even as well as most dogs.

The only alternative remaining was for him to join a freak show. A freak show was a traveling exposition filled with a collection of strange plants, animals, and people. Some entrepreneurial type with low morals would accumulate his freaks for display and charge the public an admission price to view them. Freak shows were commonplace in Victorian England, but they have since gone the way of the workhouse. The taunting in the show was as bad as it had been on the streets, but at least Joseph again had some modest form of bed and board.

After some years of this, and with Joseph grown into his mid to late teens, he finally caught his first real break in life since the death of his mother. A distinguished physician from the renowned London Hospital, Dr. Frederick Treves, attended Joseph's freak show and quickly gained a dual interest in him. The first was as a unique medical specimen: *What's wrong? What condition does he have? What caused it? How can we cure and prevent this?* The second interest was that of one human for another who was obviously adrift and victimized by an unsympathetic urban society.

Dr. Treves used his influence and position to acquire two adjoining rooms in the basement of London Hospital, where he planned to house Joseph on a permanent basis. Joseph was at last off the streets and out of the cruel reach of the public. Since the loss of his mother, he'd never enjoyed this level of security or comfort. At first, the maintenance staff and nurses held the commonly accepted view that he was retarded or dangerous. However, because Joseph was not going anywhere and could no longer be driven away, they gradually began to accept him and to correct their initial misconceptions. With more regular exposure and after his facial operation, they were also able to better understand Joseph's less-mumbled speech.

What they eventually discovered was that under the rough exterior was a pleasant and engaging personality. Joseph had a good heart and mind. This was primarily the result of a gift his mother had given him during their short time together. His mother had read the Bible to Joseph and encouraged him to memorize many of its verses. Joseph was amenable to this and began a lifetime habit of reading and memorizing Scriptures. He had internalized the Word, and it yielded and preserved good fruit in his spirit, helping him to accept his harsh lot and to absolve his persecutors. Through it all, he had retained goodwill and avoided holding malice.

People began to enjoy visiting Joseph in his small apartment. First it was just the hospital staff, but eventually a broader visitation developed. It became a popular activity throughout London society to call on Joseph. Actors, writers, artists, and politicians became regulars on his schedule. Eventually Edward VII, the future king of Great Britain, was a part of his inner circle. Joseph even developed sufficient proficiency in a hobby. Using paper, light pieces of wood, and cardboard, he constructed small architectural models, such as a church. Joseph would frequently give these as gifts to those who visited him, and it became coveted in high society to acquire one of Joseph's models as a souvenir gift of the visit or as a token of his friendship.

Joseph died suddenly during the Easter season of his twenty-eighth year. He wanted to attend the worship service held in the hospital chapel, but after having done so, he returned to his apartment exhausted from the effort. He told the nurse in attendance that he wished to take a nap. He added, however, that he intended to do so like everyone else sleeps. By this, Joseph meant that he planned to lie down in a bed on his back. His usual position was sitting up propped against a wall or wedged into corner. During his nap, the weight of his great head snapped his fragile neck and Joseph passed on in his sleep.

By his manner of life, Joseph has left us a legacy of enormous value. During his time in London Hospital, he completed his written autobiography and permitted himself to be photographed. Both the autobiography and the photographs survive to instruct us further, as well as to supplement our memory of his unusual life. Joseph did not offer these two permanent artifacts so that we might gawk or snicker; he already had more of that than anyone else during his lifetime. I believe he bequeathed these to us as substantive reminders of what, and how much, he overcame. Joseph was a true victim of a fallen earth and an unregenerate population, but he never adopted a victim perspective. He sought to be, and was, an overcomer. He had an exceptional number of reasons to become bitter, but he chose to become better instead. This does not happen absent a conscious determination to do so.

It's very unlikely that anyone reading this story has experienced a combination of handicaps and persecution remotely approaching the level of Joseph's. Therefore, by comparison, we have no standing to claim victim status. We may look in the mirror and be dissatisfied with the color or texture of our hair, the shade of our skin, the set of our teeth, the size of our feet, the shape of our nose or ears, or the weight and height of our body. Joseph's legacy – the facts of his life, his autobiography, and the photos – serves to remind us to *get over it*.

Now, those are obviously my words and not Joseph's. In his lifetime, Joseph's was not a story of heroism; he was as human in every way as we are, while clearly not endowed with as many physical proficiencies. Nevertheless, he made friends at every level, developed a skill, forgave his numerous tormentors, and refused to feel sorry for himself.

Some of our dissatisfactions with self and with our lot in life are based on real circumstances, and some are false and simply perceived to be real. The perceived must be sorted out and discarded. The real will either fall into the *changeable* or the *unchangeable* classification. If it's in the latter, we must strive to accept it. If it's in the former, then we have the alternative to strive instead to remove, exchange, or modify it. All of us have a unique purpose in life, and all of us are gifted, just differently gifted. It's not an argument about whether it's fair or unfair to have been given one, five, or ten talents; it's about what we have done with our talents. It's about how well we have invested those we have been given. If one holds on to the outlook that their life is unfair, then that's really holding an offense against God.

Whether our dissatisfactions are real or perceived, changeable or unchangeable, they all originated from the same single source: comparison. Anytime we compare ourselves with another, we will either feel inferior (not as good as) and envious, or superior (better than) and prideful. Both are losing responses. The winning response is to remove acts of comparison from our lives and replace them with patience (the hope that improvements will come) and contentment (accepting our present circumstances). The apostle Paul once said that when comparing each other to each other, we are found to be fools.

Learn from Joseph; take a lesson from him in being an overcomer. Life shouldn't be lived as a victim, no matter what challenges are faced. It's not what's on the outside that counts; it's what's on the inside that counts – what's in our head and heart. Put in the good stuff, and take out or leave out the bad. Joseph did not live his life as a victim, and neither should we as we follow the path he walked.

Every examination of Joseph's life – and there are many – has concluded that he was a humble, God-fearing man who knew and believed the Scriptures. He must have had his view fixed on something greater than and beyond his present situation. That something enabled Joseph to love God, to love others, and to love himself despite rejection and difficulties beyond anything that we will personally experience. All men in totality – body, mind, and spirit – are made in the image of God. Joseph, especially, reflected God's nature.

> "Tis true, my form is something odd but blaming me, is blaming God. Could I create myself anew I would not fail in pleasing you."

In addition to his autobiography and photographs, Joseph left us with the quote above, which seems to summarize the nature of his unusual life. The borrowed lines are from the poem "False Greatness" by Isaac Watts. It is often said that Joseph ended his correspondence by quoting these lines; others say they were used as advertising in his freak-show pamphlet. Both uses may be accurate. Joseph was fond of them and was known to quote them often.

> *Who am I, … that You have brought me this far?*
> (1 Chronicles 17:16)

Arland D. Williams Jr.

Lost in the Water

I would have lost heart, unless I had believed (Psalm 27:13)

Two bridges stand today as monuments to this story. One is located in Mattoon, Illinois, at the T-intersection formed where Lakeland Boulevard dead-ends into Charleston Avenue. It's visually insubstantial, and can barely be described as a bridge. It is more like a viaduct over a broad excavation – essentially a large, open ditch. The formation beneath the street grade is punned as a *chunnel* – a composite of *tunnel* and *channel*. Its primary purpose is to carry east-west-bound vehicle traffic over the north-south-bound yards underneath. Early in Mattoon's history, the city fathers demonstrated significant foresight by excavating a channel below the urban grade to avoid ensnarling the increasing volume of vehicle traffic with the diminishing volume of rail traffic, thus preventing delays to either transportation method.

The wisdom of this design and subsequent investment is commendable and not to be taken lightly. By comparison, a similarly sized city a hundred miles from Mattoon failed to take such action, and today suffers sixty-five trains per day intersecting catty-corner and snake-like across the city, while completely severing and shutting down all urban activity including emergency vehicles. Nonetheless, in contrast to its vital role, the Mattoon

Bridge is not very imposing, rising to a maximum height of less than ten feet, and can be crossed with barely a notice.

The other bridge could not be more different from the first. It crosses the mighty Potomac River at a wide portion not far from where it passes the stately Mount Vernon Plantation, and then, downstream, it pours its considerable waters into the Atlantic Ocean. The bridge's primary purpose is to carry high volumes of surface traffic between Washington, D.C. and Arlington, Virginia, while functioning as the terminus and origin of I-395. It has, over the years, grown into a series of multilane, bi-directional bridges of varying architectural styles and purposes, with some carrying rail and others vehicular transportation. This series of bridges was collectively known by the nondescript name "Fourteenth Street Bridge." Regardless of the insignificant name, there is no way a bystander could fail to notice them. Many pedestrians are drawn to the nearby riverside parks, inclined to relax while idly observing the frenzied activities and attractive designs on this network of bridges.

On January 13, 1982, at approximately 4:20 p.m., the status of these two very different bridges began developing something in common, eventually becoming linked immemorially. Beginning around noon, the nation's capital experienced an uncharacteristically severe midwinter blizzard. In response, the area's manifold federal offices closed early. Before the sun set, the day would record storm-related accidents that shut down or gridlocked the entire metro area's subway, road, and air traffic systems at the cost of many lives. It was to be a day of tragedy as well as a day of related magnanimity.

On the west bank of the Potomac River, less than one mile south of the bridge and tucked up tight against the shoreline, is Washington National Airport (now Ronald Reagan Washington National Airport). It was here, in close proximity to the nation's capital, that Air Florida prepared a Boeing 737 for takeoff to its intended destination in sunny Tampa, Florida, via Flight 90. The passengers were boarded on time, but the plane was delayed on the runway at length as it underwent the occasional de-icing procedures required to offset freezing, slushy buildup while awaiting the hoped-for break in the nasty weather – the break that never arrived that day. After some time and for an uncertain reason, the plane was given departure clearance. Days later, the air transportation authorities realized that several critical standard safety procedures had been ignored or misapplied.

The 737 only traveled westward one mile before failing to lift and clear the Fourteenth Street Bridge. The crash resulted in the death of four motorists after seven vehicles were damaged, along with significant portions of the bridge. The Boeing landed on the far side of the bridge, broke through the thick surface ice, and quickly sank (all but the tail section) beneath the cold waters. Only six of the seventy-nine occupants escaped the submerged and mangled wreckage, emerged to the surface gasping for air, and then clung helplessly in the oily water to a broken tailpiece.

Rescue attempts from the water were not possible as the river was solidly frozen, and the only capable icebreaker was already engaged in a rescue downriver. Rescue attempts from the bridge, which were already compromised by the concurrent vehicle-related injuries and the bridge damage, were not possible either. Professional emergency teams were blocked from arriving due to the snarled traffic backups. Rescue attempts from the shore using ladders and makeshift ropes were admirably attempted, but proved wholly inadequate even as those assisting struggled for balance in the two feet of fresh snow. All potential air support was suppressed by the blinding weather, the same conditions that had already downed the 737.

The six survivors were in grave danger of perishing in clear view of the large host of assembled bystanders. Their bodies had all been injured to some extent during the crash, and two were near-blind after being exposed to the jet fuel accumulated on the surface. But their most immediate threat was hypothermia. This condition takes hold in minutes, with death resulting when a combination of basic life-sustaining metabolic processes shut down due to a severe decrease in body temperature.

A small National Parks Department helicopter with a two-man crew risked departure from Anacostia Park and successfully traveled the three air miles to the bridge in near-zero visibility. Upon approaching the survivors, they released personal floatation devices with little success. Their attention was focused on removing the survivors from the water, but their efforts were limited by the capacity to proficiently rescue only one victim at a time. The extraction harness was a simple loop on the end of a suspended rope.

It was first offered to a man who handed it to nearby flight attendant Kelly Duncan, who was then partially lifted and partially dragged to the shore, where emergency help had gathered to assist. The harness was offered a second time to the first man. He again handed it to another passenger, who was also successfully removed to the shore. On the third return, the chopper crew correctly estimated that their rescue window was drawing to a close, so they fashioned a second makeshift rope and attempted a two-person rescue. Again, the first man declined the opportunity and instead assisted two other survivors, a man and a woman, each suffering a broken hand. Once he had both the man and the woman reasonably secure within the two harnesses, the man in the harness grabbed hold of a third victim, another woman, in an attempt to drag her with him to safety. During this impromptu three-person rescue procedure, both of the women slipped back into the open water. The resulting complications consumed precious time, and ultimately forced the two helicopter-based rescuers to engage in exceptionally courageous separate actions.

From the shoreline, Lenny Skutnik shunned his heavy outer clothes, dove into the water, swam out, and pulled one of the totally exhausted women to shore. Simultaneously, paramedic Melvin Windsor stepped out without protective restraints onto the chopper's landing skid, in order to grab the other woman by her wet clothes and pull her from the water to the relative safety of one skid. This action, while ultimately successful, resulted in the skids becoming submerged. Such a condition held a potentially disastrous outcome for all aboard, had it not been avoided by pilot Donald Usher's quick, evasive maneuvers.

By the time the rescuers were able to execute another return, the first man was no longer visible. After a thorough search, it became certain that as he awaited this last opportunity for extraction – the one that was undeniably his alone to accept – he'd suffered the lack of muscle coordination and sluggish thinking characteristic of advanced hypothermia. Consequently, when the tail remnant of the plane finally broke through the ice and sank, he lacked the strength and willpower to push away and resist its dangerous undertow. He slipped beneath the surface unto sure death, and into anonymity at the muddy bottom of the river. His sequence of selfless actions was soberly and admiringly recorded by the news reporters via their cameras and notepads, later to be commemorated in numerous publications, one film, and a song. There was not a single eyewitness among the many gathered who failed to be deeply impressed by the dauntless scene played in real-time before them. Heroic action was in fashion that hour.

The five rescued survivors were hospitalized, and all lived. There was a disturbing catch, however; no one had been able to get a good look at the final survivor, the one who came to be known as the "sixth man in the water." Even those whom he saved were not able to identify him beyond a simple "I saw a man's hand pass the rope to me." The man's face was also blocked from the view of both those on the bridge and on shore, and daylight dimmed even as operations were still underway. The best description came from the pilot, who confirmed it was a man and that he appeared to be "middle-aged and maybe balding."

Once attention shifted from the five survivors, there were seventy-four victims who needed to be located and identified. Of these, one was the unknown sixth man. Many wanted to know who he was, but there didn't seem to be any means to satisfy their curiosity. Several days later, a coroner made a conclusive discovery: Only one of the male victims had lungs completely filled with water. It was determined from this unique status that he must have surfaced and then drowned. This body was associated with the role of the sixth man, and was later identified as that of Arland Dean Williams Jr., the mystery rescuer.

> "I was the last man in the water. I was the one who saved your sons and daughters. And when they finally sent down the last shred of rope, I saw my last hope wave good-bye."
> ~ Commemorative song by Sarah Hickman

At the time of the crash, Arland was a forty-six-year-old federal bank examiner living in Florida, but born and raised in Mattoon, Illinois. After undergoing a recent painful and unwanted divorce, he was once again dating his high school sweetheart, Peggy, who still lived in Mattoon. His objective was to finally marry her. His chosen profession had him diligently engaged in cleaning up the notorious savings and loan financial scandals of the early 1980s. This employment required frequent air shuttle between his home in Florida, his children and office in Atlanta, the District of Columbia, and his hometown in Illinois. To those who knew him well, he was just *Chub*; not because he was overweight – he was not – but because he seemed so average, naturally content, and even-natured.

The move into banking was a natural for him, as his father, Arland D. Sr., was a bank president in Mattoon. The most uncharacteristic part of his life was his decision to leverage his high school ROTC into four years of college at the famous Citadel, The Military College of Charleston, South Carolina, and then to proceed with his two mandatory years of army service, which he spent as a stateside officer during the era of the Vietnam War. The Citadel is well known for its all-encompassing educational severity, as demonstrated by less than a third of the candidates being able to complete the associated requirements. Ironically, and perhaps prophetically, the demands that concerned Arland most deeply were those related to swimming and water safety, as he'd had a lifelong fear of water.

Not all who heard the news of Arland's heroic self-sacrifice received it with joy. His father and his son and daughter have understandably expressed regrets that Arland traded his life for others. It's not that they aren't proud of him; they are very proud. It's because of the seemingly unfair trade, in that a stranger gained, while they suffered deep personal loss. All three relatives believe some of the tragedies later afflicting the family are traceable to Arland's unfinished roles as father and as son. Such is nearly always the double-edged destiny of heroic action, especially when it ends fatally, as it so often does.

I learned Arland's story firsthand during my tenure in Mattoon. After leaving the area, I shared it regularly. I always concluded the telling with the observation that in order for Arland to have been so altruistic during a time of grave, sudden, and unpredictable personal crisis, he must have already been well prepared to do so. By this I don't mean he had any inclination or premonition his life would take such a final dramatic turn on that particular winter's evening; he certainly did not. There is no way to prepare at the last moment for a crisis circumstance, especially an unanticipated one. What I intend to communicate is that the uncompromising, decent, thoughtful way he lived his life every day had unknowingly prepared him to take the high and unselfish route when an unexpected and unusual event suddenly engulfed him. Daily, he had to be doing right in the frequent, small things as well as in the occasional, large things. He fed his heart and head healthy food on a regular day-in-and-day-out basis. If he had fed them with the garbage of cheating, cutting corners, and compromise, then his natural reaction would have been to continue looking out for himself, first and last.

Great Britain's conservative champion, three-term, and only female prime minister, Margaret Thatcher, stated this supposition as: "Watch your thoughts, for they become words. Watch your words, for they become actions. Watch your actions, for they become habits. Watch your habits, for they become your character. And watch your character, for it becomes your destiny. What we think, we become. My father always said that. And I think I am fine." Yes, she was, and so was Arland.

It would not have been sin or selfishness for Arland to have accepted the rope at any opportunity between the first and the final time, and no one would have thought any less of him for such an act. But it was his nature to serve others before himself. If we could have observed his life, we could have predicted the altruistic outcome, because every day we would have seen him putting in the good stuff. What you put in is what comes out in a crisis. No one can put in junk and expect any satisfactory outcome.

After about four years of sharing my personal conjecture on why Arland acted heroically during the terror of uncontrollable moments of horror, someone from the audience approached me afterward and stated that he'd known Arland well. My first thought was that my summary point was about to be challenged. Rather, I received the following confirmation: "I knew Arland, and when I heard about what happened I thought, *Why, there's no surprise. That's exactly the way I remembered him living his life. He was always putting others first and doing the right thing.*" An old computer industry expression sums it up simply as GIGO, or "garbage in, garbage out." In other words, if you input questionable or challengeable data, then expect questionable or challengeable results as the processed output.

Scripture offers a number of succinct ways to communicate the same principle. Here are four illustrations: First, it's not what a man takes into his body that corrupts him, but what he takes into his heart. Next, we must be faithful in the little before we can be found faithful in the great. Third, as a man thinks in his heart, so is he. And finally, anyone may give his life to save family or friends, but true love will do it for a stranger or even an enemy.

> "So the man in the water had his own natural powers ... he
> could hand life over to a stranger, and that is a power of nature,
> too. The man in the water pitted himself against an implacable,
> impersonal enemy; he fought it with charity; and he held it to a
> standoff. He was the best we can do."
> ~ Publication by Roger Rosenblatt

Reflecting again on those two bridges, the small one in Mattoon was immediately dedicated in Arland's honor after the accident, and it became the Arland D. Williams Jr. Memorial Bridge. It's the little bridge with the big name and the big story. In doing so, Mattoon named its only available structure in memory of Arland; it was essentially all they had to work with, as the small prairie town lacked anything of greater significance. Two decades later, Mattoon built a new elementary school and named it after Arland as well.

Several years thereafter, President Reagan dedicated the previously damaged Arlington-to-D.C. bridge in Arland's honor, making it the other Arland D. Williams Jr. Memorial Bridge. All too often tax-funded public structures like bridges, buildings, highways, and monuments are named after or by some politician for personal aggrandizement and political party gain. Every so often a name hints at an awesome story in which a person of integrity, like Arland, resides and is remembered. His name is what both bridges have as a common bond. His final acts of generosity are what turned GIGO into "goodness in, goodness out."

That I would see the goodness of the Lord in the land of the living.
(Psalm 27:13)

Rose Valland

The Art of War

*And he took away the treasures of the house of the Lord
and the treasures of the king's house;* (1 Kings 14:26)

There was an obscure, middle-aged woman of plain appearance who quietly and nearly singlehandedly went about the risky business of saving Europe's art treasures from the destructive and greedy Nazi hordes who occupied her French homeland and most of Western Europe. Her activities took place during the time of the more encompassing events depicted in the acclaimed nonfiction books *The Rape of Europa* by Lynn Nicholas and *The Monuments Men* by Robert Edsel. I was inspired to tell her story before finding these books, and well before the film productions that bear the same titles were released; but I delight in the subsequent exposure this deserving heroine is now receiving. Her full Catholic name was Rose Antonia Maria Valland (1898–1980), and throughout the Second World War, she worked at a small art museum in Paris, France.

Rose's life is the valiant story of an unpaid, untitled volunteer who secretly recorded the shameless German art pilfering of Europe, and thereby helped track and recover thousands of stolen art objects. Her role was like that of a spy; its successful execution was of incalculable historical, cultural, and monetary value. Paintings by Rembrandt, Vermeer, Monet, Pissarro, Degas, and many more masters passed literally under her caring oversight. Rose loved art so much she willingly volunteered at French art museums for almost a decade before the Nazi subjugation of France. Her greatest joy was just to be near the precious masterpieces and to assist with their display and preservation. She performed these labors of love while she patiently waited for a more permanent, paid appointment with its concurrent authority, benefits, recognition, and monetary compensation.

France's greatest national fine arts institution is the Louvre, and it's located in the center of the capital city of Paris, along the Seine River. In 1940, as German forces began their occupation of France, Nazi officials quickly exercised control over the Louvre proper, as well as its outlying Jeu de Paume museum, a modest gallery housing an exhibit of Impressionist works, located near the far more famous Tuileries Gardens and Place de la Concorde. The Nazis utilized the Jeu de Paume's unimposing facility to execute a key step in their overall sinister plan to systematically plunder the art treasures of all Europe. It was used as a centralized collection, storage, and transport facility for the priceless art confiscated from museums and Jewish-owned private collections throughout Europe. Hitler prized the artwork, but his intentions went deeper than simple collection. He wanted to permanently erase the cultural heritage of the countries he conquered while simultaneously adding stolen glory to Germany's.

Rose was a simple volunteer at the Jeu de Paume for several years prior to the war; but after the Nazis' occupation of Paris, she was asked by her former supervisor and mentor, Jacques Jaujard, to take on the added responsibility of overseeing the daily operations. Nearly all other museum staff had been dismissed by the Gestapo so that their dubious actions could not be observed. From the Jeu de Paume, the stolen art was transported mostly by train to the homes of Hitler, Goering, and other Nazi officials, as well as to German museums and to massive underground and rural hiding places. The dual attraction for the Nazi selection of the Jeu de Paume was its atypically low profile in that the museum and its sole employee, Mademoiselle Valland, were both unpretentious.

The Germans viewed Rose as a bland, methodical, minor functionary who was occupied with simple tasks like maintenance and inventory. Therefore, they assumed she would not concern herself with attempting to pierce the veil of secrecy over their deceitful operations. They saw her akin to a custodian, someone who would be sufficiently compliant to obediently perform whatever was demanded of her without any further curiosity or resistance. After all, she held no title or paid position. Among the many of Rose's attributes they didn't suspect, was that she had a fine grasp of both art history and the German language. Her memory for details was exceptional, as was her dedication to the culture of her homeland, a dedication sufficient enough to risk her life to preserve it. Rose assumed the role of the demure house mouse who closely observed the stray alley cats.

The Nazis – acting on an executive order from the chancellor of Germany, Adolf Hitler – set up a repository in the Jeu de Paume for nearly twenty thousand looted art objects. Hitler, himself a failed painter who was turned down by the academy in Vienna as a young man, arrogantly sought to facilitate the seizure of nearly all European cultural treasures. He particularly coveted those pieces owned by the Jews whom he'd come to spitefully hate, mindlessly blaming them for Germany's failures. Hitler intended to supplement his private collection – he fancied himself the supreme arbiter in determining worthy art – and to transform his provincial and industrial hometown of Linz, Austria, into the art capital of the world. To facilitate this, he established a special task force, which operated as the ERR (Einsatzstab Reichsleiter Rosenberg) *Special Task Force* under the protection of the Gestapo. The Jeu de Paume soon became the ERR's European headquarters, even though Alfred Rosenberg (the third R in ERR) only rarely came to visit the museum (he was eventually tried at Nuremberg for his crimes, found guilty, and hanged.)

The Nazis first retained Rose for mundane tasks like watering the plants, eventually assigning her to more substantial ones like cataloguing art objects. As she quietly worked, she eavesdropped on the Germans and made secret lists of the more substantial plundered treasures in a diary-like book hidden at her home (not unlike Irena Sendler's lists and jars in an associated story). As much as possible, she tracked the destinations and manifests relating to the art shipments. The Nazis – as was the German nature – had meticulously identified and recorded Europe's artwork even before the start of hostilities. Maintaining this approach after their occupation, the Nazis photographed every object they stole. Rose secretly borrowed their documentation in order to produce photographic or hand-written duplicates at night, in her home, before replacing the originals the morning.

With America's entry into the war, the Nazis began to panic and their plundering accelerated. In turn, Rose applied herself more diligently, now listing nearly all of the thousands of pieces of art forwarded to and through the Jeu de Paume. The related details of the shipments were communicated to the French Resistance movement, to which she belonged. By doing this, she was able to have the artwork immediately spared from accidental Allied bombing or sabotage, and thus hopefully available for recovery and restitution later. Often, Rose made deliberate, dumb *mistakes* in an effort to both delay the processing and to maintain an air of calculated personal ineptitude, whenever it served as a profitable strategy.

On one occasion, in May of 1941, Rose *the mouse* observed Reichsmarschall Hermann Goering when he arrived to personally select some of the more priceless paintings for his massive private collection, a habit of many lesser Nazis officials as well. Second in command only to Hitler, Goering was an extraordinarily vain, brutal, and greedy man. Goering's personal art collection contained seventeen thousand confiscated items, making it larger than the holdings of many public museums then and now.

During her long tenure, Rose occasionally lost the confidence of one of the many Nazis passing through her museum. Even when not under immediate suspicion, she was habitually followed by Gestapo agents. Four separate times someone specifically became skeptical and accused her of suspicious activity. Each time, she was dismissed, only to again find a way to ingratiate herself and be recalled for further duty. The Nazis were stretched thin and had few available proficient art technicians. The potential consequence during any of these moments of wariness could just as easily have been death, rather than dismissal. That Rose had no close family or friends worked in her favor, since there was little beyond firing or killing her that the Nazis were able to threaten or do.

The final months of the war were the most risky for her. When the Germans realized they were losing the conflict, witnesses to their actions were regularly eliminated without hesitation or regret. As an Allied victory became more apparent, Hitler despaired and issued his infamous Nero Decree, which instructed his architect, Albert Speer, to destroy German landmarks and the stolen European artwork. Speer disagreed with the order and mitigated its execution as much as he could, but many art treasures were still lost. There was an accompanying minor order also issued, but fortunately never enacted, which instructed that Rose be subjected to "deportation [to a death camp] and execution upon arrival."

The Nazis, meanwhile, had grown anxious to evacuate the museum and fully ship out its remaining precious cargo. Rose reacted by undertaking even more dramatic and desperate efforts in her desire to thwart the thefts. An art train bound for Germany, and hastily loaded with many boxcars crammed to capacity with paintings and other valuables, never made it out of Paris – thanks to Rose. She forwarded her accurate and detailed information to the French Resistance. The underground partisans then sabotaged the train sufficiently to stall it on the tracks. It remained immobile during the several days that were necessary for the Allies to liberate Paris and the surrounding countryside.

Rose described the noble effort to save the art train in her personal memoirs, *Le Front de L'Art: Défense Des Collections Françaises 1939–1945*. These inspired a 1964 movie based on the real events relating to the art train. The film is titled simply *The Train*. When the hero, played by Burt Lancaster, begins feeling desperate about the paltry means available for stopping the train and preventing it from a return to Germany, he asks in frustration, "What do they expect us to do, stop the train with our bare hands?" Factually, it was stopped by a young French lieutenant and six volunteers who used explosives to destroy the tracks. In a life-is-stranger-than-fiction circumstance, that lieutenant was Alexandre Rosenberg. Among the stolen items found on the train were paintings belonging to his father, Paul Rosenberg, a prominent Paris art dealer and of no known relation to the Rosenberg who headed the ERR. Not all of the art was evacuated by rail. In their last-moment rush, the Germans forced the French truckers' union to supply 150 men, and then coerced the few Jews not yet sent to the death camps to provide the labor; thus, the Jews unwillingly helped steal their own artwork, furniture, valuables, and collectibles.

Surviving those final days under her Nazi overlords didn't place Rose above risk because most of the local Paris population, as well as some Allied personnel, viewed her as a German collaborator rather than as a heroic spy who risked her life for the benefit of future generations. As the war closed, collaborators frequently faced ostracism, property seizure, prison, beating, and death at the hands of fellow citizens. On the day of liberation, Rose had to protect the remaining contents of her museum even from her fellow Parisians, some of whom stormed the entrances, apparently intent on looting it while bearing arms and threatening violence.

After the war, Rose continued to cooperate with her government, as well as with the Allies' American-based specialized artistic works division, titled the Monuments, Fine Arts, and Archives (MFA&A) – also known more famously as *The Monuments Men* or *The Venus Fixers*. It remained necessary to sift through the bombed ruins of Europe for the many cherished art treasures hidden by the Nazi thieves and scattered throughout Germany and the other Reich nations in caves, mines, and castles (most notably the remote and awesome Neuschwanstein Castle of Bavaria's Mad King Ludwig). The Allies gradually uncovered one thousand repositories just in southern Germany. Further complicating the effective recovery and restitution work based on Rose's records was the fact that Nazi personnel often stole the Fuhrer's confiscated artwork; in other words, some of the art was twice-stolen and secreted to unrecorded, personal hiding places.

Eventually, Rose received the position she so long desired and had worked so selflessly to earn. She was appointed a conservator of the French Musées Nationaux, and in 1954 was named Chef du Service de protection des oeuvres d'art. Rose retired in 1968, but continued to work on restitution matters for the French archives. Her valor and devout service resulted in many lifetime awards from her homeland, as well as from other countries. The French government honored her with the Légion d'honneur, Commandeur of the Order of Arts and Letters, and Médaille de la Résistance. In 1948, she was recognized by the United States, and in the 1950s, was even celebrated by her former foe, then formally called the Federal Republic of Germany or informally simply West German. This was an unusually high recognition for a woman in a time before full emancipation and equal rights.

Despite her career successes and governmental decorations, Rose remained generally unknown in her lifetime and thereafter. This was mostly due to the period in which she lived; it was a time dominated by men, and further, a time when someone from a small, rural village without family name or wealth was unlikely to be granted much merit, favor, or attention. Rose was even disliked by the general French population, who were prickly about her sharing the recovery information with the famous American task force. Many were also displeased with her continued dogged personal pursuit of the recovery. Most of the population wanted to put far behind them their unpleasant war memories, with so many of them riddled with guilt and collaboration from having supported the Nazis through their puppet Vichy government and, often further, having committed anti-Semitic activities.

Rose spent the remainder of her post-retirement life diligently recovering and preserving cultural properties. She died in 1980; almost no one attended her funeral. This was the collective consequence of ill-placed and undeserved envy, indifference, and hostility. It took until 2005 for her own museum, the Jeu de Paume – the one she selflessly served and saved – to mount a pathetically small memorial plaque on one wall. The American Monuments Men felt entirely different toward Rose, however, and they freely credited her contributions as so much greater than only preserving and restoring just one museum.

At the conclusion of her career, Rose had established a résumé that came to include the following roles and positions: graduate student of École nationale des beaux-arts de Lyon, art historian, member of the Resistance, art recovery expert, captain in the French military, museum curator, published author, representation in two major Hollywood films (although one with a change of her name to Villand), and likely the most decorated woman in French history. Even if private and unheralded, hers was a very accomplished final act for one who had labored gratis so long as a volunteer worker. In the end, it wasn't degrees from famous academies, rich or noble ancestries, enviable political connections, general popularity or name recognition, or well-placed bribes that brought Rose to the pinnacle of the French art world. It was simply the demonstration of her commitment to art through tireless and unselfish deeds of dedication.

Rose's part of the story, as key as it was, has concluded. The larger story has not. It continues today with one-hundred thousand stolen World War II era art objects still either missing or unknowingly in the wrong hands. Many of these are comparatively modest items, such as silverware, books, and precious stones or metals, but some are famous paintings and sculptures. On occasion, a well-known and valuable piece of art will be identified in a public or private collection or auction. When this occurs, formal negotiations are set in motion to attempt righting a seventy-year-old wrong. Even the best intentions to return misplaced art become exceptionally difficult, however, because so many hundreds of thousands of the original owners were murdered in the German death camps. Once such story about Gustav Klimt's stolen 1907 *Portrait of Adele Bloch-Bauer* (called the Austrian Mona

Lisa) is chronicled in Anne-Marie O'Connor's magnificent non-fiction book, *The Lady in Gold* (the related film is titled *The Woman in Gold*). On other occasions, art is still discovered in a cave, a castle, or a mine. An enormous cache, engineered by and for Hitler, was found hidden seven hundred feet underground in an Altaussee, Austria, salt mine. Sometimes paintings are found deliberately obscured beneath other framed paintings of lesser interest, or in a long-neglected basement or attic.

Other masterpieces will, sadly, never be found because some of the art forwarded to the Paris-based central collecting point was deemed unworthy (many of the modern works) or degenerate (especially the Jewish works) by the Deutschland-uber-alles, fanatical and unsophisticated German minions. These pieces – mostly oil and water paintings – were first unceremoniously slashed, and then burned, in the courtyard of Rose's museum while she secretly watched unable to salvage them. As documented by Rose, some of the destroyed paintings included precious works by the modern masters Klee, Monet, Renoir, Picasso, and Miro. Other geographically dispersed storage points of looted art were spitefully ordered destroyed by the German high command when they sensed the war was lost; a few collections were ably saved, but others were destroyed. Reichsfuhrer Heinrich Himmler, head of the Gestapo and the Waffen-SS, burned his substantial personal collection of stolen art prior to his arrest and subsequent suicide.

Most likely, Rose never fully suspected the potential magnificence of the humble, instrumental volunteer role she had readily accepted – a role seemingly no greater than that of a janitor, or worse, appearing to be a collaborator serving the wanton desires of an evil Nazi overlord. Rose willingly chose to suffer the life-threatening risks of her unofficial position as spy for the Resistance, as well as the humiliation of her official position, which was essentially that of a slave to a malevolent master, all while her good deeds were potentially mistaken for Nazi sycophancy by her countrymen. Setting these rejections and unpleasantries aside, Rose had to, and did, focus on the distant vision of the far greater and final good, which was the preservation of three millennia of European culture.

Life is full of little steps that, when consistently well executed, lead slowly and unsuspectingly to great endings. Rose remained faithful in the small, early requirements of the opportunity set before her. This faithfulness led steadily and surely, just as scripturally promised, to a position where she could show her faithfulness in the larger opportunities, not unlike the lives of Joseph and Daniel of an earlier biblical time and example. She was not motivated by any immediate personal reward, and yet significant public acclaim – as well as private reward – invariably accompanied the successful conclusion of her altruism. Like so many other quiet heroes, her reputation has grown since her death and exceeds that which existed in her lifetime.

Rose accepted the work of an unpaid volunteer. The cost of doing so was especially high under the Nazi regime as measured in terms of personal risk, belittlement, and sleepless nights. In performing pro bono work, ones such as Rose demonstrate commitment, gain relevant field experience, make contacts and develop relationships, have the opportunity to do what they love, build résumés, provide community service, display their aptitudes in a practical environment, fine-tune their skills, and become well positioned for hiring or career advancement. Any one of these is beneficial; collectively, they can be overwhelmingly advantageous. Rose's example is a useful life lesson for all of us, regardless of our age. She had many natural and artificial hindrances opposing her goal of securing a significant position with a major art museum. Largely, however, through the opening she created by accepting long years of diligent service as a volunteer, she finished well. It's not the sum of frustrations, oppositions, and mistakes we have encountered that makes life rewarding; it's the continued striving to finish our given role despite them, and to finish it well. As the apostle Paul said, *I have fought the good fight, I have finished the race, I have kept the faith* (2 Timothy 4:7). Said more simply in a colloquial style: It ain't over till it's over.

And ... he took away everything. (1 Kings 14:26)

Colonel George Washington

Only One Left on Horseback

Therefore I have set My face like a flint, (Isaiah 50:7)

The patriotic deeds of a mature George Washington, the Revolutionary War general and first American president, are well known and documented, leaving little need for further examination. There's also a small canon of familiar stories about George Washington as an adolescent. One example is when he is alleged to have chopped down his father's cherry tree. When asked about the incident, the child replied: "I cannot tell a lie. I did it with my little hatchet." The promotion of this story is attributed to Mason Parson Weems. Its place in popular culture was initiated in 1800 by its inclusion in his book *The Life of Washington*. Even though this story has endured for generations and has the appearance of truth, it is actually folklore. Even so, it's morally instructive and is intended to portray Washington's constructive character – a goal it does accomplish. It tells us that how we respond to adversity in our youth often determines the nature of our character as adults. This was clearly true in Washington's life.

There is another story about Washington as a young man that leaves the impression of fiction, yet has been substantiated as fact. This true story transpired during the time of the Seven Years War (1756–1763), known in America as the French and Indian War. At this time there was no "official"

United States. What later became the States were then British colonies located in a small portion of the North American continent, where all colonists were born British subjects, not American citizens. The colonies numbered only thirteen and were clustered along the Atlantic Coast from south of British Canada to north of Spanish Florida.

West of the Allegheny Mountains to the Mississippi River was a vast interior, loosely occupied by France, called simply the Ohio Valley Country, which became known after our independence as the Northwest Territories, with Vincennes, Indiana, as its capital. England (aka the British Empire) and France were the superpowers of the time, and they were in competition to establish firm and, hopefully, final control of the Valley. To facilitate their position, the French aligned themselves with several indigenous Native American tribes, as the British already had a natural alignment with their colonies.

Washington was twenty-two, the age of a typical college senior today, but he already held the position of lieutenant colonel in the Virginia militia. The British Crown had just appointed General Edward Braddock to the colonies as its supreme military and civil authority. Upon hearing this, a self-assured but inexperienced Washington approached Braddock with an offer to join his forces against the French presence at Fort Duquesne (east of present-day Pittsburgh, Pennsylvania). The offer was accepted, Washington advanced to the rank of full colonel, a wagoner by the name of Daniel Boone was hired to assist, and together the crusade was launched against the French-held fort in an ambitious surprise attack.

Washington was familiar with the country around the fort due to his time as a surveyor for his mentor, Lord Thomas Fairfax, who had considerable landholdings in the area. Additionally, this was not the first time Washington was to fight the French in the hotly disputed area known as the Monongahela River valley. At age twenty, in the opening weeks of the war, he'd led and lost an earlier battle for control of the valley at Fort Necessity, located a short distance from Fort Duquesne (near modern Washington, Pennsylvania). Washington hoped that, under Braddock's experienced battle leadership, this would be his chance for redemption and reputation.

To reach the fort required a journey through thickly forested mountain terrain, some of it traversing risky valleys, where the men were exposed on the narrow paths or could be trapped without escape routes. Braddock's solution was organizing an expedition of overwhelming size in terms of munitions, supplies, and men. Subsequently, it plodded along, marking little distance daily as the way through the forest required cutting a time-consuming access of sufficient size for the entourage.

Reacting to the frustrating circumstances, Washington convinced Braddock to form a smaller fighting unit with which to make a more rapid attack in advance of the remaining support. A group of less than two thousand men was assembled for this purpose. But their plan was easily discovered by the defenders. The French immediately prepared a surprise attack of their own, placing their mix of troops and tribes in a favorable offensive position. With a force only half the size of the British force, they waited to ambush them in a narrow gorge, having assumed the high positions along the protected forest ridges. July 9, 1755, was the date of what came to be known as the Battle of Monongahela.

What transpired during the two hours following General Braddock's arrival at the gorge is more accurately labeled a *massacre* rather than a *battle*. The English troops were quickly reduced to less than a third due to the injuries and deaths inflicted by well-protected and hidden French and Indian forces. With one exception, every officer and every person on horseback, was wounded or killed. Braddock suffered a mortal shot mid-battle and died on the return route. The French forces were only mildly diminished. The favorable French and Indian position was one factor behind the disparity; the other was the British military's own formal battle tactics. They stood upright, as trained for European fighting in open formation, and, if on horseback, they remained mounted, thereby providing easy targets. (The British manner of fighting was noted by Washington, who would later use it to his advantage against the anti-revolutionary English forces.)

Colonel Washington's responsibility as aide-de-camp to Braddock required him to ride, unprotected, from point to point across the battlefield, delivering the general's orders. Singularly remaining alive on horseback, Washington's responsibility defaulted to organizing the troop disengagement and leading their hasty march back to the safety of the larger British force and then on to Fort Cumberland, Maryland.

Word spread quickly that Washington was among the dead. He promptly wrote letters to his brother and mother assuring them he was alive and testifying to his battle experience. He reported that when he examined himself afterward he was completely unharmed, but that he found four musket ball holes through his coat and more in his hat. He also reported combing lead fragments out of his hair. Somehow they had damaged and penetrated his clothing while not touching his body. He indicated that two horses were shot from under him during the fighting, but that he rode out mounted on a third. He wrote: "Death was leveling my companions on every side of me!" Colonel Washington attributed his preservation to the protective hand of a providential God. Shortly thereafter, what transpired became the subject of popular revival preaching and Sunday sermons. Everyone concluded that God had a special purpose in keeping young Washington alive. Soon, the story of the massacre at Monongahela (aka the Battle of the Wilderness) found its way into American history books, where it remained for over a century.

In 1770, fifteen years after Monongahela, Washington expressed a desire to revisit the Pennsylvania battleground. This had been the location of two of Washington's most painful experiences, and his memories of them were still disturbing. He sought closure. Washington arranged for his lifelong friend, Dr. James Craik, to accompany him back to the valley. After the men arrived, they were met by a group of Indians accompanying a great revered chief. The chief had heard about their visit and expressed a desire to meet privately with Washington. Once the time and place were determined, Washington inquired as to why the chief wanted to meet with his former enemy. The chief was old and frail, and the men wondered what special reason had motivated him to travel such a great distance to see Washington. Through an interpreter, the chief told the men that before his life ended, he felt compelled to meet the man whom God would not let die in battle.

Over a council fire, the chief shared his personal perspective on the battle, one that Washington did not fully know. The chief had singled out the tall, mounted colonial officer and instructed his men to take special aim at him. (Washington was well over six feet in height – substantially taller than most of his contemporaries.) With Washington as the only man still on horseback, the objective should have been easy to accomplish, yet the chief's men repeatedly failed to bring down their special target. The chief then raised his own musket, but after a dozen carefully sighted shots, he determined further effort was useless. He instructed his men to save their ammunition and direct their efforts elsewhere. The chief said that he and his men were well trained and experts in the use of muskets in battle, and that, save for Washington, they could hardly miss from their advantageous position. He realized the Great Spirit was protecting this young officer and that He had a special purpose in preserving his life.

Then the chief shared that he had come not only to meet the man whom God had so wondrously preserved, but also to prophesy over him. The old man said that Washington would soon fight and win a mighty war in order to found a great nation, of which he would become its chief. Sequentially therein were predictions of three significant events to soon occur in our early history. First, the "mighty war" he was to "fight and win" was the Revolutionary War for American independence led by Supreme Commander Washington. Second, Washington's "founding of a great nation" occurred when the new constitutional republic was organized and birthed postwar by the Constitutional Convention, over which Washington presided as chairman. Third, Washington did "become its chief" when he became our first president, serving two back-to-back terms.

The year 1775 – just five years after the prophetic meeting with the chief in the woods – marked the beginning of America's War for Independence. The war against the powerful British Empire consumed the next eight years and ended in unexpected victory for the fledgling nation called the United States of America. (See the story on Haym Salomon.) It was largely a military conflict, and its primary fighting force, the Continental Army, was led by General Washington, just as had been predicted by the old chief. God protected Washington at Boston, Brooklyn Heights, and the Delaware River, as well as through the battles of Trenton, Princeton, Yorktown, and the many others. After peace with Britain was consummated by the Treaty of Versailles, Washington laid down his considerable power, because he firmly believed that military authority should be subservient to civilian authority. History buffs know that act as "choosing the role of Cincinnatus over that of Caesar." It was a rare, magnanimous statement in the history of mankind, and one that set a precedent for America that we still honor three centuries later.

As the war wound to its end, Washington met with his officers in Newburgh, New York. They were depressed and in near mutiny over unfulfilled pay and pensions from the Continental Congress. As he attempted to read a letter of pacification from a Congressman, he found himself constantly stumbling.

Pulling his reading glasses from his pocket, he placed them on for the first time in front of his men, explaining, "Gentlemen, you will permit me to put on my spectacles, for I have not only grown gray but almost blind in the service of my country." He'd brought the men to tears; they no longer needed to hear the letter.

The time between the war's end until the enactment of the Constitution in 1787 marked a five-year period during which Washington played a vital leadership role as chairman of the Philadelphia Constitutional Convention. The goals were to first author the United States Constitution and then to pilot it through ratification by the states. The Constitution authorized the election or appointment of executive, legislative, and judicial leadership. Washington was asked to serve the country in yet another key capacity, this time as our first chief executive officer, the president. He did so for eight years, fulfilling two consecutive terms of four years.

Thereafter, an overwhelming majority of the country's citizenry favored appointing Washington as the king of America. This position rightly may seem strange to us today. Again, Washington is to be credited for the fact that it seems strange. He laid down his civil authority and power, just as he had earlier laid down his military power, desiring instead the plain, quiet life at his Mount Vernon estate in Virginia. This was the second time he had established a rare, but lasting, precedent and became a selfless example for future generations. Few other men have ever abandoned power, much less when it was so easily in their grasp; most violently cling to it instead, and even demand more. Having abandoned power twice, Washington is likely the only man in history with such a legacy. He simply had this to say regarding his many titles: "I hope I shall possess firmness and virtue enough to maintain what I consider the most enviable of all titles, the character of an honest man."

In *George Washington: The Founding Father*, Paul Johnson writes of the events of Washington's resignation of his command and of England's King George III's personal reaction:

> Having made peace between the civil and military powers
> of the new country – and, in an emotional ceremony, bidden
> farewell to his officers on December 4, 1783, ... in Annapolis,
> Maryland, on December 23, ... he formally handed back

to Congress his commission as commander in chief, which they had given him in June 1775.... He had his horse waiting at the door, and he took the road to Mount Vernon the next day. No one who knew Washington was surprised. Everyone else, in varying degrees, was astonished at this singular failure of the corruption of power to work. And, indeed, it was a rare moment in history. In London, George III questioned the American-born painter Benjamin West [on] what Washington would do now he had won the war. "Oh," said West, "they say he will return to his farm." "If he does that," said the king, "he will be the greatest man in the world."

One historian I read did write that Washington was the greatest American in the history of our country due to who he was and what he accomplished. I have come to agree.

Washington is an example of the citizen-politician who goes to the capital of his state or nation, serves a few terms, and returns to civilian life – just as the Founding Fathers practiced and intended. Sadly, this has been almost completely disregarded by the pervasive career politicians of later generations. The current practice of politicians is to gain elected government positions and then refuse to honor voluntary term limits, thus obtaining lifetime security and prestige, exemption from laws legislated on others, and inappropriate padding of personal income through gifts from lobbyists, benefit increases, and lifetime pensions. Their lifestyles would shock and embarrass a selfless man like George Washington, who served eight years as commander in chief, accepting only expense reimbursements as his compensation. (See the story on Dave Roever for a recent, but similar example). On June 16, 1775, Washington appeared before the Continental Congress for the purpose of being offered the command of the new army. In his own words, he did not feel up to the task: "Mr. President, Tho' I am truly sensible of the high honour done me, in this appointment, yet I feel great distress, from a consciousness that my abilities and military experience may not be equal to the extensive and important trust: However, as the Congress desire it, I will enter upon the momentous duty, and exert every power I possess in their service, and for support of the glorious cause. I beg they will accept my most cordial thanks for this distinguished testimony of their approbation. But, lest some unlucky event should happen, unfavourable to my reputation, I beg it may be remembered, by every gentleman in the room, that I, this day, declare with the utmost sincerity, I do not think myself equal to the command I am honored with. As to pay, sir, I beg leave to assure the Congress, that, as no pecuniary consideration could have tempted me to have accepted this arduous employment, at the expence of my domestic ease and happiness, I do not wish to make any proffit from it. I will keep an exact account of my expences. Those, I doubt not, they will discharge, and that is all I desire." That demonstrates why God's favor rested on him; he could be trusted to be faithful in both the small and the great. Although largely unheeded, he modeled a high standard of public service that remains for us to emulate.

Washington's national contributions and his personal examples clearly demonstrate why God could trust him with so many critical roles. He could be counted on to deny himself and perform what the Lord laid before him. He was preserved in order to see God's plans completed through his life. The special qualities developed in an American crucible have, over the past centuries and especially since the time of Washington, become the template for countries and nationalities all over the globe. His time was unique, and the men surrounding Washington were dedicated to serving the same cause.

Washington was honored by his contemporaries, and he is remembered today by the simple description: "First in war, first in peace, first in the hearts of his countrymen." He was truly the *Father of Our Country* three times over, and thus the *grandfather* of the great men in the following generations and centuries, men like Lincoln and Reagan, who acknowledged they followed in Washington's large, clearly imprinted footsteps.

Today, few have heard this relevant story. However, it hasn't always been the obscure account it's become. This story was once printed in virtually all school textbooks. While at present removed from classrooms, it's had a resurgence in several recently published nonfiction books by respected history researchers and writers. Washington himself often recalled this dramatic event and recognized that it helped shape his character and confirm God's call on his life. I was in elementary school during the 1950s, and as an adult I retained vague recollections of this "bulletproof" Washington episode. In order to confirm it, and to recover forgotten details, I located several dated, out-of-use American history textbooks circa 1930–1940. Sure enough, the story was present and incorporated within the sections outlining the French and Indian War. There's an occasional current recognition of Washington's bulletproof stature. In the February 21, 2015, edition of the *Wall Street Journal*, Editor Jack Schwartz summarized his review of Washington's military career by stating: "And he [Washington] was lucky in battle, appearing almost invincible to the bullets whizzing around him."

If history was still taught with the fullness of these kinds of stories, it would be a far more appealing subject. It would display the whole and comforting truth of a God who holds us in His hands for a purpose greater and larger than the ones the secular humanists permit our children to see in their textbooks filled with revisionist history and outright lies – the ones in which they have censored out God and His wisdom in order to promote the foolishness of man and rationalize false goals. They attempt to control our heritage by what they include, as well as by what they omit.

For additional evidence that this story was once commonly known, primary researcher David Barton of WallBuilders in Aledo, Texas, referenced three dozen historical texts within his own limited, personal collection. The historical sources utilized by Mr. Barton include the personal records of the participants in the battle, details provided by Benjamin Franklin in his autobiography, and the research of prominent historians of earlier periods, some of which were published more than 160 years ago. I know of no man who has done more than Mr. Barton to promote the story of George Washington at the Battle of Monongahela, as well as so much more historical truth regarding America's Christian foundations.

In closing, I want to help ensure this wonderful story comes home in a personal fashion to every reader. George Washington was special to God. God created him to be different from everyone else in order to set before him a unique purpose for his life. God has created each of us to be different from everyone else in order for each of us to serve Him in our unique life purpose, if we choose to walk in obedience. If we don't play our part, it may not get played at all, and others will be negatively affected along with us. We can start on the path with small acts, and as long as we are faithful in the small, God will trust us gradually with the large.

While we're walking faithfully in either the small or large, we may very well find that we are also invincible. This is not an invitation to walk out in front of a semitrailer truck as a test; we should never put God to the test.

We must put God to the *trust* and *He* puts us to the *test*. God's faithfulness does not require testing because it never wavers. It's always available to those who walk in obedience. I am able to recognize with confidence a few times in my career when God provided me with a bulletproof vest. I was sniped at occasionally by direct reports, jealous peers, and overbearing supervisors, any one of whom wanted me vacated from my position for an unsavory purpose. But I had the confidence I was where God wanted me to be, and in remaining there, despite the temporary damage or pain, He faithfully saw me through the circumstances to victory every time. That's a personal example of what I mean when I say we are all bulletproof when we are in God's perfect will.

In the many years of his long military career, which included eight more years during the War for Independence, George Washington was never wounded in battle. Think of it! He spent more than a dozen years in the forefront of battle leadership without ever taking a bullet. *A thousand may fall at your side, and ten thousand at your right hand; But it shall not come near you.* (Psalm 91:7) When we're faithfully fulfilling the purpose God has for our lives, He will protect us and not release our purpose until it is finished. See the rest of the poetic ninety-first psalm for applicable details.

* * * *

Author's Note: My story is not the whole of Washington's amazingly full legacy. As an additional teaser, it also includes the following four substantial activities, and more, that Washington did AFTER completing his third role in my story, that of two-term president: 1) accepting the role of commander-in-chief of the Army a second time when war against France seemed imminent; 2) preparing a plan to emancipate his slaves; 3) facilitating the construction of the federal city at Washington D.C. when current President Adams refused to do so; and 4) founding three premier educational institutions.

And I know that I will not be ashamed. (Isaiah 50:7)

Parable of the Four Farmers

Bloom Where You're Planted

Do not associate with those given to change; (Proverbs 24:21)

An African farmer living in Hopetown, Africa, was hearing tales about others who'd made fortunes after discovering diamonds in Central Africa. These tales so excited the farmer that he could hardly wait to sell his farm and go prospecting for diamonds. Finding diamonds seemed like a way to get rich faster and more easily than did remaining and working his farm. So in 1867, he hurriedly sold the farm and spent the rest of his life wandering the African continent, unsuccessfully searching for the precious gems that were gaining such high prices in the world markets. Finally, worn out and in a fit of despondency, he threw himself into a river and drowned. The man's suicide may sound like the end of the story, but it was really the beginning.

Meanwhile, on one of his many crossings, Daniel Jacobs – the man who purchased the man's farm – noticed a bright flash of light coming from the bottom of the stream. Bending down, he picked up a good-sized stone. Admiring it, he brought it home, and thinking it an attractive curiosity, he placed it on the fireplace mantel.

Months later, a neighboring farmer, Schalk van Niekerk, visited Daniel's home and noticed the stone above the fireplace. Removing it from the mantel, he examined it closely, weighed it in his hands, and became exceptionally excited. He asked Daniel if he knew what he had in his possession. When Daniel replied it was probably just a piece of rock crystal (sometimes called *clear quartz*), his visitor told him that he believed the man possessed a large diamond. The farmer had difficulty believing this could be true since his stream had many such stones – not all as large as the one on the mantel – but nonetheless, they were sprinkled periodically along the bottom. After consulting with experts, however, the *crystal* was confirmed as a diamond of exceptionally large size – one of the largest ever found.

The farm sold by the first man – so he might find diamonds elsewhere – turned out to be one of the richest diamond fields on the African continent. The first farmer had literally owned acres of diamonds, free and clear. Unknowingly, he sold them as part of the farm for an insignificant portion of their value in order to free himself to look for them elsewhere. The vicinity of the farm became the site for several of the world's largest diamond finds, including the Eureka diamond at 21.25 carats and the Star of South Africa diamond at 83.50 carats. If the first farmer had only taken the time to study what diamonds looked like in their natural, unpolished state and had subsequently explored his property before looking elsewhere, he would have realized his fantasies.

Thereafter, the Hopetown area didn't remain a quiet farming community; rather, it became the focus of a worldwide diamond rush. Today, the ruins of the Jacobs house are preserved and exhibited as an African national monument.

Portions of this story have been retold many times since the discoveries on the Jacobs farm. Baptist minister and Temple University founder Russell Conwell (1843–1925) credited hearing its origins from a North African Arab whom he met while traveling in the Middle East. Conwell might have been our country's first motivational speaker, as he claimed to have incorporated portions of the story into speeches given worldwide over six thousand times. He titled his speech "Acres of Diamonds," and he summarized its fundamental message as "dig in your own backyard."

This simple historic tale about a foolish farmer illustrates three valuable personal principles for us today. They are not principles related to actual precious commodities like diamonds (or later gold, oil, and silver), but principles about other precious matters called opportunities, which have equal, or perhaps greater, value than those physical ones.

The first principle is that too often we think we must look somewhere else to find riches, when in fact, we're standing in the middle of our own productive field. Most likely we are not searching for real diamonds, but instead, we seek happiness, success, contentment, and peace. All the while, these valuables are within our grasp. It's the old idea that the grass may look greener on the other side of the fence, but it really isn't. The reality is that we are simply dissatisfied with what we already have, or we haven't thoroughly utilized all of the resources, gifts, opportunities, and blessings we've been given. It's been said that if the other person's yard is greener than ours, it's probably getting better care. And besides, while we're looking at other yards, other people are looking at ours. Before running off to those that only *look* greener, let's be certain that our own is not just as green, or perhaps even greener. Abraham Lincoln once said, "Most folks are as happy as they make up their minds to be." If we had the wisdom and the patience to explore the opportunities surrounding us, we would likely find that most of the riches we seek are already right where we are.

The second principle is that these riches could be slightly hidden, just like the diamonds in this story. Rarely will they be found out in the open and obvious. The truly valuable things in life are not the ones that seem so popular and important right now, like music, sex, cars, sports, parties, motorcycles, video games, gambling, fashion, golf, drinking, hanging out, and texting. Real riches are disguised as parents, teachers, pastors, mentors, counselors, and church leaders. They are also found in our homework, our jobs, our family activities, our volunteer efforts, books, and studies.

The third principle is that it's okay to grow, stretch, try new things, and change locations, but not at the cost of the good things we already have. We are only truly poor when we are dissatisfied with what we have at the moment.

In order to bring these three principles home in a practical manner, let's ask ourselves some warm-up *diamond mining* questions, and then finalize our thinking by completing a simple written exercise. The intent is to help unearth opportunities extant in our life, those that may be overlooked, underutilized, or unappreciated. Thoughtfully consider your *diamonds* – both those acquired and those still sought, and then answer these questions:

- What am I building my life around, spending my resources to acquire?

- Are all of these truly diamonds, or are some really just common rocks?

- Am I doing the best I can right now with the diamonds I've been given?

Now, the associated multistep exercise is as follows: Remember that often what we think is important – a diamond – is really not; it's just a rock. First, in an effort to help discern the difference between the two and eliminate confusion, list on a piece of paper all of your current priorities, opportunities, dreams, goals, resources, and projects. Be as specific as possible and avoid vagaries. Then, after careful evaluation, label each of them either as a *diamond* or as a *rock*. Now create a nonprioritized two-part list by placing the true diamonds at the top and the rocks at the bottom (or you may make side-by-side columns). The next step is to individually write each diamond on the list on a small square of paper – only a single diamond on each piece. Then, one diamond at a time, start throwing them away, beginning with the least meaningful to your life until you have only two or three squares remaining. Finally, and most importantly, heartily pursue the remaining squares (that is, the diamonds), by aligning your activities and resources in accord with the ones that remain on the page.

This will ensure that you are mining the ground already under your feet. We all have acres of diamonds – gifts, people, blessings, possibilities, talents, and helpers – right where we already are. If we don't realize this, it's probably because we either didn't recognize them or we just didn't look very hard for them. Let's go after them, work with them, give them time and attention, hold them, and share them. Working regularly with these diamonds will lead to more true riches throughout our lifetime.

In Wes Davis's *Wall Street Journal* review (April 30, 2009) of Willard Spiegelman's book *Seven Pleasures: Essays on Ordinary Happiness*, he shared the following wise observations about life: "Ordinariness can yield much more pleasure than is normally assumed. All the striving for happiness may cause us to overlook the riches of the familiar and near to us.... You find that the plainest occurrence is surprisingly rich." The idea is to slow down enough to pay attention to what is nearby and to examine the world around us – give extra time and focus to what we see and hear. This thinking substantiates everything shared thus far about the riches right under our feet, right where we are.

Even if it's only partially true, perhaps you think the story about the diamonds is an anomaly; that it's a unique, one-of-a-kind circumstance. It very well appears to be an outlier, so as a reproof, I am offering three more remarkably similar tales about foolish farmers. They all have the same theme, all occur during the same time period, and all yield the same beneficial principles.

In the first of these backup stories, a farmer living in Coloma, in northern California, circa 1847, heard that gold had been discovered in central California, near Sacramento. He became fixated on the opportunity for quick riches – often called *gold fever*. He sold his ranch to a Swiss immigrant by the name of Colonel Johann Sutter. Sutter employed a carpenter, James Marshall, to build a sawmill sluice to carry stream water closer to his crops and cattle. His little daughter started playfully dumping handfuls of dirt into it in order to watch it rush downstream. Marshall noticed that certain shiny lumps were washing out and settling to the bottom. After examining them, he suspected the bright little rocks were actually gold. During an assay, they were confirmed as gold nuggets of the highest quality. This event started the famous California Gold Rush (see the related story about Tommy Thompson in *Exploring Inner Space*), the largest gold discovery in American history, with hundreds of millions of dollars in value just in Coloma alone.

In the next story, a man who lived and worked on his farm in Titusville, Pennsylvania, for twenty-three years became dissatisfied with his agricultural lifestyle. After hearing about oil discoveries in Canada, he recalled that he had a cousin living there. The cousin was in the oil business, so he wrote and requested a job. His cousin wisely advised him to first undertake a formal study of petroleum. The farmer did so with commendable zeal and hard work. He attended well-respected Temple University and learned everything there was to know about oil at that time. As his cousin had promised, he was hired and moved to Canada in 1865, hurriedly selling his farm for a decent sum of about $50,000 in today's value. The new owner of the farm carefully walked his land in an effort to become familiar with its assets and liabilities. While checking a stream that twisted through the property, he noticed his cattle would only drink upstream of a certain point. This was a curiosity. By investigating further, he found scum gathering on the surface downstream, thus discouraging use by the cattle. Even further and closer inspection revealed that the scum was actually oil seeping to the surface. He'd discovered a portion of the richest oil field found to date. It would soon be worth hundreds of millions of dollars as the economy was fast moving from whale oil to petroleum-based products like kerosene, oil, and gasoline.

In the final story, a man from Newbury, Massachusetts, which is just north of Boston, paid his way through nearby renowned technical college MIT (Massachusetts Institute of Technology) with finances gleaned from his small farm. Upon graduating in 1878 with a degree in mining engineering, he remained at the university as a professor of mineralogy. The new job, however, did not satisfy for long. He contacted Superior Copper Mining Company in Wisconsin. The company was interested in his potential, but they could only offer him a modest salary, supplemented by a share in the profits of any new minerals he might discover. He confidently accepted, quit his new professorship, and sold his small rural homestead. However, as far as I know, he never found any significant mineral deposits. What is known is that back on his previous homestead, the new owner – who had no formal training or education in minerals – was diligently caring for and expanding the old farm. Farm implements continue to be manufactured ever larger in a successful effort to increase productivity and profits. So, in keeping with the trend, one of his first purchases was a bigger wheelbarrow.

That area of the country is very rocky. Since the time of the first settlers, rocks cleared from fields and gardens were used to mark property lines, construct houses, and form fencerows. Uniquely, and as a source of local pride, mortar is never used to bond the individual stones. Instead, the stones are carefully selected for size and shape, and then simply stacked together in firm patterns. So when the farmer's new wheelbarrow scraped the sides of the old stone fence's gateway, it was an easy matter to remove some of the rocks to broaden the entrance. In the process, he noticed a somewhat shiny rock, shaped (and sized) much like a football. Yes, it had happened again. The rock was almost pure silver and worth thousands of dollars. This was the accidental beginning of the Chipman Silver Mine. Silver mining in that area continued uninterrupted for almost a century.

At this point, we may be able to justify renaming this story "Four *Foolish*

Farmers." This series of parables was compiled for the benefit of two audiences. One was high school graduating seniors whom I often overheard saying, "I can't wait to leave this boring town; there's nothing for me here." The other group was comprised of inmates at the state prison and residents at the recovery centers who'd often tell me something like, "I can't go back home after my release; there's nothing for me there. I've got to find some newer, greener pasture."

I've made my own mistakes in this area, so I can relate to those farmers, and I can relate to both of those audiences. I've salted lessons derived from my faulty experiences into the parable's creative mix. I identified the three principles listed above only after I'd first traveled several difficult routes to my own enlightenment. I didn't learn any of them the easy way. While working my way through college, I was employed by a locally based, quality manufacturing company. The company was owned a by single and very wealthy family, and it held a great many patents. It had a long and successful history, and today it still remains profitable and respected. I was asked twice to remain in their employ after graduation. I turned them down, thinking that was a job I'd held during college; now, with a diploma, I could do so much better. It took me seven painful years to get back to where I was the day before I left that company.

Some fifteen years later, I found another quality company with a long industry tenure, owned by a single and wealthy family; this time it was engaged in telecommunications. After about five years, the grass began to look greener and I was tempted to move to other, glitzier competitors. This is what many of my coworkers were doing at the time. But I'd learned my lesson with my college employer, and I stayed where I was. At first it was painful, as I received phone calls reporting glowing comments from my associates who had left. After a year or two, however, the reports devolved into complaints; the same dissatisfactions surfaced with the new employers as they'd had with my employer. On the other hand, my satisfactions were rising as a reward for staying the course.

A similar story is told about two men who were both moving independently from Town A to Town B. At some midpoint along the way lived a farmer. The first man asked the farmer what the people were like ahead in B. The farmer responded by asking, "What were they like in A?" The man said that they were unfriendly, mean, and nosy, and that's why he was moving.

The farmer said that, unfortunately, they were just like that in B. The second man arrived at the farm a few minutes later and also asked about the people in B. Again, the farmer queried, "What were they like in A?" The man said they were friendly, good-natured, and helpful, and he was sure going to miss them. The farmer said that, fortunately, they were just like that in B. The moral is that everywhere you go, you're still there, and you bring your satisfactions and dissatisfactions along with you.

During what I call my *turnaround* time – the time when I was repairing my initial employment error – I purchased an interesting inspirational piece for my wife's office. It was a plastic potted flower about eight inches in height. On its base was a small gold plaque stating: "Bloom where you're planted." Those became the words I lived by and which I share with you in conclusion of this story.

For their calamity will rise suddenly, (Proverbs 24:22)

* * * *

Author's Note: Russell Conwell's writings were the primary source for all four foolish farmer stories. They are currently in the public domain.

Dave Roever

You Never Were That Good-Looking

You have tried me and have found nothing; (Psalm 17:3)

All of us have wounds and scars on the inside and outside, but Dave Roever's life is firsthand proof that these don't have to define us or prevent us from fulfilling our destinies. Many former soldiers are recovering from the pain inflicted in distant wars, like Korea and Vietnam, as well as from the recent and continuing wars in the Middle East. If you are a veteran, then this story is especially dedicated to your healing. This will seem like a war story, but it's really a love story.

Dave was the son of a rebellious South Texas biker who became a pastor after marrying a godly young lady. Ironically, Dave's life followed a very similar course to his dad's. The one substantial difference is due to the event that's the fulcrum of his life story. Marriage, military service, fatherhood, education, manhood, Christianity, recovery, and ministry are all vital subjects today, just as they should be, and they all merge compellingly in the telling of Dave's unforgettable chronicle.

When seventeen-year-old high school junior Dave met thirteen-year-old freshman Brenda, it was instant love, and he quickly asked her to marry him. She rewarded his forwardness with a slap in the face, and as a follow-up, he was advised, "If you really love me, then you'll wait." Dave did just that, and in the intervening period, they both remained pure and faithful. Their wedding followed shortly after Brenda's graduation. Dave had been attending Bible college full-time and working at General Dynamics part-time. As a newlywed, he began overemphasizing the earning aspects related to the job rather than diligently continuing to focus most of his attention on his Bible school coursework. His grades dropped accordingly, resulting in the receipt of a draft notice announcing he'd lost qualification for a continuing student deferment. At the time, many young men were being inducted into the military for duty in the long-running conflict in Vietnam, Southeast Asia.

Dave still had the option to apply for a surefire ministerial deferment, but because he felt inclined to actively serve his country, he didn't pursue it. He did elect to avoid the two-year army draft by enlisting in the navy for a four-year commitment. Thus began a series of three challenging, prewar training assignments in which he excelled, finishing each time at the top of his class. The culmination was a position as a Navy SEAL (SEa, Air, Land) wearing the coveted Special Forces black beret. Dave was soon ordered to Vietnam, and faced what he still calls the most difficult and painful experience of his life – saying good-bye to his bride. Considering what Dave faced in the near future, and for many years thereafter, that statement is a powerful avowal.

Once in Asia, he was assigned to the dangerous river patrol working on a PBR, a high-speed, lightweight cruiser with a four-man crew, four .50-caliber machine guns, and two massive turbo-charged engines powering jet pumps instead of propellers. His team replaced one that had just been nearly wiped out after suffering 90 percent casualties. Dave's commanding officer's name was – no joke – Lieutenant Rambo.

Dave says he had three bunkmates during his time overseas in 1969, and they all made fun of him for refusing to be unfaithful to his wife by indulging in drugs and prostitutes. Each man, respectively, gave him a different nickname: Dudley Do-Right, Preacher Man, and Dr. Dolittle. In turn, he came up with nicknames for each of them: Pervert Number One, Pervert Number Two, and Pervert Number Three! Because Dave continued to excel in his responsibilities, he was soon in command over the three men in an odd payback situation. Not long thereafter, Dave and Pervert Number One, Mickey Block, would assume each other to be dead after they were viciously maimed in separate combat situations. (Both recovered to eventually become best of friends and join hands in worldwide ministry.)

In a chilling scenario that could have been lifted from *Apocalypse Now,* Dave's crew was upriver on a mission to disengage enemies who had fortified themselves along the jungle-covered banks. From this secure position, those communist commandos had attacked a patrol the day before. Standing on the bow of his PBR and next to the foremost machine gun, Dave raised his right hand to the same side of his head in order to lob a white phosphorous grenade. (These are used like napalm to burn away vegetation and expose enemy troops, armor, tripwires, and traps.) At that exact time, the grenade detonated, likely due to being hit by a sniper's bullet fired from shore.

Instantly, Dave suffered extreme physical damage to the right side of his face and the top of his head, including his ear, eye, teeth, jaw, and lips. He also lost portions of his fingers and thumb. The front of his chest was ripped open down to the bones, exposing internal organs. Because phosphorous burns slowly until it's fully consumed, and cannot be extinguished even under water, his body continued to smolder until his flesh simply melted off and floated away. He lost sixty pounds of body weight in a few terrifying moments. Dave knew he wasn't dead because he could literally see his heart beating. There's much more to this painful ordeal, but this is enough to convey the horror of Dave's experience.

Somehow he made it over to the muddy bank, where he was placed on a stretcher by evacuation helicopter medics. As Dave tells it now with some humor, his burning body ignited the canvas and he landed headfirst on the ground. After being wrapped in wet blankets, he was placed on the chopper. In flight, the medics assumed he was dead and one of them was in the process of completing the death tag and affixing it to Dave's toe, when Dave finally was able to utter one word: "Medic!" The pilot was so shocked he lost control, and as they were falling from the sky, Dave again humorously reports he feared they'd crash and he'd be the only survivor. The pilot recovered and all aboard made it safely to the base.

Once back, Dave's painful survival experience turned into an extensive recovery period. He changed hospitals and geographic locations a number of times over the weeks before finally being transported stateside to Brooke Army Medical Center at Fort Sam Houston in San Antonio, Texas. It was there he was scheduled to see his young wife for the first time since their separation and, more importantly, for the first time since his injuries. Dave had already had several post-trauma experiences that caused him to be anxious about meeting Brenda. Earlier, he'd requested a mirror, and in it he saw the reflection of a monster where a man had once been. One side of his face was missing down to the bone; the other side was swollen to double its normal size.

He shared a hospital ward with twelve other burn victims; but Dave was the only one of them who left the ward alive. He'd witnessed a depressing situation when the wife of the patient next to him arrived for her first visit. She took one brief look at her husband, who was burned over his entire body due to a gasoline fire during a helicopter crash, and she said, "You're embarrassing. I can't be seen with you." She then removed her wedding ring, placed it on the bed between his legs, and walked out. The man died within hours of his painful wounds compounded by a broken heart. What, Dave wondered, would Brenda's reaction be to the shocking, bloody pulp of a husband she was about to see?

Here's the report in his own words (from his book, *Welcome Home Davey*): "My wife, Brenda, still a teenager, walked into my room, a girl I had respected while we dated. She was a virgin when I married her and so was I. Our relationship was built on respect, not in the backseat of a car. Two kids who had waited for each other because they respected and honored God and themselves. Now, that respect would come back, not to haunt me, but to help me. The day Brenda stepped into that room it was truth or consequences. She walked up and read the chart on my bed to confirm I was her husband. She read the tag on my arm to be certain the right man was in the right bed. Then, convinced it was me, she bent down, kissed my face, looked me in my good eye, and said, 'I want you to know that I love you. Welcome home, Davey.'" When Dave protested that he was sorry he couldn't look good for Brenda ever again, her response was, "You never were that good-looking anyway." This was not a cruel insult, but rather a coded affirmation that she loved Dave for who he was, not for what he had.

The following year was a blur of frequent, pain-filled surgeries, many of them centered on repairing his damaged face and replacing missing skin. Dave calls that time "my slow year of crucifixion." Upon finally leaving the military hospital, a new struggle became apparent. In the burn ward, Dave says, "Everyone is a freak, so no one is a freak"; but once outside, things were immediately different. Not only did Brenda and Dave need to adjust to his new appearance and limitations, but so did everyone else. Shock, curiosity, and cruelty were typical reactions – not unlike what had been bestowed on Joseph Merrick, the Elephant Man. Dave's new identity became an overwhelming issue. He would hear himself described as *it,* not *him* or *he*; there's no humanity in the pronoun *it.*

Perhaps the one who had the greatest challenge accepting Dave was Dave himself. One of the first lessons he had to learn was to receive unconditional love. This gift was faithfully administered by Brenda. It's a difficult challenge for all of humanity to accept without reservation that which is freely given, cannot be earned, and is undeserved. This is one reason that God's gift of salvation is so misunderstood and frequently rejected. Because Dave had earlier learned this lesson in his spiritual life, he was eventually able to apply it in his marriage relationship. It really is true that it can be more difficult to receive than to give, especially when you are helplessly unable to reciprocate. Accepting the care of others with simple gratitude displays a rare kind of dignity – a kind that usually is not naturally present and has to be deliberately acquired.

Dave found his way out of the medical centers and back to his former life, first through Brenda and then through a series of guest-preaching opportunities in a few small churches. As these grew in frequency, so did his confidence. For about a year, he'd received monthly disability payments. Dave decided he no longer wanted to be dependent on the government and to continue living like a victim, not earning his own way in life. Subsequently, he dialed the regional Social Security office and requested the checks be discontinued. The office informed Dave that he qualified for full lifetime income. In faith, Dave stated he didn't want to "live off the government dole" and he didn't want to think of himself as disabled. Following the instructions he received, he submitted his request in writing, and his support checks ceased coming. With this act, he proved to himself that he'd successfully found his way through all the potential entrapments available within the false roles of wounded soldier, burn victim, disfigured beast, self-pitying survivor, and lastly, lifetime disability recipient. Dave accepted his position as simply a man. While he was still in Vietnam, Dave's wife and parents had erroneously received a letter informing them of his death; his buddies back at the barracks had divided up the spoils of his possessions as per the traditional, unwritten military code. But now, with this act, Dave was fully and wholly back from the dead.

With only one ear, one eye, one thumb, and one good finger on his right hand, and with more reconstruction operations still required, Dave went out looking for the job he didn't have and the regular paychecks he desperately needed, as Brenda was well along the way in the first of their two miracle pregnancies – pregnancies the doctors had told Dave he was incapable of effecting. Afflicted with multiple serious physical handicaps – not unlike Joseph Merrick, his prospects for successfully finding a job were thin. The initial offer finally came in the form of office manager at a concrete company where his brother was employed. He gratefully accepted the position, but Dave would not stay long at that business.

He began to feel that, of all places, he was to return to Vietnam in the midst of a still "hot" war against his country and its ally, South Vietnam. Dave again visited that land, but this time with a Bible, armed with John 3:16; not like his first visit when he carried an M16 rifle and wore a black beret (he now wore a wig). He spoke a little of the native language, mostly words related to war; now he was learning words relating to peace and liberty. Dave was well received by the local population, as was the message of eternal hope he shared. Therefore, he repeatedly returned to Vietnam over the next year, right up until Saigon was overrun by the North Vietnamese Communists. Dave barely made it out of the country, miraculously catching a seat on the last flight out. As his plane taxied down the runway, the pilot was forced to evade enemy machine-gun fire directed at the plane.

Once safely back in the States, Dave became acutely aware of the way the nation had largely, and sometimes even aggressively, turned its back on the veterans of the war in Vietnam. It was widely reported, although untrue, that America was losing the military aspects of the war. What was true was that we were on the verge of a decisive win when America lost sufficient internal political support due to an adversarial press and weary population, and thus pursued its war on ever-thinning credibility. While Dave had personally heard the words *welcome home* from his loving wife, too many others were coming back to silence, rejection, loneliness, and shame. Many soldiers reacted by losing themselves in alcohol and drugs. Dave now began to focus on an outreach to help repair this situation by applying what he had learned firsthand. This led to the establishment of the Roever Evangelistic Association, which involves Dave's wife, Brenda, as business manager.

Due to extensive national and international travel demands, the Roevers became home-education parents, and their children, Matt and Kimberly, accompanied them nearly everywhere. In this role, the family came to understand the needs of school-age youth, and Dave has since spoken to millions of public high school students. The audiences for Dave's motivational speaking grew to also include veterans and active military, especially the physically wounded and emotionally traumatized warriors. He expanded his topics to include subjects of broader interest to these men, subjects like marriage and family, drug prevention, and manhood. He's shared in countless locations while never charging for his appearances. I've met him and enjoyed his presentations numerous times. He is the *real thing*. As of this writing, Dave is still very much alive and his story is ongoing.

The Roever Evangelistic Association website states:

> Because of his war-time experience of service, injury and recovery, Dave is uniquely qualified to speak to the needs of military personnel. In every setting, Dave's message is one of hope. Using his life as an example, he addresses issues relevant to his audience and presents concrete solutions to life's problems. Often drawing upon his war experiences of loneliness, peer pressure, disfigurement and pain, as well as triumphs, Dave weaves a message of courage, commitment, and survival that touches and transforms those who hear him. The foundation of his hope is his faith. (*roeverfoundation.org/ meet_dave_roever.php*)

As a gifted communicator, he's often found in a variety of settings including public schools, military bases, business and para-church conventions, television and radio studios, youth assemblies, or at his organization's Eagles Summit ranches in Colorado and Texas. No matter where Dave is, he's always certain to share a caution about not becoming conformed to culture; just because everyone else is doing it doesn't make it right or even a good choice. What's acceptable to a culture changes with time and with location; what is true does not. The truth is able to withstand the foibles and fads of today's atmosphere of popularity. He advises not looking to peers as a source on what is the right thing to do; instead, find some wise, mature counselors. For example, peers will say that saving yourself from immorality and honoring the other sex is square, out of date, or denying yourself some "feel good" fun. Respecting yourself and others is none of those things. Dave and Brenda are living proof of the benefits gained from making a choice to stay chaste and remain faithful. It's the thing to do now, and it will pay dividends when you need it later. We should all learn from Dave and not listen to our Pervert Number One, Two, and Three.

Sadly, it took the army thirty-four years (until 2004) to award Dave his several earned medals, including the Purple Heart. This took place roughly at the same time that he received an honorary doctorate degree for his lifelong contributions. Dave had victoriously grasped his life mission well in advance of any belated recognition provided by these government and scholastic awards and titles. There's really no final ending to Dave's story as of yet, but here's a chosen conclusion using his own words, as he imitates an imaginary freak-show barker: "Come one, come all! See the Human Torch who burns so brightly that the night is turned into day; a man who is ever aflame and yet is not consumed! See the living miracle who is dead yet alive, whose death is his life. But stand back when he appears. Stand back, ladies and gentlemen, for he longs that that same fire may burn in your own souls" – as it burned in his body!

> *Concerning the works of men, By the word of Your lips, I have kept away from the paths of the destroyer.* (Psalm 17:4)

* * * *

Author's Note: My wife and I visited the National Navy UDT-SEAL Museum on North Hutchinson Island in Fort Pierce, Florida, some years after I began telling Dave's story. An impressive memorial statue just to the east side of the main entrance contained inscriptions bearing the SEAL Code and Ethos. We were motivated to photograph, transcribe, and share them as an inspiring addition to the written version of Dave's story.

The United States Navy SEAL Code

• Loyalty to country, team, and teammate • Serve with honor and integrity on and off the battlefield • Ready to lead, ready to follow, never quit • Take responsibility for your actions and the actions of your teammates • Excel as warriors through discipline and innovation • Train for war, fight to win, defeat our nation's enemies • Earn your Trident every day

The United States SEAL Ethos

"In times of war or uncertainty there is a special breed of warrior ready to answer our Nation's call; a common man with uncommon desire to succeed. Forged by adversity, he stands alongside America's finest special operations forces to serve his country, the American people, and to protect their way of life. I am that man.

My Trident is a symbol of honor and heritage. Bestowed upon me by the heroes that have gone before, it embodies the trust of those whom I have sworn to protect. By wearing the Trident, I accept the responsibility of my chosen profession and way of life. It is a privilege that I must earn every day. My loyalty to Country and Team is beyond reproach. I humbly serve as a guardian to my fellow Americans, always ready to defend those who are unable to defend themselves. I do not advertise the nature of my work, nor seek recognition for my actions. I voluntarily accept the inherent hazards of my profession, placing the welfare and security of others before my own. I serve with honor on and off the battlefield. The ability to control my emotions and my actions, regardless of circumstance, sets me apart from other men. Uncompromising integrity is my standard. My character and honor are steadfast. My word is my bond.

We expect to lead and be led. In the absence of orders I will take charge, lead my teammates, and accomplish the mission. I lead by example in all situations. I will never quit. I persevere and thrive on adversity. My Nation expects me to be physically harder and mentally stronger than my enemies. If knocked down, I will get back up, every time. I will draw on every remaining ounce of strength to protect my teammates and to accomplish our mission. I am never out of the fight.

We demand discipline. We expect innovation. The lives of my teammates and the success of our mission depend on me – my technical skill, tactical proficiency, and attention to detail. My training is never complete. We train for war and fight to win. I stand ready to bring the full spectrum of combat power to bear in order to achieve my mission and the goals established by my country. The execution of my duties will be swift and violent when required, yet guided by the very principles I serve to defend. Brave men have fought and died building the proud tradition and feared reputation that I am bound to uphold. In the worst of conditions, the legacy of my teammates steadies my resolve and silently guides my every deed. I will not fail."

Parable of Instruction

Still My Favorite Teacher

Let not many of you become teachers, (James 3:1)

Mrs. Clark stood in front of her fifth grade class on the first day of a new fall term and told the students a lie. Like most teachers, she'd addressed the children during school orientation and had said she loved them all the same. At the time that she said it, she meant it; she thought she was that kind of teacher. However, slumped in the back row was a skinny boy named Johnny who was just plain difficult to like. He was soon going to unwittingly expose her inadvertent hypocrisy.

Mrs. Clark began to notice that Johnny didn't play well with the other children, his clothes were messy, and he always needed a bath and a hair washing. Communicating with him was difficult because he only spoke when spoken to, and then only responded in monosyllables like "yup," "nope," and most often a noncommittal "maybe." On the good side, his silent demeanor and standoffishness meant he was never a disruption; he didn't require admonishment for fighting and bullying, or need to be sent to the principal's office for discipline. Johnny rarely completed his assignments or turned in his homework. Her frustration with him reached the point that Mrs. Clark almost enjoyed marking his papers with a red pen, drawing bold Xs next to his errors and omissions, or marking the top of his papers with a big F.

Every teacher had access to their student's academic histories and was encouraged to review them. If she had read Johnny's school records earlier, she would have understood him better. Mrs. Clark had put Johnny's off until last. When she finally checked his file, she was appropriately surprised. His first grade teacher had written: "Johnny is a bright child with a quick laugh. He does his work neatly and exhibits good manners ... he makes friends easily and is pleasant to be around." His second grade teacher had written: "Johnny is an excellent student, well-liked by his classmates, but he's troubled by his mother's terminal illness and life at home has become a struggle." His third grade teacher had written: "His mother's death has been hard on him. He tries to do his best, but his father doesn't show much interest and his home life will soon affect him negatively if some corrective steps aren't taken." Johnny's fourth grade teacher had written: "Johnny is withdrawn and doesn't show much interest in school. He doesn't have many friends and he sometimes sleeps in class." By fourth grade, Johnny was the kind of poorly performing student that Mrs. Clark knew him to be the following year.

The school year progressed with their relationship mostly unchanged as the two-week Christmas vacation approached. On the final school day of the old year, Mrs. Clark's students followed the longstanding tradition of bringing their teacher gifts. There were many presents under the little tree in the corner of the room waiting to be opened during the afternoon party. All were wrapped in beautiful ribbons and bright, fancy paper, except Johnny's; his were clumsily wrapped in the heavy brown paper commonly used in grocery bags, and held together with masking tape. His presents were just like Johnny, not very neat or attractive.

When it was time to unwrap gifts, Mrs. Clark was a little surprised to have received anything from Johnny, so she took care to open his two gifts in the middle of the other presents. A few children began to snicker when she opened the first, containing a rhinestone bracelet with some of the fake jewels missing; and then they did so again when she opened a second containing a half-filled bottle of cheap perfume. Mrs. Clark had the presence of mind to kindly stifle the children's rude reactions by quickly placing the bracelet, followed by dabs of the perfume, on her wrist, holding it up, and exclaiming, "My, how very wonderful!"

Johnny lingered after school that day and stood by her desk. This was unusual behavior and it created both curiosity and more surprise in Mrs. Clark. He looked nervous, but sounded sincere when he said, "Mrs. Clark, today you smelled just like my mom used to, and her bracelet looks really nice on you. I just want you to know that you're my favorite teacher."

That night Mrs. Clark did not sleep well; something unidentified was deeply troubling her. She examined the day's activities, especially Johnny's participation. Eventually she began to understand the situation. She recognized Johnny's problem, and, perceiving her part in contributing to it, was ashamed of her attitude toward him. Before sunrise, Mrs. Clark determined she needed to make some immediate changes. From now on she would *really* love and help all of her students the same – especially the slow and troubled ones – beginning with Johnny. She would strive to become the kind of teacher she said she was, the kind she wanted to be, and the kind the students needed her to be.

On the first day of school after the holidays, the fifth grade students were greeted by a new teacher. It was still Mrs. Clark on the outside, but on the inside, she was different. She quit just teaching subjects like reading, social studies, and math; she began teaching students. As she had determined, Mrs. Clark paid particular attention to Johnny. After working with him for some days, his mind seemed to awaken and find a fresh spirit. The more she encouraged him, the more he responded. By the end of the year, Johnny had caught up with most of the other students and he had even begun to surpass others. Now to keep her promise of impartiality toward all students, Mrs. Clark had to keep her pride in check and resist the temptation to treat Johnny, and those like him, as teacher's pets.

The school year ended and Johnny graduated from the fifth grade with the rest of his class. This meant a move from elementary school to the middle school some miles away. Before departing for summer vacation, Johnny was found, for the last time, waiting by Mrs. Clark's desk after the rest of the class had charged out the door. He told Mrs. Clark a simple good-bye, followed by, "You're my favorite teacher."

Mrs. Clark didn't hear from him for three years. In late spring of the third year, she found a hand-addressed envelope in her assigned mail slot at school. It contained a note from Johnny reporting that middle school had gone well and he was moving on to high school. He concluded it with: "You're still my favorite teacher."

Several years passed without any contact from Johnny. Then in late spring of the fourth year, she found a familiar handwritten envelope in her mail slot. It contained another note from Johnny saying high school had gone well and he'd been accepted at the state university on a partial scholarship. The note again concluded simply: "You're still my favorite teacher."

Mrs. Clark continued to teach fifth grade at the same school. Nearly four more years passed without further updates from Johnny; that is, until late spring of the fourth year, when she found a third note in her mail slot. It was from Johnny and reported that he was graduating from the university in a few days with a degree and summa cum laude honors. This note concluded similar to the other two: "You're still my favorite teacher." That simple statement always reminded her of the long-ago Christmas party and of her renewed commitment to teaching during the sleepless night that followed it. The recollection never failed to inspire and refresh her.

The next six years passed quickly for Mrs. Clark, who had spent more than half of them enjoying retirement from the classroom. Late in the spring of the sixth year, a small package arrived at her home. It was from the office manager of her old grade school. Inside she immediately recognized Johnny's handwriting. It appeared on what was to be her final note from him. It contained another brief update indicating that he'd gone on to medical school, where he met a pretty young nurse to whom he was now engaged. But the note wasn't alone. Attached was a sealed, formal envelope. The envelope contained an embossed invitation to his wedding with another handwritten note tucked inside. This second one reminded Mrs. Clark that he'd lost his mother back in elementary school and reported that his father had passed away several years ago. Thus, having no one to represent his parents at the wedding, he asked whether she'd be available and willing to do so. This note concluded with the now-familiar words: "You're still my favorite teacher," but it had an unfamiliar signature. It was signed: Dr. John R. Mills, MD.

Mrs. Clark accepted the wedding invitation, considering it an honor to sit up front where Dr. Mills' parents would have sat. She arrived wearing the bracelet and perfume given to her on that last Christmas when she and Dr. Mills were together – when he was still known as Johnny.

After the ceremony they embraced and Dr. Mills thanked Mrs. Clark for being there for him on his wedding day, and more importantly, he thanked her for what she'd done for him back in fifth grade. Mrs. Clark replied that his gratitude was misplaced, for it was he who had honored her with the invitation, as well as he who had encouraged her to become the kind of teacher she wanted and needed to be. It was the combination of his simple trust and fidelity that acted as the catalyst for decisive growth in her life.

They were both right, because they'd been mutually influential in making substantive, positive changes in each other's lives. Johnny's unquestioning love for Mrs. Clark was the igniting spark for her change; it was her change that returned the love to Johnny, who then leveraged it to consistently improve his life. Those two small, physical Christmas gifts of the bracelet and the perfume were the first seeds sown into lives that would grow into greater gift giving. These kinds of gifts don't require shopping, money, or wrapping, yet they are gifts that will endure and keep on giving. The real gifts were their time and attention to each other. These were the best gifts they had given, and the best ones they had received.

Their gifts are representative of gifts we can all afford to give: our love, talents, kindness, attention, and time. These are the true gifts that are needed by those unlovable ones like Johnny, or by those misguided ones like Mrs. Clark. At some point in our lives, we are all like Johnny and need to receive from a Mrs. Clark; at others times, we are capably equipped like Mrs. Clark and can give of ourselves to a needy Johnny. Even Johnny, who seemingly had nothing, found something to give Mrs. Clark. We are reminded to be generous in giving of ourselves, for none of us has anything in life of real value that we have not been given ourselves.

The investments that we make in others are the best ones because they are life changing and thus pay lasting dividends to the giver and to the recipient. There are only three things we can take beyond the grave; I call them the *everlasting three*: integrity (sometimes called a good name or reputation), relationships, and faith.

> *Let not many of you become teachers, knowing that we shall receive a stricter judgment.* (James 3:1)

* * * *

Author's Note: I first discovered this story about midway through life. It's one of the earliest I recall appropriating and sharing. Over the years I have modified its structure and personalized the storyline. I've attempted to uncover two specifics related to the origins of the story. The first was determining whether it is fiction or nonfiction. The discovery data was conflicting and inconclusive, with some indicating the one, and others, just the opposite. So it is likely a mix of both. Therefore, I'm presenting it as a parable, and I've changed the names of its protagonists. Their names were selected on the basis of my preference and have carryovers from my past. It became the story of one of St. Mary's elementary school teachers, Mrs. Clark, and one of her most challenging students, Johnny Mills. To my knowledge, neither name represents a real person within the context presented. The second of the two specifics related to the origins of the story was attempting to determine who conceived the core story. Again, the discovery data was conflicting and inconclusive. I was able to find multiple, unattributed renderings of the story, but never able to confirm the original author.

Students often offer written essays to me after hearing a story. Many are very personal and moving. The following is one from a fifth grade boy: "I remember I was like Johnny. I was not doing good in school. I was sloppy because my grandpa shot his self. He was my favorite. He would take me for ice cream. My life was great [until] a couple years later [when] my mom came home crying and I was trying to cheer my mom up. She said she loved me and she said to me, your grandpa died. My life crashed, my heart was smashed, my life was dead. My dad helped me through it, but I will never ever forget." This young man recovered, like Johnny did, and is a good student today.

Rick Rescorla

I'm Taking Them Out!

Set a man ... who may lead them out and
bring them in. (Numbers 27:16-17)

His childhood ambition was to become an American soldier like the ones who had helped his country during the war and whom he later viewed in Hollywood films. Cyril Richard Rescorla was born in Hayle, England, in 1939, at the start of World War II. He grew up during the Battle of Britain and the American-led Allied Expeditionary Force. Early on, Rescorla adopted the name of *Rick* instead of *Cyril* because he thought it sounded more American; everyone knew him as Rick thereafter. Some of his earliest and most cherished recollections are of the GIs from the States who were stationed nearby. He grew to manhood, believing in the goodness of our global vision, especially our opposition to Communism.

Rick was naturally big, strong, and well coordinated. He was so good at rugby, the shot put, and boxing that many expected he would become a professional athlete. Instead, he joined the British Army as a paratrooper at seventeen. He saw four years of modest-duty action in the colonies of Cyprus and Zimbabwe (formerly Rhodesia) as a sometimes soldier, police-man, or mercenary. It was in these capacities that he came into firsthand contact with Communist-fomented insurgencies, and he converted from sympathizer to avid anti-Communist. He was not, however, fully satisfied with the direction of his life until after he turned twenty-two and immigrated to the States, signed up with the army infantry, and joined the fight beginning to stir in Vietnam. Rick served in the reformed 7th Cavalry Regiment, 1st Cavalry Division, which came to be known as the Airmobile. This was a newly conceived approach to limited warfare. It used a combination of helicopters, forward landing zones, and fast, hard-hitting mobility combined with air support as needed. These tactics were adopted for use in the jungles against an enemy who used guerrilla tactics. While serving in the Airmobile, Rick earned the rank of lieutenant and became the commander of the Bravo Company.

Vietnam was the former French colony of Indochina. Throughout the twentieth century, it was never fully independent and had become a pawn between the capitalistic West and the Communist East. France had unsuccessfully fought local insurgent troops there for two decades. After they abandoned the effort, the United States entered in their place. The purpose changed from maintaining Colonialism to containing Communism. The Ia Drang Valley had been an infamous deathtrap for the French, and now it was the site of America's first major battle in their Vietnam War, and possibly the bloodiest one of the entire conflict. At Plei Me, a Special Forces camp in the Highlands near the valley, the four hundred Americans positioned there were surprise-attacked by wave upon wave of a Viet Cong force totaling four thousand men. Rick's actions throughout the siege are legendary for the bravery he displayed. When it was over, America had not seen so high a body count, even in the Korean War.

There were two separate groups to be evacuated by airlift at the battle's end. Rick was the last man in his group to board a departing chopper. After takeoff, word came that the other group had been cut off from their extraction point, LZ X-ray. Rick requested to be flown into the entrapment. He strapped on as many ammo belts as he could, placed an M16 in his right hand and a grenade in his left, and jumped ten feet to the ground. His actions so inspired the men that they were able to survive a bloody firefight and make it through a hellish night until the morning reinforcements arrived.

In a separate tactical action just days later and again in the Ia Drang Valley, Rick's brave rescue effort helped save another group from annihilation after they too were pinned down, surrounded, and cut off by the enemy deep in the jungle no man's land at LZ Albany. Rick had now thrice demonstrated the bravery of a war hero. He was highly decorated with the Bronze Star and the Silver Star for heroism as related to these three exceptional combat actions in the Ia Drang. His actions largely made the difference between the French and the American outcomes in the Ia Drang Valley of Death.

Rick continued serving full-time in the army as a career officer, advancing to full colonel before deciding to retire. The men under his command were especially well cared for, but he could not sleep well because he keenly felt the weight of every man lost under his command, and he was consumed by thoughts of those who had died. A close friend said that a little bit of Rick died along with each man he lost. He was close to every man under his command, and he was serious about their well-being. Many commanders chose not to identify with their men, believing it kept them in a more clear-headed decision-making mode. Not so with Rick. Those who knew him said that if there was a life to be saved, Rick couldn't ignore it. So he chose retirement just prior to the standard twenty-year active-duty mark.

Details of his story are in the books *Heart of a Soldier* by Pulitzer prize-winner James B. Stewart, and *Touched By A Hero* by Rick's wife, Susan, as well as in the Hollywood film *We Were Soldiers Once ... and Young*, directed by and starring Mel Gibson. In 2006, a life-sized bronze statue of Rick was commissioned and placed at the Walk of Honor at the National Infantry Museum in Fort Benning, Georgia. The statue is based on a much-publicized iconic photo of Rick on patrol in the Ia Drang Valley. (The reader is encouraged to view the photo or the statue, as there is something compelling and timeless about them.)

After leaving the military, Rick attended the University of Oklahoma on the GI Bill. He earned a bachelor's degree and a master's degree in literature, followed by a doctorate of law. During this more leisurely time in his life, Rick – who was multilingual and certainly a modern Renaissance man – began his lifelong private practice of writing songs, novels, and plays; these works were generally founded on his international experiences. For a short season, he worked as a college professor in South Carolina. Then Rick moved to New York City, where he accepted an appointment as vice president of safety and security at Morgan Stanley Dean Witter (MSDW), which was the world's largest financial institution at the time, as well as the largest tenant in the World Trade Center (WTC). It occupied thirty floors, from the forty-fourth to the seventy-fourth. Rick immediately set about using his skills, experience, and education to introduce programs and procedures that would later be employed in saving many lives twice over.

It was in this last career that Rick again distinguished himself in the role of rescuer, although now as a civilian, not as soldier. Recognition didn't come from combat-related bravery, but rather for his accurately anticipating both of the two terrorist attacks on the WTC and subsequently dedicating himself to the associated goals of damage prevention, readiness preparation, and employee protection. He cautioned anyone who would listen that the WTC complex (consisting of more than just the two well-recognized Twin Towers) was a prime terrorist target, and he predicted an attack would come. He tried without success first to convince his employer to move to a safer location, and then tried to convince the Port Authority in charge of the WTC to better secure and provision the buildings, especially the unsecured truck delivery section under the Center.

On February 26, 1993, the anticipated terrorist attack arrived in the form of a truck filled with explosive urea nitrate-hydrogen gas. It was driven into the open basement of the North Tower, known as Tower One, with the expectation that the ensuing explosion would drive it into the South Tower, known as Tower Two. Rick was on the scene and not only survived the impact, but his related plans and on-the-scene heroic actions also saved the lives of hundreds of his coworkers and other tenants. Rick loved to sing, had a ready sense of humor, and was almost always wearing a smile. In the heat of the evacuation, Rick incorporated these personal characteristics to enhance his extradition efforts. Coworkers reported Rick calmly issuing the necessary instructions, even jumping on a desk at one point and pulling down his pants in order to get their attention and counteract the panic. Rick was acknowledged as a hero for the fourth time. *Rescuer,* if not *Hero,* had become his new middle name.

In 1998, just five years after that first attack, Rick was filmed in a documentary in his office on the forty-fourth floor of the Center. Therein he detailed probable future terrorist warfare methods and objectives. This was long before Osama bin Laden and other Islamic militants had become infamous for their threats and deadly activities. In the video, Rick correctly predicted there would surely be a second attack on America and that it could once again be directed at the WTC because it was such a large and purely American symbol. The success of the earlier attack was more likely to embolden the enemy than to deflect his attention. Rick's reputation had grown in light of his accurate and successful contributions related to the first WTC attack. So Rick took advantage of this and utilized the years between the Trade Center attacks to further train the MSDW staff in regular safety drills, as well as continue to badger the Port Authority about improving the emergency lighting, security, fire protection, and stairwells within the buildings. He was an unpopular man with the Authority, who thought him a crazy pest, but he forced them to provide many necessary safety and security measures in areas beyond those where he had direct authority or responsibility.

Rick and his new bride, Susan, booked a vacation flight to Europe, set to leave on September 12, 2001. During the time away, they intended to plan Rick's retirement. The day before their departure date, just three years after the interview for the documentary, the forecasted second attack came. What transpired then became both his life's finest chapter and his final one. Months afterward, the History Channel made a film about Rick's performance that day entitled *The Man Who Predicted 9/11*. The film follows Rick's dramatic timeline between 8:45 a.m., when the first plane hit North Tower One, and 9:58 a.m., when South Tower Two fell (after being hit at 9:03 a.m. by a second airliner just seventeen minutes after the North Tower One was hit).

Here's a brief summary of that final one-hour-and-thirteen-minute period in Rick's life. After the first hit, Rick called Susan to tell her not to worry because he was fine and would get everyone out of his building safely, and then the line went dead. After hearing the intercom announcement from the Port Authority telling everyone to stay inside his building, Rick responded in a mix of strong Cornish and American slang expressions. In summary, what Rick said was, "I'm taking them out!" Acting without authorization, he immediately began evacuating the occupants. After the second plane hit his building just above the MSDW floors, all possible escape for the 1,355 other business occupants was instantly gone. Because Rick had refused to follow the Port Authority recommendation, he had gained seventeen vital minutes of security, permitting 3,700 MSDW staff to have already safely exited the tower.

Various employees of MSDW later reported seeing him active across all thirty of the floors occupied by their company. Just as in combat, he was everywhere – calm, pleasant in the face of others' panic, and reassuring by his personal presence and charismatic demeanor. Rick was heard singing *God Bless America* as he went about directing his one-man evacuation. Because of Rick, almost every employee of his company made it out of the building; only five didn't. Think about that legacy: They left and they lived! Otherwise, the toll of the dead on that day of horror would have far exceeded six thousand instead of being limited to about three thousand.

Rick remained in the tower, and he was soon back in the stairwells, moving along the aisles, shouting into his bullhorn to gain attention, locating anyone lost or injured, giving sure directions, comforting the hysterical. As he led more survivors out, Rick continued to sing so that they would remain assured and more easily follow his lead, even when the dim lighting and smoke obscured their view of him.

When it appeared that everyone was out, Rick returned with the professional rescue workers for a final look. That's where he was last seen. He was inside Tower Two – the first one to fall – when five hundred thousand tons of steel and concrete collapsed and buried this five-time hero, ending his selfless life and concealing his body forever. Rick died exercising the virtues he'd learned and he'd lived: duty, honor, and courage. Rick died a victim of his own predictions, but he died as he had lived – watching out for others before himself.

Although he was still on the job that fateful day, Rick's body was already ravaged by a prostate cancer that had penetrated deep into his bone marrow. Few people knew of the serious condition that forced him to live in pain and diminished his physical strength. The treatments and medicine caused him to gain weight. For a man who always exercised and kept his body fit, it was an embarrassment he chose not to explain. It was not the illness and it was not the Islamic murderers that took his life that day; he laid it down in a Christlike manner for others, many of them strangers. Jesus said, *Greater love has no one than this, than to lay down one's life for his friends* (John 15:13). It was not the Muslim extremists who left the most profound impression for us to remember about that day; it was Rick Rescorla. Rick, the model soldier, chose to stay until his mission was accomplished: the first one in, the last one out, with no one left behind.

Here's a revelation about a characteristic trait found in those rare, brave public defenders and servants like Rick. It's their modesty. There are three identifiable clues in his life to sustain the point. The first is that he didn't offer or accept performance excuses related to his illness to the point of keeping it secret. The second is that although he and Susan had been together for several years, it was not until she was unpacking some of his personal items after a move that she discovered a box full of his military medals and became aware of his status as a hero with multiple decorations and commendations for exceptional bravery in battle. Rick had never mentioned these to her and had deliberately kept them out of sight. Through annual visits, Rick had always kept in close touch with his family and friends in Hayle, England, and neither did they know much of his heroic record. The third is Rick's abiding conviction that he could have done more for his men and for his coworkers, even though he accepted more responsibility for those whom he served than was reasonable for anyone else to ever expect of him. Heroes rarely think of themselves as having been heroic; they often believe they should have done more. (See the Irena Sendler story.) Rick never read his commanding officer's book about their Ia Drang Valley actions – even though it was his photo on the cover – and he never watched Mel Gibson's interpretive movie. He said he didn't do so because he never thought of himself as a hero. At his 9/11 memorial service, everyone disagreed with Rick's self-assessment. He was called a warrior, friend, leader, and the bravest man they ever knew. That's exactly the kind of attention Rick would have avoided.

The life of Colonel Cyril Richard "Rick" Rescorla, JD illustrates that in a crisis, there isn't much difference between soldier and civilian, war and peace, defense and offense, professional and volunteer, survivor and victim, prevention and reaction. A hero's objectives and motivations within the crisis are always the same: the protection of others more than self. When we see someone in uniform, such as a soldier or a sailor, a nurse or a paramedic, a firefighter or a police officer, we should tell them, "You're appreciated for your good work." In doing so, we may be thanking yesterday's hero or encouraging tomorrow's hero-in-the-making. Someday, perhaps that uniformed hero might save you, me, or someone close to us. Perhaps that uniformed hero may even be you. (As of my writing, the police and other positions of public safety in society are being maligned and attacked – even physically assaulted – by segments of the general population and even by community leaders and officeholders as high as the federal executive branch. Consequently, open displays of support increasingly serve to satisfy a growing need.)

> *That the congregation of the* Lord *may not be like sheep which have no shepherd.* (Numbers 27:17)

* * * *

Author's Note: The following are lyrics from a Johnny Cash-Dave Matthews song titled *For You* as it was used in the film *We Were Soldiers Once ... and Young.* The film covered battle actions in the Ia Drang Valley. I offer it as a poetic tribute to Rick's heroic and selfless life – both his military and his civilian periods.

> I will drink the cup, the poison overflowing. I will lift you up, watch over where you're going. The first one in the last one gone, I'll be the rock to stand upon for you.

Phoebe Ann Mosey

Aim High

The helpless commits himself to You. (Psalm 10:14)

The collective imagination of the early American West is populated by dramatic, near-mythological portraits of native Indians and home-steaders, endless buffalo herds, explorers and mountain men, cowboys and cavalry, stage coaches and rattlesnakes, bank and train robberies, cattle drives and feral broncos, Wells Fargo and hanging judges, gold and silver discoveries, wigwams and war dances, gunfights and outlaws, rugged individualism, saloons and gambling halls, vast prairies occasionally carved by barbed-wire fencing – primitive, untamed, and lawless, and hosting ghost towns named Deadwood, Tombstone, and Dodge City located near rivers like the Pecos and Red or on trails such as the Santa Fe and Chisholm. Thoroughly woven into this colorful scenario is the myth and the reality of the rifle. Especially remembered are the names of those individuals who capably handled their rifles in service to themselves, their community, and greater history – names like Wild Bill Hickok, Kit Carson, the Earp Brothers, and George Armstrong Custer, as well as the names of their nemeses, those who used them to prey on decent society like Butch Cassidy, John Wesley Hardin, Jesse James, and William H. Bonney (Billy the Kid.) City slickers, gamblers, outlaws, and marshals carried a revolver or derringer; practical ranchers and hunters carried a rifle. Handling a gun of any nature often made the difference between eating or going hungry, between protection or loss of property, between life and death – often without warning.

In our modern society filled with its incalculable selection of round-the-clock sports, theme parks, movies and plays, gaming casinos, virtual reality, and digital games, we find it nearly impossible to understand the high interest engendered by a nineteenth-century shooting competition, or by a traveling Wild West Show with its exhibitions of marksmanship. The few recreational sports that existed in the West were more pragmatic and less leisurely in nature. What could be more grounded than demonstrating your practiced skill with the very same device that provided your livelihood and ensured your safety? This was the passion and allure of marksmanship.

The word *marksmanship* very much expresses the correct gender originally associated with this skill. It was an avocation dominated by men firing rifles for the most part, less so for shotguns and handguns. Just as most readers are able to readily name several of the NFL's top quarterbacks, a person living in the nineteenth century could name the country's top shooters, and the big salaries and advertising dollars followed them just as they presently do our athletes and celebrities. The fashionable promoters and suppliers weren't Adidas, Nike, or Spalding; they were Winchester, Smith & Wesson, and Colt – the guns, as they said, that won the West. Nearly everyone owned and used one or more of these, but only a handful of men were good enough to make their living exclusively from related showmanship. In the vernacular of the times, they were referred to as champions; today, we would call them *stars*.

The careers of two of the most popular and capable of these sharpshooters were often linked in a common endeavor. Both would easily have earned the modern top-notch label of *superstar* because they were better known and more respected for their abilities than were their peers. Even more substantially, their careers had a tenure lasting a half-century each. One was Buffalo Bill Cody; the other, Phoebe Ann Mosey – yes, a lady who shone in a man's world while retaining every degree of her femininity and modesty. At a time when it was universally agreed that a woman's place was in the home and that women were indeed the weaker sex, she was America's first female superstar, and most likely also the world's, beating men at their own games. All things being equal, she never lost to a man.

Unlike most female (as well as male) entertainers today who shamelessly engage in bad behavior in their private lives, and who are even known to deliberately exaggerate it publicly for the extra attention it generates, Phoebe's long career was morally flawless; she was consistently a paragon of good behavior, and thus a positive role model. After meeting her, it was often said that she was both much more of a shot and much more of a lady than expected. Every photograph ever taken of her – and there were many – reveals the same thing: a conservatively dressed woman in an ankle-length skirt with a long-sleeved blouse buttoned tight to the neckline. This was her private and her public persona; there was no disconnect. What the photos generally fail to reveal is the very capable world-class athlete within the modest clothing, who was able to ride a horse or a bike, tumble or flip, run or jump, all the while armed and nailing her targets.

The lore of the old Wild West is full of familiar names of once-living legends such as Calamity Jane, Bat Masterson, Geronimo, Pancho Villa, Judge Roy Bean, and Belle Starr. Most of what's recalled about these personalities is more fiction than fact. If you find that Phoebe's name isn't familiar to you, it's okay, as that's expected and not uncommon. However, by sharing the facts about her life – which are sufficiently exciting so that no fantasy need be added – I hope to make her name, reputation, and personal character into character memorable by the time you complete this story. A couple of generations ago, writing this story about Phoebe would have been unnecessary, as everyone in America and in much of the world knew about her life intimately. Like so many others, passing time has changed that, and she is now mostly forgotten or dismissed. Miss Mosey is arguably America's single-greatest woman athlete within her sport and within her times as measured by dominance, achievement, longevity, and personal integrity. All this while only five feet high, under a hundred pounds in weight, and bearing no formal education or professional training; she was wholly self-taught. She was variously known in the press as *Rifle Queen*, *Maid of the Western Plains*, and *The Western Girl*. Befriended by Indian Chief Sitting Bull, who attempted to buy her (and failing that, to adopt her), he settled for fondly renaming her *Little Sure Shot* and just being a friend.

Phoebe's relationship with a rifle, ironically, did not come from being raised in the West. It was born of dire necessity in Darke County, Ohio, where her Quaker family lived the hard life typical of pioneers. During the exceptionally rough winter of 1866, her father, Jacob, was caught in a blizzard. He was returning to the farm on foot from his day job at the mill fifteen miles away. He made it back to the family's log cabin later than usual, and his extremities were frozen and his speech was gone. Never recovering the full use of his hands after the exposure, he died a few months thereafter. Without his supplemental income, the farm was soon lost.

Although only six years old at the time, and the fifth of six siblings, Phoebe was inspired to help meet the family's needs for survival. It began with what she always credited as one of the best shots she'd ever made. Propping her father's heavy, forty-inch-long muzzle-loading Kentucky rifle on the windowsill of the home, she took aim at a rabbit, pulled the trigger, and marked it through the head – a critical method because it left more eatable meat than a body shot. Phoebe said of that shot: "I know we stuffed in enough powder to kill off a buffalo.... I got the rabbit but my nose was broken."

That rabbit kill would be the first of three defining events in her life. Through it she gained a confidence with guns that never left her and served her well throughout her life. Her family was uncomfortable with the young girl assuming so much risk and responsibility. In her favor was a natural gift for using guns combined with an avid interest in them. What gradually developed was a regular pursuit of wild game for the family's consumption: rabbits, birds, and the occasional largesse of a deer.

The second defining event in her life was not in any manner as pleasant, or as brief, as that first exhilarating shot. On such experiences as the following one, a lifetime of success or failure is often founded, as one subsequently chooses to become bitter or better. Over the next three years, the family's situation did not improve. Phoebe's mother made the decision to board her at the county poorhouse in the nearest town, Greenville, a practice and an institution unknown today but common for the times. At the institution known as the Infirmary, a local farmer arrived, seeking a helper for his wife and new baby; in exchange, he promised to provide an education. Ten-year-old Phoebe was sent to live in their home. That's when the horrors began in such an egregious fashion as to make her previous difficult years at home and at the poorhouse seem idyllic in comparison. It would be two long years before twelve-year-old Phoebe again tasted freedom, then another three before seeing her mother and reestablishing the woodland life she had enjoyed so much.

The farmer and his wife both misused and abused Phoebe. It's unknown whether sexual misconduct was involved because her modesty prevented her from ever confirming it. It's certain they administered significant physical and emotional hardships. The wife was especially cruel. They would drive her extremely hard, feed her only enough to keep her alive, deny her love and compassion, beat her around the neck and head, and lock her in closets. Phoebe said that they were "wolves in sheep's clothing." She determined to never speak their name again, and for the rest of her life she would only refer to them as the *He-Wolf* and the *She-Wolf* or *Mr. and Mrs. Wolf.* The educational part of the bargain was never provided. She was, instead, guarded as a virtual prisoner and used as a slave.

This ill relationship climaxed one winter day when the wife repeatedly struck Phoebe on the ears, then locked her outside in the deep snow, barefoot and without a jacket. Her offense had been falling asleep in the evening while darning the She-Wolf's clothes. Phoebe said, "I was slowly freezing to death. So I got down on my knees, looked toward God's clear sky, and tried to pray. But my lips were frozen stiff and there was no sound." She nearly met the same cruel fate that took the life of her father, but after she passed out, the He-Wolf brought her inside despite the ranting of his wife. Finally, the sought-for escape opportunity presented itself and Phoebe hopped a train back to Greenville, returning to the life offered by the poorhouse. For the next three years, she worked as a seamstress. Later, fifteen-year-old Phoebe left on foot to make the twenty-mile trip home to reunite with her mother for the first time in five years.

By then, her mother, Susan, had remarried, but financial circumstances hadn't improved despite the new relationship. The most immediate risk was a contractor's lien against the home, which seriously threatened their right to continue living there. Phoebe again left her mother and siblings to live on her own, this time as a professional hunter, supplying game to Cincinnati restaurants and hotels. Her meat was sought for its top-quality condition related to her clean, select shots. In time, she earned and saved enough money to pay off the lien and guarantee her mother a debt-free home for life. This was the third, and likely final, defining event in her young life.

Barely into her teen years and already a full-time wage earner, she'd learned priceless lessons in hard work, budgeting, and frugal living from which she never departed, regardless of the amount of money she earned. Earn it she did – unheard-of big money for a woman, or even a man, in those lean and chauvinistic times. At the peak of her career, Phoebe was earning around one million dollars annually. Always consistent with her comfortable, but never ostentatious or conspicuous living standard, was an abiding sense of caring for society's needy elements, especially widows and orphans. Throughout her lifetime, she contributed a portion of her earnings to poor farms and orphanages, always remembering her own humble origins and difficult childhood.

Career marksmen of the period traveled from location to location to participate in shooting contests for cash and other prizes. The host community rarely failed to promote their local champions and wager them against the visiting challengers. Irishman Frank Butler arrived in Darke County when Phoebe was still fifteen, after she had already solidly established her reputation with a rifle. At age twenty-five, Frank was one of the more proficient and better-known traveling professionals, so it was only natural that he challenged Phoebe to a Thanksgiving holiday match after the locals backed her as their hometown favorite. Phoebe won the match with a perfect score to Frank's double miss. Afterward, Frank wrote: "I was a beaten man the moment she appeared, for I was taken off guard. Never did a person make more impossible shots than did that little girl. It was her first big match and my first defeat."

She'd won his respect, but even more, the always gracious and demure teen had won his heart. He was ten years her senior, but significant age differences in relationships were standard fare for the times. Frank held great appeal for Phoebe as well. He was handsome, had an Irish accent, and they shared a common interest in marksmanship. Frank didn't smoke, drink, or gamble – all of which complemented her Quaker values and quickened her mother's approval. After a season of courtship, she became Mrs. Frank Butler – a position she held for the next forty-six years without a hint of scandal or unfaithfulness on either side.

As their relationship matured, Phoebe's shooting took on greater importance and Frank's became less so. Instead, he assumed increasing responsibilities as her manager and agent – a reverse of nineteenth-century roles. Their union produced no children, and both of them happily continued their professional careers in tandem throughout their lifetimes, while readily admitting neither had any capacity for, nor interest in, domestic life. In their middle age, they liked to say that their young friend Johnny Baker was their adopted son, but it was not legally so and it was only said out of fondness, as he was a long-term recipient of their loving support.

Shortly after marrying, the couple joined what was then the greatest traveling show on earth, Buffalo Bill Cody's Wild West Show. *Colonel* (an honorary title) Cody had been an Indian scout for the U.S. Army Calvary, a Pony Express rider, a Plains hunter and guide, and an agent of the railroads during their western expansion years. He was also at the top of the list as a popular and capable marksman. His career hit its full and satisfying stride at early middle age, with him as the premier entertainer. He had a commanding and attractive physical presence, combined with a natural sense for high showmanship. By luck or intuition, his entrepreneurial timing was perfect. He brought the best of the Wild West to the eastern states and to the world, just as its popularity was at its peak and just as the real West was being tamed by barbed-wire fencing, Indian reservations, loss of game (especially buffalo), gold and silver discoveries, Ned Buntline's dime-store novels, cattle drives, transcontinental railroads, courthouses, and territories qualifying for statehood.

The Wild West Show was a unique mix of rodeo, broad dramatic plays, and circus. It offered a taste of life on the old frontier to an America that was rapidly industrializing. Residents of the crowded urban centers flocked to Buffalo Bill's show in order to live for a moment in the Wild West. Within his show, Cody established the modern superstar system more than anyone before or since. For a short season, Cody fulfilled that superstar role singularly, but he soon found his equal in a female star with whom he profitably shared the world stage during the final decades of the nineteenth century and on into the first decades of the twentieth century. Cody's very capable and personable manager-agent, Nate Salsbury, *discovered* Mrs. Butler (aka Phoebe Ann Mosey), and signed her to a prominent role in the show. The two weapons experts had different natures, but they liked each other and worked well together. Cody might have fulfilled a role as a type of surrogate father figure to Phoebe.

Once on board the Wild West Show, Mrs. Butler adopted a stage name, *Annie Oakley*, with the *Oakley* possibly taken from a district in nearby Cincinnati or from a relative. She dropped *Phoebe* altogether in favor of her middle name, which she modified into a soft and friendly *Annie*. Annie Oakley stepped out professionally for the first time in Louisville, in front of seventeen thousand paid viewers. Thereafter, she only missed five performances in her career (much like the iron men Cal Ripken and Brett Favre), four of them due to an incidence of blood poisoning that nearly took her young life.

The show's transportation entourage was comprised of eighty-two railcars holding a retinue of five hundred live animals and actors. Performances numbered more than a hundred annually. They featured reenactments of the Battle of the Little Big Horn and an attack on a settler's cabin, the Grand Entry of the Rough Riders of the World, and the Deadwood stagecoach robbery, as well as riding tricks and, of course, several demonstrations of shooting skills. Remarkably, Indians elected to participate at a time when the Indian Wars and Uprisings were still in progress, some of them well known then and now, such as Sitting Bull and Crazy Horse. Some of the Indians had even recently been present with General Custer at Little Big Horn in the Montana Territory. The show's popularity could readily be seen during the 1883 World's Columbian Exposition in Chicago – the *White City*. Cody opened directly across from the fair's main entrance, thereafter easily holding his own against a world's fair that drew twenty-eight million paid visitors when the population of the nation was well under one hundred million.

Neither a housekeeper nor a liberationist, Annie was a professional performer who practiced high standards of personal femininity, morality, and fashion. She stated: "God intended women to be outside as well as men, and they do not know what they are missing when they stay cooped up in the house enjoying themselves with a novel." She successfully avoided being manipulated by advocates of either of the extreme beliefs of what a woman should be. She was a career high-achiever, as well as a reserved Victorian lady, and she moved the bar higher for womankind when she tastefully, uniquely, and subtly combined the two roles. An example of Annie's practical, middle-of-the-road position is that she favored only educated women being allowed to vote rather than full suffrage, but at the same time she advocated that all women be trained in the handling of weapons. Her advocacy on behalf of women and guns went as far as providing women's firearms training, and then encouraging her graduate students to remain armed beyond the classroom.

Her life was a living defense of the Second Amendment. She taught 15,000 women, free of charge, how to shoot a gun during her seven years of "retirement" living in South Carolina. Although I was unable to find any direct quotes on the subject, Annie lived the Second Amendment and could not have conceived of a time in America when it would be under threat of extinction or severely restricted by misguided regulation. She openly said that all schools should have a firing range and provide firearms lessons in sport and self-defense for both sexes (unlike today's gun-free zones). The easiest killing fields today are our unarmed schools, where the good guys are banned from having access to prevention and containment weapons. Instead, schools are forced to rely on an inhospitable maze of internal and external locked doors. This approach is today's lame *duck-and-cover* (related to atomic bomb survival in the 1950s) equivalent to reducing the casualties inflicted by heavily armed mass killers. We would still benefit from adopting many of her perspectives.

Annie was especially concerned with living above reproach and projecting an image of modesty; some say she was obsessed with maintaining that image. Her motivations had multiple sources: the shame from her abuse by the "wolves," living a man's role in a man's world, engagements in seedy venues like burlesque and vaudeville establishments, a job that was literally under the lights and open to public scrutiny, and finally her natural sense of decency formed during a Quaker childhood. She sewed her own conservative stage outfits, avoided the noisy nightlife, rarely drank, and even left instructions in her will that her body be prepared only by a female undertaker. She scrupulously guarded her reputation from suspicion. The most overwhelming challenge to her legacy blindsided Annie in 1903, when she was no longer traveling with the Wild West Show. Sensation-seeking Hearst-owned newspapers reported the incredible. She was said to have been arrested in Chicago for stealing a black man's trousers in order to finance a cocaine purchase! In actuality, it was a seedy woman who foolishly used Annie's name during the arrest. Without any fact-checking, Hearst ran the farcical story nationally.

Annie was devastated, but she was not incapacitated. Unsatisfied with quiet letters of apology and simple retractions, she sought full absolution through the court system from all fifty-five responsible newspapers. Hearst aggressively resisted providing any remuneration and further attempted to dig up dirt to smear her and thus discredit her court testimonies. He found none. It took six years and most of her savings, and it required personal appearances in every courtroom, but she won all except one suit. Because of her earlier experiences, she hated injustice and anything that came against a person to keep them down. She was fueled by a righteous anger. This series of legal actions remains the largest personal injury tort in American judicial history. It was the most intense battle of her career and visibly aged her. Throughout her life she was determined never to lose her reputation and never to return to poverty. The fight against Hearst newspapers involved elements of both of these things, but in very real terms she demonstrated that she emphasized her name above her purse.

Decades prior to events like Farm Aid or the Concert for Bangladesh, and well before there were celebrity spokespeople representing every imaginable disease, Annie was supporting tuberculosis victims through personal financial contributions and heightening its visibility through public appearances. She had a vast collection of precious metal awards earned over a lifetime of competition; that is, until she melted them and used the proceeds to build a sanitarium in memory of her two sisters who died of the disease. Annie's roles as benefactor, philanthropist, and teacher were always performed quietly and with discretion. It's for these reasons they are often overlooked or underplayed by biographers, who mostly focus on her overarching fame as a sportswoman. After her death, it was discovered that Annie had given away her entire fortune to assist family, finance girls through college, support orphans, and fund charities. Frank once summarized their charity work in the following manner: "It is the brotherhood of mankind to find what the grief is and help where you can."

I've not offered any specifics regarding her many adventures with Cody's show, but one is illustrative of Annie's gentle politics. While she was touring Europe with the Wild West Show, a royal command performance was ordered by Britain's Queen Victoria. After the show, the Prince of Wales, Edward Albert, desired to meet her and summoned her to the royal box. He was widely known as an immoral wife-cheater. Annie deliberately broke protocol and shook long-suffering Princess Alexandra's hand before his. In doing so, she stated, "I'm an American and in America, ladies come first." A possible second motivating factor might have been that Annie was frequently snubbed at the British men's clubs; thus, she would have seamlessly executed a subtle double point.

During the Spanish-American War, she made the following offer to

President McKinley: "I for one feel confident that your good judgment will carry America safely through without war. But in case of such an event I am ready to place a company of fifty lady sharpshooters at your disposal. Every one of them will be an American, and as they will furnish their own arms and ammunition, will be little, if any, expense to the government." During Teddy Roosevelt's presidential term, she made another offer to organize a women's regiment in which she was willing to actively serve. T.R. declined, which is somewhat surprising and inconsistent, because later during WWI, he approached a reluctant President Wilson with a similar request for himself. As an alternative during the First World War, Annie began attending the army camps on her own initiative as a volunteer, inspiring the troops with a combination of skill performances and training sessions. After the war, she raised money for the Red Cross, visited wounded soldiers, and gave charitable exhibitions for their entertainment. She said later in life that this time was one of greater fulfillment for her than her time spent with the Wild West Show.

The professional lives of Annie, Frank, and Buffalo Bill demanded almost continuous travel by all available means of transportation – train, auto, and ship. In October of 1901, one of the show's two extensive trains collided head-on with another, unaffiliated train. The cost to the show was nearly incalculable even though there was no loss of human life. After some delay, the show was performing again, but the financial losses from the accident – when combined with the declining interest from changed times – eventually led to its closure. During the wreck, Annie was violently thrown from her berth as she slept. Initially reported as having died in the crash, she had actually been carried by Frank to a temporary hospital. She suffered some paralysis, required several surgeries, and lost a year and a half of her life to convalescence before returning to her career. Stress related to the accident had two immediate effects: her hair turned white and she retired from Cody's show.

A second serious travel-related accident occurred in November of 1922, when a car the Butlers were driving flipped over and crushed Annie's hip and leg. She was forced to wear a steel leg brace and to walk with the aid of a cane the reminder of her life. Nothing short of death seemed able to slow sixty-two-year-old Annie for long. Beginning late that year, she was again setting marksmanship records and winning competitions against much younger opponents. On a summer afternoon in Long Island, the petite sharpshooter gave the last public exhibition of her skills, and she never missed a shot.

Death did claim Annie four years later while at home, in her sleep. She'd returned to the area of her youth in North Star in Darke County, Ohio, where she was cared for until the end by several nieces. The home is gone now, but a marker has been placed at the location. Her tombstone in Brock Cemetery reads simply: "Annie Oakley, At Rest, 1926." When death separated Phoebe from Frank at age sixty-six, Frank stopped eating and, in just over two weeks, joined her in a companion grave setting. They died that November with their integrity fully intact and their fame still operative; neither life nor death had diminished their reputations.

Will Rogers later remarked of Annie's life: "Nobody took her place. There was only one ... And, when I think of Phoebe Ann, I remember it's not what you do that makes you, it's what you are." During her lifetime, she was idolized globally by millions. Educators considered Annie Oakley a role model of character and success. I offer her life as one with value for today as well. Liberals speak sneeringly of Sarah Palin "doing her Annie Oakley thing" as an attempted insult, when, in fact, it's a high compliment, proving that it is best to know backgrounds before expressing related negative sentiments. (Their misuse of the name of Harriet Beecher Stowe's protagonist, Uncle Tom, as an intended slanderous insult is another example of uneducated, negative labeling, as he is a Christlike martyr of noble character.)

Annie is universally remembered as a symbol of the Old West, as one who epitomized the capable, independent frontier woman, yet she never permanently lived farther west than Ohio, the place where she began and she still remains. Larger than her associated Western legacy is her life motto, which she lived and shared: Aim high. Les Brown, the author of *Live Your Dreams*, wasn't speaking directly of Annie when he wrote: "Most people fail in life not because they aim too high and miss, but because they aim too low and hit ... shoot for the moon, because even if you miss, you'll land in the stars." His words surely support her admonition and her legacy.

You are the helper of the fatherless. (Psalm 10:14)

Russell Stendal

But You Care, Don't You?

When a man's ways please the LORD. (Proverbs 16:7)

The window for openly evangelizing in Colombia, South America, began to violently slam shut in the late 1970s. Farming, which was still the country's largest industry, became committed to the production of cocaine, marijuana, and heroin. Drugs were fast on their way to becoming the dominant factor in the nation's economy, and shamefully, the primary market was not domestic; rather, it was the United States. Simultaneously, the country's population experienced severe fractionalizing and headed into anarchy, and things are still the same today. The sociopolitical breakdown consisted of primitive indigenous Indians; rural subsistence farmers; national military, paramilitary, and left-wing factions like FARC (which translates to Revolutionary Armed Forces of Colombia); tribal-based anti-Christian terrorists; narcotics-trafficking cartels referred to as *the Mafia*, with corrupt police officers and bribed drug enforcement officials in tow; and insurgent anti-government guerrillas backed by Communist immigrants from Cuba. Colombia has been described as an ideological jungle with each group striving against the other – often through violent means – for control and power in order to impose its own rapacious agenda on the national whole and to appropriate whatever monies are available. Drugs were the source of substantial loose cash, and thus an easy means to finance the conflicting ideological ends.

Nearly a thousand pastors, priests, and missionaries were forced out of the country at this time. Entire denominations abandoned Colombia; the few that stayed became tangled in deep compromises with various elements of the pervasive drug trade. One guerilla leader was confirmed as responsible for the deaths of four hundred pastors, holding the deadliest record in modern Christian history. It's believed the torture techniques used by some of the criminal factions were handed down from the time when the Spanish and Portuguese Catholic Inquisition operated in Colombia and its neighboring regions.

A single Christian family remained uncompromised and, despite the threats, refused to leave. By staying, one family member in particular eventually achieved the rare status of modest acceptance by all the factions, and was thus able to move relatively free among them. The ease of access and general acceptance had not come easily, and it had not come without exacting considerable personal cost. Once this status was acquired, he was able to maintain that bearing for a long tenure, despite the ever-shifting political landscape. The unique trust was extended to a man of many talents and tasks: writer, electronics technician, commercial fisherman and farmer, pilot, missionary, publisher, land developer, Bible translator, radio broadcast personality, pastor and preacher, lecturer and teacher, ministry founder and executive president, corporate board member, filmmaker, and always, family man. He was a gringo from Minnesota by the name of Russell Martin Stendal.

How Russell arrived in Colombia has become the stuff of family legend and missionary lore. At the age of four, he viewed a picture book about South America titled *The Awakening Valley*. Photos depicting the hard life of Indians in Colombia arrested his attention. Russell questioned his dad as to why things were so bad and what they could do to help. Then came the most challenging question, a personal one: "You care, don't you, Dad?" As a response, his dad told Russell about people referred to as *missionaries* who were called by God to provide foreign assistance. Without waiting for bedtime prayer, Russell immediately knelt in the family room and prayed for God to call his family to become missionaries committed to helping the Colombian Indians find a better life. Upon rising from his knees, Russell wondered if they would be able to leave the next morning. Departure day did eventually come, but it was four years later. At the age of eight, Russell – the oldest child – and his four other family members were on their way to Colombia as missionaries with Wycliffe Bible Translators. Soon the Wycliffe jungle pilots were young Russell's heroes. Fifty years later, four generations of the Stendal family are still in Colombia, continuing to fulfill their ever-expanding objective.

Their missions outreach began with the primitive Kogi Indians of the rugged Sierra Nevada Mountain Range in Northern Colombia. The Kogi were one of the first tribes to make contact with white Europeans, the Spanish explorers of the sixteenth century. They were consistently overlooked, however, for the next four hundred years, leaving their ancient way of life undisturbed. This was due to a combination of their harsh, remote location and a culture that forbade communication and contact outside of the tribe on penalty of death. Until recently, they were still living a Stone Age lifestyle. The Stendals' first attempted contact with the Kogi was through a non-Kogi Indian who was multilingual and willing to act as interpreter. True to the tribe's ancient reputation, he was poisoned when the Kogi learned of his work. The Stendals eventually gained acceptance through a combination of two unique circumstances with key tribe members, both involving miracles of God's healing and timing. God had to open the door that no man could open.

Missionaries are often accused by secular anthropologists of displacing the natives from their supposed idyllic paradise-like lifestyles. They are, however, rarely living in anything close to Eden; more often they are barely subsisting under barbarous circumstances. Kogi life has been characterized by extremely high infant mortality, short life expectancy, numerous serious diseases and worm infections, malnutrition, and drug addiction to a cocaine-based traditional concoction. They were the poster children for the deprivations that first motivated four-year-old Russell after viewing the geography book. In light of the chaotic political situation existing in Colombia since the 1980s, the Kogis' living standard was left unimproved. Had the Kogi managed to evade their primitive conditions, they would have been subject to elimination, manipulation, or exploitation by the many warring factions swirling around them – all of them having far more power and consequence then a primeval tribe could have withstood. Missionary assistance from the Stendal family provided the Kogi with a level of aid and protection not otherwise available, even from their government when it was intentional about providing it, and it was rarely so disposed.

The Stendals believed in ministering to the Indians' bodies as well as to their spirits, and ministering to their bodies meant helping them acquire education and skills in farming, hygiene and health, fishing, and safe drinking water. Improving the lives of the Indians was their original and continuing primary focus, but being able to minister to the Kogi and other tribes first meant gaining their acceptance. Once accomplished, it meant helping them find their place within all the competing group identities of modern Colombian society. As has been so true in other times and locales, the native Indians were at the distant end of society's pecking order. The Stendals, however, gave the Kogi a singularly great gift: Russell's dad completed the translation of the Bible into their language. He delivered it to the chief and proceeded to read certain passages. Upon hearing it, the chief proclaimed to his people that they had just received the truth, and that the word-of-mouth myths passed down among them for generations had become distorted and were no longer accurate or acceptable to follow.

Young Russell gained his missions-related jungle skills early by regularly helping his parents, especially his dad, and by living at times with the tribe. As their aid progressed, they noted that the Kogi were maturing, and, on a larger scale, that Colombia was changing. For their missions work to go deeper into Colombian society beyond the Kogi tribe, Russell's ministry would require a change of means and direction.

Russell became a bush pilot while still in his teens, and a series of small planes served to assist him with several of his varied new undertakings. At times, these included transporting people or supplies. Later, they developed into dropping parachutes containing Bibles, radios, and medicine into remote village locations, or delivering parts for transmitters, towers, or antennae on any one of forty mountaintops within his private (radio evangelism) network. One plane served for four years and came to be fondly known as the Pink Panther for its color and its animated exploits. The 1953 Cessna has since been retired and can be viewed in restored condition at the Voice of the Martyrs campus in Bartlesville, Oklahoma.

Flying small, low-powered aircraft in the mountains – often alone, at night, and in areas known for tropical storms – served to yield a series of nearly unbelievable death-defying experiences from which Russell was safely delivered. These would be difficult to accept without factoring in divine intervention. They include being targeted in a crossfire by two jet fighters, multiple engine failures, midair fires, automatic weapon hits from the Mafia, frequent collisions with chickens and trees, crash landings, night landings in the jungle, and hazardous grass landing strips, all with unfailing, miraculous safe endings, and all transpiring with used parts installed by unqualified mechanics. These close air escapes continue to be the status quo, as the ministry still employs the use of small planes in dangerous conditions on into its fourth generation. Russell says that his jungle pilot experiences are the fulfillment of his boyhood dream of an exciting life, but that there are times when it just plain gets too exciting.

Early on the morning of August 14, 1983, the twenty-seven-year-old bush pilot was planning to depart the rural village of Canyo Jabon in southeastern Colombia. He thought he'd be leaving the same way he'd arrived, by flying out in his Cessna 170. Russell was there for a business meeting to transfer his startup fishing business to the local Indians as a benevolent gesture. It was then that his life went on a 142 -day unscheduled sabbatical. It was the time and place of his first kidnapping. He'd often been threatened with kidnappings, but he had successfully avoided them thus far. This day he was unable to do so, and he was held longer than any of his subsequent captivity experiences. Marxist guerillas sold drugs, fleeced the locals, and kidnapped Americans in order to finance their long-running anti-government rebellion. Now they'd set another trap and marked Russell as their target. They mistook the young pilot for a rich North American gringo who could be cashiered for some big money.

Russell was forced to lay down his fully loaded, double-barrel twenty-gauge shotgun and surrender without a fight in order to save his captured friend from being killed in retaliation for any lack in his cooperation. After securing Russell, the insurgents spitefully sprayed his cherished Cessna with automatic weapons fire to ensure he'd never fly it again. They then raced upriver into a secure jungle area under their control. Unknown to his Communist captors, Russell had a .38-caliber Smith & Wesson revolver strapped to his left ankle under his pant leg. With the first distraction, he fired the handgun at his captors until depleting the cylinder. It was a brief firefight that wounded his guard, but failed to gain his freedom. From that point forward, he was always partially tied and vigilantly guarded. His home became remote hideaways with frequent moves to secret new locations.

Constantly looking for escape opportunities but never finding them, Russell switched to a long-term strategy. His new plan was to make the best out of a bad situation. He would take his captors captive! The empty days and nights of captivity became times of prayer and meditation. As he closely observed his captors, he realized their lives were more prisoner-like than was his own. Russell was free inside, even if tethered on the outside, and there was a good chance a cash ransom would be paid and he'd be released to return to his wife and children. By contrast, most of his kidnappers were men and women who'd been taken from their families as young boys and girls, given weapons, and expected to dedicate themselves to a terrorist lifestyle, always with the distant promise of a worker's paradise after the final victory. They were threatened with death themselves, or death to their families, should they try to quit the movement. The guerillas were physical captives, but more importantly, they were spiritual captives. Russell was at liberty inside because he'd embraced the truth of the good news, which had given him real freedom. He came to realize God's immediate resolution for the guerillas' painful predicament was him.

Russell determined that taking his captors captive could be done by a two-point personal approach. First, he would quietly engage the insurgents in personal conversations on controversial but substantive issues of interest to them. He readily found those issues to be creation, America, President Ronald Reagan, the Bible, Christianity, God, Communism, and capitalism. But, of course, his positions were always the polar opposite of his captors, so caution was a vital convention to honor so as not to push too hard too fast. Second, he would begin to share his life experiences, and he determined to be candid with them about every aspect. His approach gained immediate acceptance, and he was provided with writing materials. Russell began committing his story more formally to paper. It would be the book he'd always intended to write, but had never started.

In the book, he emphasized his life purpose, his beliefs, and most importantly, his mistakes. Doing so engendered a certain aspect of human frailty to which his kidnappers related. The mistakes shared included the times when he let his father fully blame a failure on his partner even though Russell shared the guilt; compromised his piloting with a drug operator; was angry at God;

overextended his credit, got deep into debt, and presumed God would fix it; made key decisions without sufficient prayer preparation; and agreed to the promise of some big money in exchange for transporting a mafia personality in his plane. Russell even shared about some of the critical disagreements he'd had with his native Colombian wife, Marina.

When the past caught up with the present, Russell was writing of daily experiences with his captors. The book became completely coincident with his captivity and contained diary-like dialogue current with the unfolding events and emotions of his ongoing captivity. The Communists became so engaged in monitoring his book – even noting the inclusion of their names – that they built a desk and obtained a typewriter for his use. They asked to read the pages while still fresh, and they guaranteed they would preserve the whole of it for him if he would also translate the English version into their native Spanish. Russell likened his experience to Scheherazade and her alleged storybook titled *One Thousand and One Nights*. It helped assure him of a daily grant of life, just as it did for the fictional Scheherazade, who was able to extend her life one night at a time by entertaining the Persian king with her ongoing storytelling before he slept.

Russell was now permitted occasional gift packages from his family, and early on he received his Bible. He immediately began filling much of his day with Bible reading, but he also developed a unique practice of mediating on one psalm each day. He tied the number of the psalm to the number of his captivity day; for example, he read Psalm 96 on his ninety-sixth day of captivity. Russell told his captors repeatedly that they had kidnapped the wrong man. They assumed his having an airplane made him a rich American businessman instead of a poor missionary just living among them while trying to help their people. After many passing weeks with no ransom forthcoming, his captors attempted to break Russell psychologically; this is a technique called *brainwashing*. During this process, he was fed continuous lies about his family in addition to stories designed to cause fear, all the while being denied sufficient sleep.

He informed them that they had two choices: to kill him or to let him go for whatever small amount his family could afford. Asked by the guerillas if he was afraid to die, he replied he was prepared for it. The day Russell reached Psalm 142, he was blindfolded and taken in the middle of the night some several hours away to an unknown location. After stopping and having the blindfold removed, he saw his younger brother, Chaddy, with a mediator. His release had been negotiated for fifty-five thousand dollars, not the million originally demanded. The Communists claimed they'd lost money by holding him. Russell had consistently warned his captors that God would not reward them because they were interfering with His work. In addition to his freedom, Russell received two more pleasant surprises: The guerillas extended a promise that his family could continue to operate in their areas – known as red zones – without any further trouble from them, and his family had been able to repair his damaged Cessna.

Russell's redemption wasn't a conclusion; it was a beginning in disguise. He'd come to know many of these men personally, even winning their respect and friendship. It was these relationships – and later those additional ones gained through other kidnappings and difficult experiences with drug cartels, military, and other factions – that eventually led to the free hand he gained in traveling throughout Colombia and in accessing all people groups. Later, some of his captors became Christians and joined him in witnessing to those still in spiritual bondage. The truth of this situation was well illustrated in the title of a Richard Wurmbrand book that Russell had read and that he was applying in his ministry: *Jesus: Friend to Terrorists*. By working His will through Russell in unexpected ways, God was taking the captors captive, one person at a time and one faction at a time. It was not Russell's idea or plan after all; it was God's. God had placed Russell in a teachable position and accepted his willingness to be used in any circumstance. Russell could not be fully used when he was still running with his own big missionary plans and projects; he had to learn to discern where God was moving and simply move with Him. He learned to do what Henry Blackaby calls "experiencing God."

Russell says, "God taught me how to be a true missionary for Him. I began to react toward problems and adversity as opportunities to learn important things and as opportunities for God to use me to bring glory to Himself. My life changed to one of victory in Jesus Christ. I still have problems, difficulties, and even an occasional defeat, but now I can clearly see the design and purpose that God has for my life. If I have the right attitude, God can reign over everything that happens in my life and teach me something useful from even the most difficult experiences."

During this first kidnapping, as well as the others to follow, Russell was a pawn between several conflicting ideologies. He sometimes must have felt

like Elijah on Mount Carmel as he demanded of the compromising multitudes: *"How long will you falter between two opinions? If the LORD is God,
follow Him"* (1 Kings 18:21).

Russell titled the book written during his first kidnapping *Rescue the
Captors*. It's still regularly printed, distributed, and read, and presently it
has two sequels, which are often referred to as simply *Rescue II* and *Rescue
III*. The *Rescue* books, and the many others he's since written and continues
to write, are serving as a bridge to those many lost, captive, and confused
men and women in Colombia and beyond, including the Kogi Indian tribe
whose plight first attracted the Stendals' attention. His writings, along with
the success and admirable example of the Stendal family, were noticed by
the international church. Collectively, these things helped to draw other
Christian workers back to Colombia; however, the men and women who
are converted from within the warring factions of Colombian society often
develop into the most effective and motivated team members.

The quality of life in the Kogi Indian tribe has greatly improved in many
ways, just as young Russell prayed for; but they remain resistant to the gospel, with most retaining their primitive spiritualist beliefs and continuing
to persecute Christian believers. Additionally, the long internal conflicts
and ongoing drug trade have created new problems for the Colombians,
with millions of refugees displaced from their homes, villages, and lands.
Death threats, selective assassinations, kidnappings, and extortion are still
prevalent, and, in fact, seem to be growing toward that degree of violence
experienced by Christian workers in the late 1970s. One former FARC guerrilla, who had served the Communist cause since the age of fourteen, said:
"My indoctrination led me to think that everything relating to Christianity
needed to be abolished, so I killed many Christians. I displaced them from
their lands and persecuted them, and I wouldn't allow them to come together
in their churches."

The Stendal family remains in Colombia and continues to expand its
ministry despite their staff and family experiencing the likes of regular
kidnappings, death threats, and aviation failures. Their story is ongoing, as
illustrated by two fresh newsletters sitting on my desk. In the first, Russell
states matter-of-factly: "We were twice lined up to be shot by unidentified
irregular forces since the last mailing." In the other: "I expect to be released
from the kidnapping soon." The ministry has benefited by linking many of its

projects to two organizations: Voice of the Martyrs in Bartlesville, Oklahoma and Spirit of Martyrdom in Clarkdale, Arizona. VOM is the much larger of the two and has as its mission finding and helping people – like Russell's family – who are in the midst of persecution, but who are willing to stay despite everything they encounter. Meanwhile, Russell continues dropping Bible parachutes by the thousands from his plane, building radio stations to broadcast the Word into hard-to-reach jungles, airing Bible studies, translating the Scriptures into native languages, mediating truces, and working his God-ordained relationships within the societal factions.

Even though many seemingly insurmountable obstructions remain, Russell effectively leverages his unusual earned immunity. First Corinthians 9:19 and 22 serve well to summarize the path chosen by Russell and his family: *For though I am free from all men, I have made myself a servant to all, that I might win the more; I have become all things to all men, that I might by all means save some.* Their long dedication is presently being rewarded as they witness a strong regional revival in Southwest Colombia and a general revival throughout the national military. That same guerilla quoted above has now met Jesus and he says, "Instead of being a messenger of hatred, I am now a messenger of peace."

The Stendals do the possible: sharing the gospel. God does the impossible: softening the hearts of men to receive it. When the Stendals arrived in Colombia in 1964, less than half of 1 percent of the population was considered evangelical Christian; as of the end of 2014, evangelical Christians comprised 25 percent of the population.

> *He makes even his enemies to be at peace with him.*
> (Proverbs 16:7)

* * * *

Author's Note: Prior to *Stories of Uncommon Character* going to print, I received a newsletter from Russell wherein he reviewed the previous year's projects, which was his fifty-first year of Colombian-based ministry. Among other updates, he shared the following points. The man he called his worst enemy (some say the worst terrorist in Colombia) because he had been attempting to kill Russell for thirty years, has become his friend. More than five hundred of Russell's friends and coworkers have disappeared during the last five years, all presumed murdered. Russell has won sufficient favor with the FARC guerilla leadership and Colombian government officials that he is accepted as their spiritual consultant. As such, he has induced both sides to declare a nationwide ceasefire with no expiration date while he meets with them in neutral Cuba to discuss the details of a larger peace agreement. More developmental narrative on these points can be found in Russell's recently released third and most recent book in his ongoing *Rescue* series, *Hidden Agenda*.

Kimberly Munley

The Training Takes Over

I will surely go with you. (Judges 4:9)

"Where does America get these heroes?" This question was asked by a navy admiral in the movie adaptation of James Michener's 1953 Korean War novel, *The Bridges at Toko-Ri*. The admiral was reflecting on airmen who – at the cost of their lives – had just destroyed several heavily defended bridges. It remains a valid question, given our continued history of providing the world with so many heroes. Since this century's Middle Eastern wars, the answer has to include Killeen, Texas. It's similar in many ways to other heartland cities recently platted from former farm land. The city is home to a hundred and twenty-five thousand residents. It's been described as having quiet cul-de-sacs and peaceful neighborhoods connected by wide, tree-lined streets. Killeen once differentiated itself as a train crossing – taking its name from railroad man Frank P. Killeen; today it does so by hosting Fort Hood army base. This is where twenty-two year old Private Elvis Presley received his tank and sharpshooter training prior to being assigned to Germany; it is presently populated by men and women who've displayed bravery in Afghanistan and Iraq. The mood in the town and on the base is often somber, with flags at half-staff in honor of brave, deceased defenders who were stationed at the base and whose families often still live in the city.

On Thursday, November 6, 2009, the flags remained in this honorary position for an extended period as fourteen dead and thirty-two wounded victims of a traitor turned mass murderer were mourned and remembered there, as well as across a nation that was, thankfully, still not immune to terror-induced shock. Deadly acts of hatred had been premeditated against innocent soldiers by radical Islamist Nidal Malik Hasan. His actions proved again that errant political correctness not only distorts truth and disguises evil, but it also kills. His beliefs were well known but deliberately overlooked or excused. The cowardly domestic terrorist's killing spree was stopped by a petite, long-haired blond mother who lived near the base in one of those pleasant neighborhoods. As a result, Killeen is now recorded in our history and registered in our memories with opposing acts of violent hatred and extreme heroism, where the former abounds, by the grace of God, so does the latter.

Killeen resident Sergeant Kimberly Munley is a Department of Defense police officer and an army veteran. After moving there, she took on much more than the usual *soccer mom* responsibilities. Before Killeen, she spent five years as a police officer in Carolina Beach, North Carolina, where her hero, Kim's father, was mayor. Possessing a small build like Annie Oakley and Rose Valland (just over five feet tall, one hundred pounds, and the mother of two young boys), thirty-four year old Kim was also an advanced firearms instructor and a civilian member of Fort Hood's Special Reaction Team (SRT). She completed prevention training for *active shooter* scenarios after the April 16, 2007, mass murder of thirty-two at Virginia Tech, where on HaShoah Memorial Day, Holocaust survivor Liviu Librescu saved many of his students' lives at the cost of his own.

Kim was nearby having her patrol car tuned up and washed, when a 9-1-1 call reported shots being fired at Fort Hood's Soldier Readiness Processing Center (SRPC). The SRPC was not on the sergeant's regular beat, but she was familiar with the facility as it was located only five minutes from her home. Without waiting for backup or authorization, she headed directly for the base, thus becoming the first law enforcement official on the scene. Kim arrived in just three minutes, including the time required to cover the final distance on foot.

As she approached the SRPC building, the sound of shots were heard ringing in the air. Immediately, a soldier ran out a door with a gunman pursuing him with automatic weapons engaged. The shooter, who was wearing the uniform of a United States Army major, was still fully occupied with executing his planned killing spree. Before Kim arrived, he had sprayed more than two hundred bullets, scoring thirteen innocent kills and thirty additional hits in subservience to his bloody god. Still on a rapid, open approach, Kim fired at Hasan, who wheeled around and charged her while emptying his two handguns with reckless intent to kill. Kim took bullets to a wrist and both thighs, but she stood her ground, willing herself not to fall. Managing to remain calm enough to aim numerous times, she placed four rounds into the terrorist's center mass – perfectly executing her training under conditions that should have caused anyone to pale or err. She fired until Hasan dropped, and then Kim dropped. But the killing ended.

It was like a showdown from a Texas-based Wild West movie, and indeed the time was just past high noon. Three-time Academy Award winner Gary Cooper, who played multiple film heroes, would have been humbled by Kim's authentic execution of his *High Noon* performance. That day in Killeen, reality surpassed fiction. Studies verify that for someone in Kim's position, time seems to shift into slow motion, and more time seems to pass than actually does. From the first shot to the last, authorities say the whole foul play lasted under ten minutes, and the final showdown less than a minute.

The radios and scanners around Bell County quickly announced: "Officer down." Brooke Beato, a close friend of Kim's whose husband is an army captain stationed at the base, said she was not surprised as she heard Kim's name broadcast. "I couldn't believe what happened, but when I heard what she did, I believed it because of who she is – I know her. It was just like her; she carries herself with confidence." The base commander, Lieutenant General Robert Cone, summed it up as "an amazing and an aggressive performance by this police officer; she walked up and engaged him." Kim executed a tactic in sync with the lessons that emerged from the Virginia Tech shootings. At VTU, first responders erroneously waited for additional backup before interacting with the shooter. As a member of the base SRT, Kim was taught that aggressive action against a shooter results in fewer victims. Hers were straightforward procedures intended to be executed by one or more groups; Kim performed them alone. That's how she acquired her nickname: *Mighty Mouse*. (The original, diminutive Mighty Mouse was a popular 1950s after-school cartoon. Although much smaller in stature, he was like the other 1950s weekly televised hero, *the man of steel*, Superman. (See the associated story on Stetson Kennedy.)

Hasan survived Kim's bullets and was quickly apprehended when her backup arrived. Although court-martialed and condemned to death, he waits on death-row for the time when his sentence may be fully executed, generally looking like a bearded Muslim imam and writing solicitations for a position in ISIS. He remains non-contrite, thinks himself a hero, and continues to support radical Islam. After two surgeries, Kim was out of the hospital in a week and was once more "to the rescue, ready to save the day," as in the animated superhero's slogan. The real-life Killeen hero described for the media what she called a "confusing and chaotic" day. Detailing the day's events, she added:

> When I got shot, it felt like a muscle being torn out of my leg. I never lost consciousness. I wanted to stay awake and know every-thing that was going on. Things are getting better day by day. Emotionally, I'm just hoping the rest of the officers, the injured, and the families of the deceased are healing as well. The training does take over. In that particular incident, we didn't have much time to think. I know it's going to be a slow process to get back to my nor-mal life, but I know that I can accomplish it and get back to what I do and love to do on a daily basis.

Like so many of the heroes in this book, Kim wishes she could have acted even faster to save more lives. From the hospital, she modified her Twitter bio to read: "I live a blessed life and thank the Lord every day for it. ... [It's] a hard one, but I go to sleep peacefully at night knowing I may have made a difference in someone's life." She knows life's secret: Live one day at a time and as though it may be your last. For thirteen solders, that day was unexpectedly their last.

Fast-forward to April 2, 2014: same base, town, and hospital, but different killer, different victims, and another hero. This time, unfortunately, it was a hero whose performance day was his last. Unarmed, Sergeant First Class Daniel M. Ferguson blocked the door that otherwise would have admitted Puerto Rican-born Specialist Ivan Lopez into the heavily occupied room beyond. In so doing, Daniel became the second fatality in Lopez's spree, but he'd prevented many easy kills of his coworkers. He forced Lopez to take his spree to the streets, first on foot, then in a car where his hatred eventually claimed nineteen victims before he added himself to the list of the dead with a self-inflicted shot to the head.

Daniel had recently returned to the States after surviving multiple duty rotations in Iraq, Kuwait, and Afghanistan, where he earned a Bronze Star. He was delighted to be back with his fiancée, enjoying the relative ease of a quiet position on a clean, stateside base. In his small hometown in rural Florida, Daniel was known as a "quiet, very respectful, bright young man who was just a well-rounded, wholesome, nice person." He was remembered as a member of the Letterman's Club, qualifying in five sports, and active in the Fellowship of Christian Athletes. In contrast, the man who killed Daniel was a self-proclaimed victim who faked his service injury while being jealous of those who had earned them. Again, the flags around the otherwise quiet, close-knit community of Killeen were forced to half-staff in honor of their fallen heroes. Days after Daniel's murder, Kim posted on her Twitter address, @hope2forget30: "Never forget November 5, 2009 and April 2, 2014. God bless the victims of Fort Hood!"

In closing, I borrow the words allegedly spoken by U.S. District Judge William Young after passing a guilty judgment on another domestic terrorist serving the Islamic-fascist cause:

> It seems to me you hate the one thing that to us is most precious. You hate our freedom; our individual freedom to live as we choose, to come and go as we choose, to believe or not believe as we choose. Here, in this society, the very wind carries freedom. It carries it everywhere from sea to shining sea. It is because we prize individual freedom so much that you are here in this beautiful courtroom, so that everyone can see, truly see, that justice is administered fairly, individually, and discreetly. It is for freedom's sake that your lawyers are striving so vigorously on your behalf, have filed appeals, will go on in their representation of you before other judges. We Americans are all about freedom. Because we all know that the way we treat you is the measure of our own liberties. Make no mistake, though. It is yet true that we will bear any burden, pay any price, to preserve our freedoms. Look around this courtroom. Mark it well. The world is not going to long remember what you or I say here. The

day after tomorrow, it will be forgotten, but this, however, will long endure. Here in this courtroom and courtrooms all across America, the American people will gather to see that justice – not war – individual justice is, in fact, being done. See that flag? That's the flag of the United States of America. That flag will fly there long after this is all forgotten. That flag stands for freedom. And it always will.

Special thanks to Kim Munley and Daniel Ferguson for their proactive defenses of our soldiers and our way of life at Fort Hood, Killeen, Texas – a home to heroes.

So she said, "I will go with you; nevertheless there will be no glory for you in the journey you are taking, for the Lord will sell Sisera into the hand of a woman." (Judges 4:9)

* * * *

Author's Note: I opened this story with a reference to a paraphrased quote from the film *The Bridges at Toko-Ri*. The idea of applying it to Killeen was borrowed from a newsletter by Newt Gingrich dated Wednesday, November 11, 2009, and titled "Where Do We Get These Men and Women?"

I generally reserve the telling of Kim's story to middle school age students and older, but once I adopted it for a fifth grade class, primarily because its length fit our open timeframe. I was uncertain how it would be received, so I asked for short essays at the conclusion, inviting them to share their impressions. To my pleasant surprise, a new sticky-point emerged; one that I had over-looked until then, but which is worth noting. Several students related to Kim's small stature, i.e. light-weight, small, young, and short. They wrote of wanting to develop the Mighty Mouse potential within themselves; that is, to become prepared to do big things even if physically small, to let the training take-over when the circumstances require.

Parable of Overnight Success

All It Takes Is Everything

Whatever your hand finds to do. (Ecclesiastes 9:10)

What did these people have in common before they became rich and famous: Bill Gates and Andy Grove (computer technology); Tiger Woods, Brett Favre, and Michael Jordan (professional sports); Joshua Bell, Itzhak Perlman, and Vladimir Horowitz (virtuoso instrumentalists); Lennon-McCartney and the Beatles (world's most successful songwriting team and rock band combination); Bobby Fischer (chess grandmaster); Warren Buffet (outstanding investor); and Wolfgang Mozart (young and prodigious classical composer)? What was the shared key to their superb accomplishments?

Of the following possible factors, which of them, if any, is the unknown catalyst: intelligence, luck, wealth, education, opportunity, aptitude, family, timing, coaching, talent, locale, biology, or something else? Each person possessed one or more of these criteria, but no single one was common to all of these paragons. Therefore if there is a common trait to success, and there does seem to be one, it must be something else.

There is something held in common by these superior performers, as well as by most or all others who exhibit remarkable proficiency in their professions. It has been called the *shared rule of accomplishment*. Several studies of successful people have uncovered that guideline, and much about the answer is surprising. Some of the finer points of interpretation resulting from those studies are, however, debated. For simplicity, I refer hereafter to the identity of the singular element of success as simply *the rule*.

The *American Heritage Dictionary* defines *world-class* as being among the best or foremost in the world, someone or something having an international standard of excellence. The rule states that ten thousand hours of practice are required prior to achieving world-class expertise in the many fields of life skills performance, especially those of music (composing and playing an instrument), games, and sports. On average, ten thousand hours of practice equates to a ten-year period of preparation in the life of one dedicated to mastering a performance goal.

The ten-thousand-hours factor seems to have first been clearly identified by University of Colorado/University of Stockholm professor Dr. K. Anders Ericsson and two of his colleagues, Ralf Krampe and Clemens Tesch-Romer. These men expanded on the affiliated research of two German analysts who studied the practice habits of violin performers. Dr. Ericsson concluded that "many characteristics once believed to reflect innate talent are actually the result of intense practice extended for a minimum of ten years." The concept was popularly labeled the *10,000-hour rule of success* by sociology writer Malcolm Gladwell in his thought-provoking book *Outliers: The Story of Success*. Conviction about the rule is uneven, with a range of professional nuances offered by these men, as well as by a host of others; a few of the most prominent ones are neurologist Dr. Daniel Levitin, sports authors David Epstein and Daniel Coyle, and economics author Geoffrey Colvin.

Referencing the rule in *Outliers: The Story of Success*, Gladwell provided a fundamental quote, which he attributed to Dr. Levitin. It was this quote that became the catalyst for the detailed, and still unfinished, discussion of the rule. The quote is as follows:

> The emerging picture from such studies (of highly successful people) is that 10,000 hours of practice is required to achieve the level of mastery associated with being a world-class expert–in anything. In study after study of composers, basketball players, fiction writers, ice skaters, concert pianists, chess players, master criminals and what have you, the number comes up again and again. Of course, this doesn't address why some people get more out of their practice sessions than others do. But no one has yet found a case in which

true world-class expertise was accomplished in less time. It seems it takes the brain this long to assimilate all that it needs to know to achieve true mastery.

Understanding of the rule is furthered by acknowledging its close relation to, and endorsement of, several commonly accepted and well-polished maxims such as "practice makes perfect" and "there's no substitute for hard work." This is a premise about human achievement not dissimilar to last century's sociological debate regarding the shaping effects on human nature of heredity versus environment. To illustrate: Is a person successful due to having exceptional intelligence, appearance, or strength, or because he was born into privilege, location, or wealth? The rule can be simplified as essentially promoting practice as the dominant factor over innate talent in people who display ultimate expertise in a skill or practice. Of course, there may be a host of lesser influences involved, such as timing, mentoring, or opportunity. When considering an application of the rule, it is essential to always bear in mind that it's intended to apply only to those who have risen – or those who want to rise – to the pinnacle of their field; that is, acknowledged achievers of world-class expertise. It does not fully apply to those who are – or who want to be – simply good at what they do or those who consistently exercise their skill only for quiet, personal satisfaction off the world stage.

To further understand the rule, let's review one recent, well-known example frequently cited as usually successful in the field of popular music: the Beatles. Much like many of the other examples of dominance, they appear to have suddenly been *discovered*; that is, recognized by the public, with massive acceptance quickly following. The Beatles are generally reported as having burst upon the American scene in 1964 after being modestly known in England only a short time.

Gladwell and other researchers note that closer examination reveals far more. Prior to arriving in America, they had already been together for seven years and had completed multiple extended trips to Hamburg, Germany. Beginning in 1960, they played eight-hour sets, seven days a week, during which they had to overcome the twin handicaps of foreign language and a noisy work environment. It's estimated that the band played over a thousand engagements, not including practice sessions and jamming. The total number of acquired practice hours prior to 1964 and their American debut exceeded ten thousand hours. That's the rule, and that's what the successful overachievers have in common: ten thousand hours of practice at their trade prior to supposedly becoming suddenly famous (aka *overnight successes).*

Studies of world-class experts yield two more significant revelations noted again by Gladwell. First, the researchers didn't discover any *naturals* with above-average ability who had floated effortlessly, cream-like to the top while not having to practice as hard as their peers. Second, they didn't discover any *grinds* who had below-average ability, but who worked twice as diligently as their peers in order to succeed. They only found people of average or slightly above average ability who just kept practicing without quitting until they surpassed ten thousand hours. Success followed thereafter (as determined by name recognition, income, peer appraisals, industry standards, or fame). Other factors like wealth, family support, physical stamina, and education may have permitted them to practice more hours in a shorter timeframe or with less interference and greater ease, but these weren't the reasons they excelled; it was the practice itself.

Once more in *Outliers,* Gladwell states: "Practice isn't the thing you do once you're good. It's the thing you do that makes you good. The people at the very top don't just work harder or even much harder than everyone else; they work much, much harder. Achievement is talent plus preparation ... and the preparation part of the formula looms far larger than we normally assume."

We may safely conclude that an attention-grabbing career, that is, achieving extremely high expertise in a field, is not the result of random chance over which we have no control; rather – like so much in life – it's based on our deliberate choice. It's a choice regarding our desired level of dedication: how much we are willing to practice, how willing we are to complete all the required preparations.

Early in my career I was a commuter; among the audio books I enjoyed while commuting were several by Earl Nightingale. I recall him sharing a story about an accomplished pianist. After a particularly fine performance, the pianist was approached by someone from the audience who exclaimed, "I'd do anything to play the piano like you do!" The pianist replied, "No, you wouldn't." Explaining further, he said: "If it were so, you would play at my level. But first, you'd have to commit the time. Time in practice is the one thing it takes – hour after hour, day after day, year after year." Doing the hard things that most people are unwilling to do is frequently the difference between the successful and all the rest.

It's okay not to practice the required ten thousand hours or ten years at some endeavor; there's no condemnation in not doing so. We must, however, realize and accept that this is our own decision, our own choice. We're able to achieve whatever level of success that we're willing to commit to and then follow through to completion. Success comes to those who are committed to practicing especially hard. If our goal is to be consummate in our field, then be encouraged. We now have insight into how to achieve it. The one factor that may be more important than any of the others, including even natural talent, is readily available to all takers: practice.

Do it with your might. (Ecclesiastes 9:10)

Tommy Thompson

Exploring Inner Space

For they shall partake of the abundance of the seas.
(Deuteronomy 33:19)

On Saturday, September 12, 1857, a double-sided paddle-wheel steamer nearly the length of a football field was caught in a life-and-death struggle with a *perfect storm* hurricane off Cape Hatteras, North Carolina. It was the steamship S.S. *Central America*, under the care of the very capable and likeable Captain William Herndon. Aboard were 578 passengers and crew. Nearly all of the passengers were miners departing the gold fields of Northern California en route from a Panamanian port, pausing in Havana, continuing northerly up the expanse of the eastern seaboard, exiting in New York City, and then returning to homes they hadn't visited for several years.

Also on board was the single-largest shipment of gold in the history of the world – more than any of the legendary Spanish treasure ships that traveled the Caribbean seas for two centuries. The thirty thousand pounds of gold aboard was in every conceivable form: dust, flake, chunk, brick, jewelry, and coin. Most of the thousands of coins were freshly produced by the new San Francisco mint. The source of the gold was the fabulous wealth that had been found and accumulated during the ten years since its discovery on January 24, 1848, by James Marshall at Sutter's Mill in Coloma, near today's California state capital of Sacramento. The resulting massive gold fever came to be known as the California Gold Rush, and the three hundred thousand participating prospectors were called *Forty-Niners* – as in 1849, the peak year. (See the related story, "Parable of the Four Farmers.")

Captain Herndon and his crew fought the 105-miles-per-hour, category-two storm winds valiantly, but despite their frantic maneuverings, the big ship was quickly blown far off course. On the second day, the crew's survival efforts were hampered by lost or shredded sails, a broken boiler, and severe physical exhaustion from hours of fruitless bailing. That evening at 8:00 EST, the steamer surrendered to the high seas and relentless waves; it sunk in international waters about 160 miles from shore in 8,000 feet of water – a depth of two miles. The captain and crew went down with the ship, but 153 passengers were rescued and able to report their accounts of the tragedy. Hundreds of millions of dollars in gold sank with the ship to the bottom of the Atlantic Ocean, where it lay in surprisingly tidy piles for 130 years.

Regardless of whether the gold was owned privately, corporately, or governmentally, most of it was intended to reach the financial markets of New York City. The loss of this extremely valuable cargo was of such dire magnitude that it helped trigger the nationwide financial panic that ensued only one month after the sinking. At the time, gold and silver reserves still backed the credibility of the country's currency.

A deep, saltwater environment is very damaging to nearly every material, natural or man-made, including iron, books, wood, food, and clothing. Uniquely, it's not a problem for gold, a chemical element assigned the symbol "Au" and the atomic number 79. This property extends beyond saltwater corrosion to also protect gold against high pressure and water penetration. Additionally, it can resist corrosion from acids, chemicals, impact, and time, all the while retaining its usefulness and bright yellow luster. Comprehensive resistance is one of the key reasons gold is so precious, useful, and sought after. Gold is also very dense, with a brick-sized amount weighing nearly thirty pounds. It's universally utilized in jewelry, currency, and manufacturing, as it's also malleable, bondable, and conductible.

There are plenty of treasure hunters in this world, and gold holds a fascination level at the pinnacle of their fantasies. So, what's the problem? Just travel to where the ship sank, scoop it up, and become fabulously rich, right? Not so fast. At least three big challenges accompany that goal and block the way to becoming instantly wealthy beyond imagination or need.

First, water weighs 8.35 pounds per gallon; therefore, for every foot of ocean floor, 67,000 pounds of water sat on top of the gold. Swim to the bottom of a pool only twelve feet deep and you will quickly feel the resulting pressure generated by the weight of the water. Most things, including submarines, will implode beyond a depth of two hundred feet – that's shorter than a football field.

Second, the technology for reaching, exploring, or even viewing the strange and unfamiliar ocean bottom simply did not exist prior to being invented by the hero of this story. At two miles' depth, the gold from the S.S. *Central America* is relatively close to the ocean's average depth of two and a half miles. Just below the surface, things start to change radically. The majority of the ocean is perpetually dark and just a couple of degrees above freezing.

Third, the ocean is unimaginably vast and underexplored. The saltwater ocean – not counting the other sources of water – constitutes 71 percent of the earth's surface, and due to its depth, is 97 percent of both the earth's biological habitat and its source of water. Yet we still know very little about it. Just a century ago, we thought that the ocean floor was bare and lifeless. One science reporter wrote that perhaps today we have only researched a billionth of the available sea. Consider the overwhelming task of finding a ship that sank deep into such vastness, during a hurricane, with no surviving crew or maps, in an unknown location.

The few things we know about the oceans are compelling: They contain enough dissolved salt to cover the earth with a 500-foot layer; 80 percent of all life resides there; a half-cup of ocean water holds millions of bacteria, hundreds of thousands of phytoplankton, and tens of thousands of zooplankton (half of all life-sustaining oxygen comes from just the zooplankton; the other half comes from plants); the combined flow of all rivers is equal to only 1 percent of just the Gulf Stream; the largest living structure known is Australia's Great Barrier Reef; the tallest mountain, Mauna Kea, is located underwater and has a height of 33,400 feet, and it's 4,400 feet higher than Mount Everest; the longest mountain range on earth – known as the mid-ocean ridge – is also underwater and has a length of 40,400 miles, making it four times longer than the Andes, Rockies, and Himalayas combined;

and one point in the Mariana Trench is 6.8 miles deep, making it the deepest spot on earth, with a pressure 1,100 times that at sea level. The many things we don't know about the oceans are overwhelming by comparison to what's known about terra firma. Humans have spent more time on the moon's surface than in the deepest ocean realms.

In 1961, President John F. Kennedy convinced Congress to explore space and place a man on the moon. It took 8 years, $100 billion, and 400,000 people to complete the task of getting Neil Armstrong there. Since that event, our knowledge of earth's atmosphere has grown incalculably. By contrast, it's commonly accepted by scientists that we still know less about inner oceanic space than we do about outer atmospheric space. The surface of the oceans is a busy place known to commerce, travel, and sport, but just hundreds of feet under, the oceans remain as distant and remote from man's reach as does the outer space beyond our solar system. Arthur C. Clarke said, "How inappropriate to call this planet Earth when it is clearly Ocean."

In October of 1989, a bright, young engineering genius named Tommy Thompson did the impossible: He accomplished what had never been done before and what everyone on the planet thought couldn't be done. Tommy painstakingly pinpointed the *Central America*'s location far out in the Atlantic Ocean, and then he began inventing ways to reach the gold and recover it. Through an innovative combination of research, mathematics, computer forecasting and modeling, engineering, and invention, Tommy was able to solve a mystery that had baffled, frustrated, and misled others for many years. More remarkably, he did so without technical or financial support from Congress or any governmental agency, and he did it in only five years with a $12 million budget and a team of only thirty people.

Tommy developed and utilized tools both great and small. Three of the more prominent were a specially retrofitted ship, rechristened *Artic Explorer*; his deep-sea recovery invention, the now-famous remote operations vehicle (ROV) known as NEMO (equipped with cameras, articulating arms, and lights); and a clever maritime GPS system that could keep the ship on target despite tides, wind, and drift. The ship was creatively designed to handle his vast array of scientific equipment, an articulating crane, the twelve-thousand-pound NEMO with its massive cables, and the unique GPS system.

After locating the sunken ship, he first fought off other treasure hunters who hoped to capitalize on his brilliant mapping data and recovery methods. Next, he was forced to assist with establishing clear, new rulings in international maritime law. Because the ship was located beyond the traditional three-mile territorial waters of the United States, clarity in this area was necessary to gain a solid green light for operations and for uncontested ownership of any findings. Past legal procedures were often conflicting from nation to nation when the activity transpired in international waters. These two challenges were anticipated, so Tommy was prepared to meet them. He skillfully and quickly outmaneuvered both the gold-seeking claim-jumpers and the legal pariahs that his find instantly attracted.

By employing Tommy's three new resources, his crew successfully lifted a substantial amount of gold to the surface in the fall of 1989. The event concluded a project of five years' duration from its dubious beginning to its victorious end. He wasn't able to reach all the gold; quantities even larger than what he recovered remained at the bottom of the sea at the completion of his extraordinary project. Even so, his accomplishment was called thereafter the greatest successful treasure hunt in history. In total, 7,000 newly minted, solid gold coins were recovered from the ocean bottom near the wreck, along with 500 gold coins of other origins, 20 pounds of gold dust, and 530 gold ingots – altogether about 17 tons of pure, refined gold. The largest single piece from the ship was called the *Eureka* bar. It weighed 80 pounds, was shaped like an oversized brick, and was stamped with an 1857 currency value of $17,433.57. In 2001, the Eureka bar was purchased for $8,000,000! Value estimates for all of the gold recovered from the S.S. *Central America* were generally around $100,000,000 in 2001 value; one source placed the amount closer to $150,000,000. (The values of non-minted [raw] and minted [numismatic] gold are not the same, and the values of both are influenced by a number of volatile factors. Consequently, it's not possible to fix the value of gold for an extended time or in a consistent manner; that is, it's not as simple as just calculating monetary-based inflation over time. A snapshot price is the best that can be provided for any given date.)

Tommy's biggest challenge turned out to be something unexpected, and it didn't occur during the difficult planning or operations phases as he anticipated it would. The most serious challenge took place after he'd recovered the treasure; it was keeping the treasure. Even as the commissioned Brinks Security Company trucks moved the gold to an undisclosed storage location, the companies that had originally insured the S.S. *Central America* and its cargo greedily blindsided Tommy. Specifically, thirty-nine insurance companies immediately filed suits contesting his ownership of the treasure. They respectively alleged that all or portions of it belonged to them because they'd paid the associated loss claims a century earlier. Tommy's fate depended on the courts upholding the maritime salvage *law of finds*, or as colloquially called, *finders-keepers*. This rule has a long international common-law history. More succinctly, it meant that when property is abandoned, it no longer belongs to anyone, so ownership defaults to the finder. Tommy fought an assortment of related, costly lawsuits with the overall litigation lasting more than seven years. While he preferred being at sea or in an engineering lab, he was forced to spend most of his time in courtrooms. He finally prevailed over his many adversaries and the treasure was fully released to him for his discretionary retention, sale, or distribution.

On a cursory examination, the secrets to his success don't seem that unusual. In fact, they are actually quite simple, except that most people don't follow them. It's been said that the secret to any success is to do the difficult things that no one else wants to do. That seems to have been Tommy's natural inclination. He worked very hard, with lots of energy, while maintaining a positive outlook in the face of severe challenges and frustrations. He repeatedly refused to accept that something could not be done. He always looked at situations from every possible angle in a deliberate effort to see things differently from the way others before him had seen them. If he needed something and it did not exist, he studied circumstances thoroughly and then he made it. He asked lots of questions of a host of bright people. Finally, once he made up his mind to begin, he would not quit nor be dissuaded until the task was successfully completed. That's how Tommy did the impossible several times over and earned wealth beyond most imaginations as his ultimate reward.

It's estimated that twenty or more tons of gold from the S.S. *Central America* remained unrecovered on the ocean floor after Tommy concluded his operations. That treasure waits for the next Tommy Thompson from a future generation. Is that you? Even if it's not, you're still able to be a treasure hunter. There's a biblical parable that exhorts us to seek the *pearl of great price*, using all of our resources and strength to do so. Once we find that pearl, we are to sell everything we have to purchase it. The pearl represents Jesus, mankind's greatest hidden treasure. The treasure Tommy diligently dedicated his life to finding was lost gold; in a very real sense, he sold everything to acquire it. Gold, indeed, does not tarnish or decay, but we can never take it with us; it can't save us or serve us beyond the grave. The *pearl of great price* will last for an eternity, and we *can* take it with us. We can profit by observing Tommy's successful life lessons, but we profit best when we apply his work ethics to finding items of eternal value. After death, there are three treasures – if we have found them – that can go with us into eternity because they are everlasting. They are: a good name, relationships with others, and our faith in Jesus Christ. If either of the first two are debatable, then throw them out and hold tighter to the last one.

And of treasures hidden in the sand. (Deuteronomy 33:19)

* * * *

Author's Note: Greater detail about Tommy Thompson and his gold recovery from the S.S. *Central America* is best available in Gary Kinder's nonfiction book *Ship of Gold in the Deep Blue Sea.* After being recommended to me by my son, his book became my initial source of inspiration for further study of related segments via various libraries, marine research centers, and the Internet, and then compiling the end result as "Exploring Inner Space."

Eva Kor

We Are More Than Our Pain

And you shall know the truth. (John 8:32)

Hitler's Nazi regime murdered eleven million people during the rule of its Third Reich. At a single location, the Auschwitz death camp in Poland, over one million Jews were imported, processed, and disposed of like so much refuse. Through many deliberate efforts since the war, the world came to remember and commemorate those who died, but some, mostly forgotten for a couple of decades, lived. Reduced to skeletons, six thousand survived the camp, with many having to be carried out in the arms of their rescuers. These numbers are so large that it's difficult to find a workable mental framework to fully grasp them. Reducing the numbers to a single individual helps us understand the severity of what took place. The victims who lived were overlooked by the numerical force and sheer horror of the many victims who died. Eva Mozes Kor is one who lived.

Eva, like most survivors, deliberately buried the memory of those desperate years and instead focused on establishing a new beginning. This attitude held sway with most survivors until 1962, when Adolf Eichmann was brought before an international court while an anxious world followed its outcomes. The trial was followed in 1978 with the airing of the celebrated NBC miniseries *The Holocaust*. Together, the trial and the program forced survivors to begin reconciling their past with their present. Both of these events brought painful Jewish memories to the forefront, while helping Gentiles understand the wartime experiences of the entire European Jewish population. Only one generation earlier, Jews were persecuted by Hitler's Nazi Party and the acquiescing anti-Semitic European populations. The world generally exhibited a lack of sympathy – displaying only blind eyes, deaf ears, and hands unwilling to help. For Eva, her reconciliation began with NBC's *The Holocaust*. She noted that the former death camp occupants were addressed as though all had died and, further, that no one referenced the unique subset to which she and her sister, Miriam, belonged – the Mengele Twins.

Three thousand child twins were forced through the infamous "Arbeit macht frei" gate of the Auschwitz death camp during the WWII war years. Without exception, all were used as human guinea pigs in sadistic experiments by the Nazi doctor known as the *angel of death*, Josef Mengele. Most were slowly murdered and then dissected when their brutal testing was completed. While an estimated 150 twins survived the combination of cruel medical procedures and general deprivation of the concentration camp, none escaped permanent physical and psychological damage. Among the survivors were Eva and Miriam. After her arrival at the camp, Eva says that when first seeing the bodies of dead and distorted children, she firmly resolved not to become one of them. The odds against her survival were incalculably poor, but for twenty-one months she successfully held on to a thread of life.

Eva and Miriam Mozes can be seen in an iconic photograph – now widely available on the Internet – taken by the Russians at the time of their liberation campaign on January 27, 1945. The stark black-and-white image shows the two of them holding hands as they lead a procession of emaciated children along a narrow barbed-wire-lined corridor. Their path would take them out of the hellish enclosure into the seeming heavenly freedom hard-won by the Allied forces. They look reasonably plump in the photo, but what is not easily revealed is that they're wearing multiple sets of clothing – all they could rapidly acquire – and they've hidden their possessions beneath the layers. After liberation and before departing camp, they *organized* everything available from the remnants abandoned by the escaping guards. (*Organized* was a word commonly modified in meaning during WWII to surreptitiously indicate acquiring anything necessary for life by stealth; e.g., food, matches, clothing, shoes, medicine.)

Eva's successful determination to live through the horror and pain led her, decades later, to an amazing series of redemptive acts that culminated in an international calling with a universal message. Regardless of race or religion, a world that's filled with suffering victims, martyrs, and refugees needs more than ever to hear Eva's story and to receive the power of the healing words she shares. Told in its fullness, her story would contain significant elements of horror, deprivation, and pain; I'm not sharing it in that manner. I have the deepest respect for what the Mozes family suffered during the events of 1940 through 1945. Being reasonably familiar with their travails, I agonize over what a multitude of humans were capable of inflicting on this family and on so many like them. I am sickened in my soul over the needless suffering that came to these families because of unthinking prejudice and unfeeling persecution. The specifics of the Mozes family's tribulation are revealed in Eva's books and videos, as well as revealed in others detailing the Holocaust and the even-larger record of Nazi Germany's countless oppressions and atrocities. The goal is to center my story on Eva's indomitable character and the living legacy of her life's work; she has accomplished the near-impossible by generating light from darkness. Hers is a positive message of fresh beginnings and new life. I say in humor that Eva often expresses the other "F" word – forgiveness; read on for the full revelation.

Eva and Miriam were born in Portz, Romania, in 1934. Eva was the firstborn twin. Although only minutes Miriam's elder, being the big-sister-in-charge was a role she accepted and acted out during the entirety of their exceptionally close relationship. From her father, Alexander, who was a successful farmer with little education, Eva learned to be tough and strong, and to resist and outsmart authority, a skill she would need to facilitate their survival. From her mother, Jaffa, who was well educated and had a reputation for helping everyone in need, Eva learned to be kind to the less fortunate and to care for others.

In 1940, Hitler gave the northern part of Romania, which contained Portz and which was known as Transylvania, to his close ally, Hungary. At the time, the area was divided equally by those favoring Romania and those favoring Hungary. (See the related story on Sabina and Richard Wurmbrand.) Along with the acquisition, pro-Nazi Hungarians gained a strong advantage and commenced enacting German-favored policies, including a purge of the Jews. Eva's father felt forewarned by these activities and made a visit with his brother to Palestine (later to become the independent Jewish state of Israel). He returned convinced it was wise to move his family there, but Eva's mother resisted. His brother did make the move, resulting in the family surviving the war. Eva's was the only Jewish family remaining in Portz's population of five hundred Gentiles.

Despite the former goodwill engendered by the Mozes family, no one in the city displayed any support as the local Nazi über-collaborators, the Iron Guard, harassed and denied them. Eventually, the Iron Guard refused to permit the family to leave the country. Instead, they were forced into the Şimleu Silvaniei ghetto after having their property confiscated. Thereafter, the family of six (including Edit and Aliz, Eva's two older sisters), were loaded onto a railway freight car and transported with far less care than that afforded cattle, as they were packed standing-room-only for seventy hours without food and water. Their destination was the largest of the many death camps in Poland. Upon stepping onto the Auschwitz station platform, the family was immediately separated without good-byes or explanations. Jaffa and the older girls most likely went to the left, along with the old and frail, for whom an immediate mass murder by poison gas was followed by incineration in one of the massive brick ovens. Alexander would have gone to the right, with the healthy and stronger for whom a temporary life of slavery, deprivation, and persecution would – upon his physical emaciation – be followed by a similar impersonal mass murder simultaneously shared with hundreds of other doomed inmate workers.

Eva soon realized her parents and two older sisters were gone, never to be seen by her again. Eva believes no other section of land in the world has ever seen as many families ripped apart as occurred for years on that rail platform. The twins had their own uniquely perverse fate awaiting them.

It was then that they had their first encounter with Dr. Josef Mengele. He first confirmed that Eva and Miriam were twins, and then had them sent with the other newly arrived twins to a special housing unit near his laboratory. Eva and Miriam became part of a group of children used as human guinea pigs in genetic engineering experiments under the direction of Mengele (twins represented a natural treatment control group). Approximately fifteen hundred pairs of twin (three thousand children) were abused, with most dying as a result of the experiments. Twins as young as five years of age were subjected to medical experiments of unspeakable horror at Auschwitz.

They were usually murdered after the experiment was over and their bodies dissected to ascertain all causes and results related to the experiments. Mengele performed experimental surgeries without anesthesia, transfusions of blood from one twin to another, isolation endurance trials, reaction tests to various stimuli, injections of lethal germs, sex change operations, and the removal and swapping of organs and limbs. His goal was to uncover biological advantages for the benefit of Hitler's *super-race* of Aryan soldiers.

First, Mengele injected chemicals into Eva's eyes in an attempt to change their color. Later, he injected other chemicals into Miriam's kidneys, which caused them to stop growing, ultimately determining her painful death by bladder cancer at age fifty-nine. After injecting Eva with a poisonous toxin or deadly germ, she became acutely ill. When Mengele observed she was failing, he told her, "Too bad, you only have two weeks to live." She presently rebuts: "I proved him wrong. I survived." She knew that if she died, Miriam would also be killed, because she would no longer have any comparative experimental value. Remembering the dead children she had observed upon arriving at camp and her subsequent vow not to let herself become like them, Eva stayed alive through sheer determination and a motivation to help Miriam survive as well. Eva refused to become a *Muselmann,* the camp term for someone who had lost the will to live.

The girls persevered beyond Mengele's lab experiments, and lived to see the American planes circling the camp in the weeks prior to their liberation. All Holocaust survivors said it was necessary to tenaciously cling to someone or some hope. Eva had Miriam. After liberation, the girls still had no one other than each other. They lived in three different refugee camps over the following year before returning for a short time to Romania to live with an aunt. Although released from Auschwitz, their struggle to attain true freedom had not ended. The USSR maintained control over Eastern Europe and continued its longstanding anti-Semitic practices in the conquered satellite nations, with Romania developing perhaps the most oppressive and corrupt puppet Soviet satellite government. Eva and Miriam briefly joined the Romanian Communist Party in order to survive as postwar refugees and orphans. Eva describes the motive as joining a club, the *in* thing to do. Ever so discerning, Eva quickly realized they were being brainwashed. She says, "Even today when I meet someone who leans to the left, I always tell him, go, try it out if you like, for everyone to tell you how to breathe, what to wear, and what time to go to bed; then maybe it is the right place for you." They left the party, accepting instead the dream of their father – life in Israel.

With her street smarts, fifteen-year-old Eva obtained emigration papers from the Romanian government and settled by 1950 in the newly founded nation of Israel. Her ship was the next to last to be permitted to leave Romania before all exit visas ceased; as such, it had a capacity for three hundred passengers, but departed with three thousand aboard. After her arrival, she attended absorption training, living in a youth village (a specialized kibbutz). There she was employed as a full-time milkmaid while serving part-time as a draftsperson with the Israeli Defense Forces (IDF) for eight years. Attaining the significant rank of Sergeant Major in the Army Engineering Corps, she provided support services during the 1956 Suez Crisis defensive war. The subsequent military victory helped Eva and Miriam relax sufficiently enough to accept that persecution related to their Jewish heritage might have finally come to its end.

In April 1960, Michael Kor from Terre Haute, Indiana, visited Israel as a tourist. He was a Holocaust survivor from Latvia who was freed by the United States Armed Forces, so he decided to move to the country of his liberators. While in Israel, he met, dated, and proposed to Eva. After marrying in Tel Aviv, the couple moved permanently to Terre Haute, where Eva became a U.S. citizen, was licensed as a professional realtor, and mothered two children, Alex and Rina. I met Eva while she was lecturing at an area university. After becoming familiar with her vision, I was sufficiently impressed to begin sharing her story in my classrooms.

After *The Holocaust* aired, Eva speculated on the outcomes of other children who'd survived the Holocaust, especially the Auschwitz twins. She searched for information and found that none was readily available. Eva then partnered with Miriam, who had remained in Israel. Together, they undertook a related discovery project. They had two aims: one of locating other Mengele twin survivors, and the other of finding medical records or Germans having knowledge of the nature of the experiments – especially which chemicals were used. In 1984, Eva formalized their effort by founding an organization called Children of Auschwitz Nazi Deadly Lab Experiments Survivors (CANDLES). The acronym was especially appropriate, as their purpose was to bring illumination into one of the shadowy chapters of Holocaust history.

On January 27, 1985, six Mengele twins (three pairs) met at Auschwitz

II–Birkenau to observe the fortieth anniversary of the camp's liberation. The twins continued on to Jerusalem, where they and seventy-four other twins staged a mock trial of Mengele. Attention to these activities created worldwide publicity, which, in turn, helped to locate more Mengele twins. One hundred and twenty-two living twins were located in twenty countries, but sadly, no medical specifics were uncovered. The U.S. Congress was sufficiently influenced by the results to pass a resolution authorizing a formal search for Mengele, thus enhancing the related activities by famous Nazi hunter Simon Wiesenthal of the Mossad, the Israeli Secret Service. There were a number of disappointing near-misses, which meant Mengele was never brought to justice. He last lived in several South American countries under the assumed name of Wolfgang Gerhard. He died of a stroke while swimming at home in 1976.

In 1987, Miriam's kidneys failed due to complications related to her Mengele experiments. Eva, the always-vigilant older sister, traveled to Israel and donated a kidney to Miriam. The surgery prolonged Miriam's life for eight years, but she succumbed in 1995. Had medical records been found, they may have mitigated her complications and extended her life. In response to Miriam's death, Eva founded the CANDLES Holocaust Museum and Education Center. The goals of the Terre Haute-based museum are to educate on eugenics, the Holocaust, and the power of forgiveness. There is a modest admission charge, and volunteer docents are always available to freely share on these three vital matters. In November of 2003, the museum was seriously damaged by neo-Nazi-inflicted arson. This didn't stop the mission of CANDLES, and by generous local and international donations, the museum was rebuilt to better-than-original standards. It reopened a year later and has since undergone continuous refinements.

For the fiftieth anniversary of the liberation of Auschwitz in 1993, Eva returned to Germany. She'd made contact with a German doctor who had worked at Auschwitz, though not directly with the always-secretive Mengele. His name was Dr. Hans Műnch, and he had agreed to sign an affidavit documenting the practice of Mengele's experiments at Auschwitz. To offer something of equal value in return, Eva determined to provide Dr. Műnch with her personal letter of forgiveness. That's when Eva says the healing first began. The keen realization was that she had the power to forgive; subsequently, she found that forgiveness is for the victim as well as the perpetrator. Eva took that first step and provided a heartfelt letter of forgiveness to Dr. Műnch.

A friend subsequently asked if she could also forgive Mengele. This was yet another monumental step – one far greater than Eva first anticipated, but one that she came to accept. After half a century of carrying the weight of hatred for Mengele, she forgave him. Eva also realized she'd held bitterness against her parents for not protecting her, for letting her down. This might seem inappropriate at first, but not when seen through the experiences of a six-year-old child. She became free of her past and free of her pain; she was no longer the victim she'd been for half a century – most of her life.

Eva received unexpected international attention when she publicly forgave Mengele and the Nazis. Not all of it was positive. Many felt that it was morally wrong to do so; others felt that she had no right to do so. These oppositions came down on her even though she explained that the acts were personal; she was only offering forgiveness for what happened to *her*, not on behalf of what had happened to all Jews. Eva further explained that forgiving the tormentors did not mean forgetting about the larger experience; in fact, it was important to remember and to share so that the horrors would not be repeated. Much of the opposition and controversy to her forgiveness experiences came from the other twins she'd identified and befriended through CANDLES. Eva further explained she had been healed through the act of offering forgiveness, but that it didn't mean she had forgotten the events or that doing so denied anything that had happened.

Eva's reaction to the opposition was fully positive; she further committed herself to another worthy effort, that of sharing the need for and benefits of forgiveness. Eva's forgiveness was the catalyst for broadening CANDLES' focus to include peace (in Hebrew, *shalom*) on both a personal and societal level. Eva sees forgiveness as the summit of a very tall mountain. The side up is dreary and difficult; however, after reaching the summit, the sunny, flowering side can be seen for the first time. She asks, why go back down from where you came, when you can continue on to the summit of forgiveness and enjoy the beautiful side? Eva shares that she learned the following three life lessons by pushing through the pain:

- Never give up on yourself or your dreams; you can do good in life;

- Only judge people by their actions and their character (see the Irena Sendler story for similar advocacy); and

- Forgive your worst enemy. Forgive everyone who hurt you. It will heal your soul and set you free.

The following is borrowed from Eva's website:

> Forgiveness means many things to many people. To adequately describe Eva Kor's journey to forgiveness and the ways survivors of trauma can heal themselves, we define it like this: To forgive is to renounce anger and resentment against those who have caused you harm, without the expectation of apology or compensation. Forgiveness is not a pardon to those who have caused the injury, nor does it excuse the acts they used to cause it. These things are no longer the problem for the person who forgives. Forgiveness is the release of bitterness and indignation for our own personal healing. Forgiveness does not require forgetting. It only asks that we refuse to accept our pain as a part of ourselves. We are much more than our pain.[1]

I see that position as wholly compatible with what was written on the subject centuries earlier in the Bible.

A publicity release (now also appearing on her website) on Eva summarized her personality as: "Powered by a never-give-up attitude, Eva has emerged from a trauma-filled childhood as a brilliant example of the human spirit's power to overcome. She is a community leader, champion of human rights, and tireless educator."

And the truth shall make you free. (John 8:32)

Author's Note: The war delineated people into distinct categories: partisans, collaborators, liberators, participators, rescuers, survivors, and victims. There were no *good* Germans still alive and free in Germany at the end of the war because all who rightly opposed the evil had been killed or imprisoned after choosing to resist rather than yield to Hitler and his Nazi evils. There's no record of Germany producing any partisan-like countermovement against the machinations of the Third Reich. Capitulation was the choice of the German nation throughout the decade-long Third Reich. Even the internal military plots to assassinate Hitler were largely performed by men in full-time service to his war objectives – men who had a personal distaste for their supreme leader, their Führer, but who still hawkishly served the German

---

1   www.candlesholocaustmuseum.org/about/eva-kor.htm

national goals. Every other country suffering under Germany's dominance produced active partisan counter-movements, but not so Germany. Many Germans claimed the *good* German status after the Allies won the war. Whether civilian or military, all Germans still living and residing openly in Germany, or still serving in Hitler's military at the end of the war, were *participators*; their degree of participation was inconsequential after more than ten years of Nazism. At the war's conclusion, they attempted to present the world with a situation that it should accept as colored gray, when, in fact, it was always black or white; the truth and the lie, good and evil, are never gray. Year by year, the choice became clearer. Those few who chose the good, suffered and died along with their families for making the right choice well before the war concluded.

The word *participator* is Eva's; I borrowed it and embraced it, but the opinion offered about it herein is solely mine. So what should be done with all these not-so-good Germans regardless of whether they're dead or alive, whether their whereabouts are known or they're in hiding? Eva has the right answer, the only real answer, and that is forgiveness. It's a timeless answer; that's to say, executing the related action is not bound by time or any fashion. Forgiveness can be offered on a one-way initiated basis as Eva did and as she advocates doing. Eva, the victim, took the first step, and in doing so she fully liberated her soul and partially liberated the soul of the transgressor. Some whom she forgave were long dead, others yet alive. Forgiveness is best, however, when the offending party admits guilt and requests to be forgiven followed by the offended party granting it. This was the higher way chosen by Dr. Münch. The iron arch over the gateway of the entrance to the Auschwitz concentration camp proclaims to all entering that "Work makes [one] free" (in German, "Arbeit macht frei"); it was a lie at that location and it is a lie whenever and wherever it is presented. Only truth makes one free. Accepting the eternal truth of forgiveness set Eva free.

The year *Stories of Uncommon Character* was ready for first publication was also the seventieth year since Auschwitz was liberated. Many individuals and national representatives traveled there to pay their respects, to remember the lessons, and to negate the depraved Holocaust deniers. Eva led a group back there herself, never one to miss an opportunity to teach, to forgive, to research, to heal, and to bring light out of darkness.

Christopher Langan

Peanut Butter for Every Meal

Now give me wisdom and knowledge. (2 Chronicles 1:10)

The prize money was the best financial break that ever happened in Chris Langan's life; he used it to purchase a horse farm in Missouri. His act does not appear to be out of the ordinary until it's revealed that Chris is likely the smartest living man in the world. He won $250,000 during a guest appearance on the fifth episode of the trivia-based television quiz show titled *1 vs. 100*. On his way to securing the top prize of a million dollars, he exercised the option to simply quit competing and depart with the winnings accumulated thus far. It was January 25, 2008, and Chris was fifty-four years old.

It's not surprising that a man of obviously superior intellect would accept an invitation to showcase his talent and take home some easy money. But why quit after only a few correct answers and a quarter million dollars? He hadn't missed a question, and the opportunity to win another $750,000 remained open to him. Chris offers the following explanation: They were asking him trivia questions. He doesn't know trivia. Trivia deals with such peripheral minutia as who was awarded an Oscar or what team won an NCAA championship. Chris's mind is occupied with data of far greater gravitas, such as the special relativity theory, DNA or planetary structures, and quantum mechanics. The show's host wasn't asking questions of that nature, so Chris chose to depart with his secure winnings, which was a wise strategy because one wrong answer meant the loss of every dollar he'd earned. In an August 20, 2001, *Newsday* article titled "The Smart Guy," freelance writer Dennis Brabham quoted Chris as saying, "A high IQ is more about problem solving than knowledge of trivia. A lot of people think, 'Wow, that person has a 200 IQ so he'll do great on Jeopardy!' But it doesn't necessarily work out that way." A man with Chris's intellect has the means to earn a salary of $250,000, or far in excess of that amount annually, so why was the prize money the best thing that ever happened to him? And for what reason would he retire to a horse farm in Missouri when he could be and should be solving world hunger, placing a camera on Jupiter or a man on Mars, discovering the cure for cancer or Ebola, perfecting alternative energy sources, preventing hurricanes and tornadoes, or finding the next big technological application for digital programming?

An examination of Chris's early childhood development is a reasonable place to begin looking for the answers to these questions. He's been reported to have spoken in sentences at six months; taught himself to read at three years; and asked encompassing what-is-the-purpose-of-life kind of questions at age five. He also undertook a study of God at an early age, decided He exists, and committed to believe in Him, which Chris continues to do in accord with his own unique and thought-provoking theories. In his K-12 educational season, he rarely did the assigned reading and home-work, mostly showed up at school only to take the exams, skipped grades, and was consistently far in advance of his peers academically. On test days, he'd arrive just minutes early to review the textbook, and then proceed to quickly ace the exam. Chris studied in accord with his challenging private agenda, which included reading and understanding the classic *Principia Mathematica* before age sixteen. As further proof that his unique methods were scholastically compatible for him, Chris slept on and off while taking the extremely challenging SAT, finished early, and still delivered a perfect score.

Nevertheless, the full scope of his childhood and teen years also reveals some serious negative factors. Chris grew up in extreme poverty, with only one set of clothes, rarely lived in secure housing, and ate free government-surplus peanut butter. At times, there was little doubt about what to expect for meals: breakfast likely involved peanut butter, as would both lunch and dinner. His family never stayed in one location for very long; on occasion, his home was just a tent. Chris shares that when his clothes were washed, he would have to hide somewhere naked until they were ready to wear again.

His mother's first husband, Chris's biological father, is alternatively said to have either died of a heart attack or skipped to Mexico before Chris was born. His second temporary "dad" was murdered; his third committed suicide; and his fourth – who became his legal stepfather – was a cruel alcoholic who physically and emotionally abused Chris, the oldest of the four boys. Unfortunately, the stepfather remained around until Chris's early teen years. To avoid his drunken rages, Chris stayed away from home most of the time. He suffered the combined effects of being smart, poor, and bruised, in addition to being picked on at school through ridicule and bullying. Avoiding home by being at school thus became another unpleasant experience, so he began hanging out at fitness centers and lifting weights. Chris began to complement his naturally large physique with additional strength and bulk. Photographs well into his middle age reveal a solid body with the broad shoulders and chest that would satisfy any pro football player. Prior to his fifteenth birthday, Chris was in bed asleep when he awoke to his stepfather beating him about the head. He ended this final abuse by rising to his feet and delivering a knock-out punch that rendered his stepfather briefly unconscious. Dad number four – the last in the series – was thereafter permanently unwelcome in the family household and wisely chose to remain away.

Chris attended small Reed College in Oregon on a scholarship. After the first year, the scholarship was lost when his mother failed to correctly complete the paperwork over the summer break. He was forced to return to Montana and live with his family. Chris began his second year of college at Montana State University, but after only a few weeks, his schooling was terminated due to transportation problems, as neither he nor his family had a decent car, and the walk to school was fifteen miles one way – often in the snow. Both school departures were thus related to poor financial circumstances. His formal schooling resulted in less than one and a half years of higher education.

At only twenty years of age, Chris was finished with all formal school education. He spent the thirty-four years between Montana State and his appearance on the quiz show performing manual labor. Chris shuffled between construction worker, cowboy, line assembler, forest ranger, fisherman, fireman, lifeguard, farmhand, and longshoreman, but most consistently, he was employed as a bar bouncer. These various jobs were all occupations where a strong physique served as an asset and none required an exceptionally fine mind. With the ability to bench-press more than five hundred pounds, he's a believer in combining intellectual labor with physical labor; his philosophy is that the best approach to creativity involves a regular mix of both. Finally, at nearly fifty-five years old, he came into the $250,000 prize money and became the owner of a rural Midwestern horse farm. As stated, this was perhaps the best thing that ever happened to him financially.

At this point, it would be acceptable to question whether Chris was really that brilliant. To have potential is a positive, complimentary attribute early in one's life, but potential becomes a waste or even an insult after sufficient time passes and there are still no results to show for the endowed ability. Regarding this matter, Einstein said, "A person first starts to live when he can live outside himself." Commenting on Einstein's statement, Armand Hammer added to the end of this line: "in other words, when he can have as much regard for his fellow man as he does for himself. I believe we are here to do good. It is the responsibility of every human being to aspire to do something worthwhile, to make this world a better place than the one he found."[2] At mid-life, Chris began to seriously consider where he could make his positive mark on the world.

Intelligence quotient, or IQ, is a measurement of one's potential capacity to learn, to think, and to create. It isn't a measurement of your ability to apply the capacity; it isn't a measurement of the degree that the capacity has been successfully utilized in practical applications; and it isn't a measurement of how much you have learned. It's only a scaled measurement of an individual's potential – whether realized or unrealized.

The average individual IQ score across the world is 100; the average for college graduates is 120, not because they have more education than the world average, although that is true, but because people with higher IQs naturally gravitate into environments of higher learning. Einstein had an IQ of 150; with it he contributed theories and formulas that, without which, it would arguably not have been possible to attain such practical achievements

---

2   http://quoteinvestigator.com/2014/03/30/aspire/

as atomic energy, rocket science and space exploration, or the Hubble telescope. Some experts believe the ability to measure IQ hits a ceiling at 195; an individual may be able to score higher, but it's not accurately measured with the current tools. Christopher Langan's IQ score is 195 (some place it at 210) – forty-five or more points higher than Albert Einstein's!

So it is reasonable to puzzle over why Chris seemingly wasted his gifts. Further complicating our understanding are the facts that Chris is both in good health and not lazy. He has kept himself in excellent physical condition and has toiled hard in demanding occupations all his days; he is neither a couch potato nor an entitlements recipient, although he lived humbly for many years on an income well below the poverty line. Chris thinks his main problem is that he could never catch a financial break in order to obtain a decent higher education with its incumbent degrees, privileges, and opportunities. There are more appropriate reasons, however, that explain why his life has apparently been so undistinguished and devoid of any lasting accomplishments.

More likely, the real explanation is that Chris lacked two critical resources. First, he had no one to provide mentoring, modeling, counseling, guidance, and/or role modeling. This resulted from not having a caring, involved father. Neither did he have a surrogate-father figure to replace the series of failed dads. There was no teacher to fill the role because he was rarely at school; he was the oldest of the four boys and thus had no older sibling; and there was no pastor because he didn't have a denominational church home. Consequently, Chris developed no mentoring relationships. No one can successfully make it completely through life on their own, especially if they lack the other of his missing critical resources.

The second critical resource he did not have was practical intelligence. Chris was book smart, but life dumb; that is, he had no street savvy. He had natural intelligence, but not the learned grasp or inherent understanding or practical perspectives that we collectively call *common sense*, the comprehension of how to apply information in real life for his own good and for personal problem resolution. Chris never realized, for example, what was obvious: he qualified for a full-ride scholarship to any university of his choosing based on his grades, test scores, and IQ. The nation's top institutes of learning compete hard to attract students of his caliber and then continue to compete after graduation to retain them as staff. Conversely,

Chris attended two minor colleges, paid many of the associated expenses personally, and finally just walked away in frustration without a formal education, never to return. Had he applied to the best schools nationally, or abroad, they would have aggressively offered him attractive program choices reaching beyond the doctorate level. Chris attributes the loss of his education and his subsequent hard life to just being the guy who got the bad breaks; no hard feelings, that's just the way it went down.

Missing both critical resources is a deadly combination for anyone, no matter how high their IQ, because sometimes raw intelligence isn't enough. This explanation is not a justification so that I can speak of Chris in demeaning tones and phrases. That's far from the point. Many of us lack one or the other of these life skills and to be both *book smart* and *street smart* is a double blessing only bestowed on a minority. Nearly all of us have one or more people in our lives to hold our hands while guiding us, or to provide timely advice, or to offer a caution, or to point a helpful finger in the right direction when we are faced with a confusing juncture. It may be a youth pastor, a teacher, a mother or father, an older sibling, a coach, a grandparent, a supervisor, or a guidance counselor.

We all need someone with practical gifting and life experience to offer a word of discernment or wisdom when necessary, to provide direction along the way, to encourage us when things go right, and especially when they go wrong. Study after study confirms that young people seek the advice of peers while ignoring the advice of their close elders; they foolishly accept peer advice, even when it violates established law or custom. They look to their peers for counsel on key life decisions, even though their peers have no more information or experience than they do. Guidance from peers may feel right, but it contains no understanding of life's big picture. It's far more likely to be wrong as well as harmful, leading to regrets. Each of us must live tomorrow with the outcome of decisions we make today.

Throughout much of Einstein's life, he labored on his unified field theory (UFT). Loosely stated, he intended to explain gravitation, electromagnetism, light, energy, and subatomic phenomena all within a mutually comprehensive and compatible set of laws. He came very close to doing so. However, each time he approached a reasonably successful conclusion, his parallel pioneering explorations in the area of quantum physics would create a complication that challenged him to resolve any seeming contradictions that kept surfacing. At the time of his death, a conclusive theory still eluded him. He died believing his theory was correct, but theories have to be proven through pragmatic means like research, experimentation, observation, and mathematical proofs. Einstein knew and accepted this parameter and he subjected his results to it.

The pièce de résistance in Chris's life is that for a long time he's been working quietly on his own (perhaps with some likely assistance from his wife, Gina LoSasso – IQ 182 – a clinical neuropsychologist), developing a comprehensive theory he calls his Cognitive-Theoretic Model of the Universe (CTMU). It is not yet complete, but those who have reviewed it thus far have been impressed and have called it the *theory of everything* and the *theory of theories* due to its absolutely comprehensive scope and nature. It's a new reality theory of the universe, not unlike Einstein's UFT in its comprehensive scope. It contends with relationships in complexity-information-design (surpassing anything that Darwinists and Neo-Darwinists are able to offer.) The Cognitive-Theoretic Model of the Universe develops the integrated and progressive relationship between intelligence, energy, and matter like DNA. It's all the more striking to realize that Chris is developing this well-received theory entirely on his own and he is demonstrably self-motivated. His endeavors are without the usual benefits of education, degrees, grants and scholarships, laboratories, analysts, associates, research facilities, colleagues, and monetary compensation. Writing for *Esquire* magazine's "Genius Issue" in 1999, Mike Sager describes Chris's approach as "the double life strategy," where in the morning you go to your manual labor day-job, and in the evening you work equations on your laptop at home without pay and for personal satisfaction.

Chris's story is, hopefully, far from over. If he lives only as long as Einstein, who died at seventy-six, which is relatively young by current averages, he will, as of this writing, have many more years to complete his theory. It's important to realize that Chris still hasn't overcome or eliminated his twin handicaps. He has to continue to push through to a successful outcome with those resources still absent from his life. As we continue to study so much of Einstein's contributions and to reap their practical benefits, we may yet do so – and maybe even more so – with Chris Langan's.

The lessons of his life are readily available to us, and are as follows:

Everyone needs help and a community, because no one makes it totally on his own. Intelligence alone is insufficient, especially without the ability to practically apply it in everyday life situations. Very few people get ahead in the world without someone in their court to mentor them; we all need encouragement and guidance, and it's important to surround ourselves with good advisors.

The need for a mentor is not limited to young people. In a June 19, 2012, article in *U.S. News & World Report*, Lindsay Olson wrote: "One of the best ways to reinvigorate your work life, boost your job search, or help guide your career path is to work with a mentor. A mentor can help guide you through common problems and make recommendations on how to improve your job performance." Socrates compared a mentor to a midwife in helping to birth good people and good ideas.

American psychologist Lewis Terman's study of gifted children provided research indicating that IQ helps an individual be more successful, but only up to a certain point. Terman sets that point at 120. Thereafter, other factors become helpful, such as determination, character, mentoring, and common sense. The importance of having someone as a mentor, or of being a mentor to someone, is the most vital takeaway from Chris's story. We're likely unable to overcome either a natural lack of street smarts or book learning, but employing the principle of maintaining good mentors will greatly help substitute for what's missing. Consider how much more positively different Chris's life might well have been if he'd been mentored early, as well as periodically, along the route. Some argue that mentors can help us fix our weaknesses; others argue that they help us develop our strengths. I don't see why the two approaches need be mutually exclusive; benefits can accrue from both approaches as we receive good advice and remain teachable enough to embrace them. Recognition of the vital roles that mentors play is as old as, or older than, the Bible. Qualifications, functions, and benefits associated with good mentors are clearly set out in the New Testament book of Titus in chapter two, verses 2 through 10.

A characteristic of Chris's that I find endearing is that he has not deducted God from the large picture. Many so-called brilliant scientists and philosophers are educated beyond their intelligence. They begin to substitute everything and anything, including themselves, for God's rightful place. They falsely claim they'll pursue an understanding of nature, man, and the cosmos anyplace it leads. What they consistently demonstrate is that they always force one large exception. If anything leads to a Supreme Creator – or even to intelligent design – then they avoid it and find a replacement answer, no matter how preposterous, narcissistic, or speculative. Not so with the world's smartest living man.

One of Chris's brilliant predecessors in the field of physics, Erwin Schrödinger, gave balance to the study of the physical universe when he said, "The scientific picture of the real world around me is very deficient. It gives a lot of factual information, puts all our experience in a magnificently consistent order; but it is ghastly silent about all and sundry that is really near to our heart and that really matters to us. It cannot tell us a word about red and blue, bitter and sweet, physical pain and physical delight; it knows nothing of beautiful and ugly, good or bad, God and eternity. Science sometimes pretends to answer questions in these domains, but the answers are very often so silly that we are not inclined to take them seriously."[3]

That I may go out and come in before this people.
(2 Chronicles 1:10)

* * * *

Author's Note: Chris Langan was introduced to me by Malcolm Gladwell in his book *Outliers: The Story of Success*. The concept of Chris's having two missing critical resources (practical sense and helpful mentors) in his life, and the statements related to his four "dads," were borrowed from Mr. Gladwell as he first proposed them in his *Outliers* book.

---

3   en.wikiquote.org/wiki/Erwin_Schr%C3%B6dinger

Captain Plumb

How Well Did I Do?

Curds and honey He shall eat. (Isaiah 7:15)

U pon graduating from the Annapolis, Maryland-based naval academy and completing his stateside flight training, the twenty-two-year-old flyer underwent combat missions over Vietnam, piloting an F-4B Phantom jet, then the navy's newest supersonic interceptor. He expected his final mission to happily terminate with a ticket home to the States, as his active combat duty would be completed in just five days. Instead, as he was held on the ground in enemy territory, his service time extended 2,103 days, or nearly six more years.

He says of those added years, "I found myself a long way from home in a small prison cell. As a prisoner of war, I was tortured, humiliated, starved, and left to languish in squalor for six years ... Try your best to smell the stench in the bucket I called my toilet and taste the salt in the corners of my mouth from my sweat, my tears, and my blood. Feel the baking tropical heat in a tin-roofed prison cell." These are the words of United States Naval Pilot Captain Joseph Charles Plumb, better known as Charlie. He was shot down midway through his seventy-fifth mission in a very unfortunate location – just south of the enemy's capital, Hanoi, and on a very unfortunate date – May 19, 1967, the birthday of opposition leader Ho Chi Minh. The takedown of a jet and the capture of its pilot were two rare events, both highly celebrated in Communist-held North Vietnam during its war against South Vietnam and the United States.

Charlie served a portion of his prison time as pastor to his fellow prisoners. He believes it was his strong Christian faith combined with his belief in the goodness of his country that permitted him to remain sufficiently unbroken and able to encourage others. He credits both of these saving qualities as being instilled in him as a young man in Kansas by his parents, pastors, youth leaders, and teachers. After his release and repatriation on February 18, 1973, the then-thirty-year-old pilot was rightly recognized as an American hero and awarded the following formal honors: two Purple Hearts, the Legion of Merit, the Silver Star, the Bronze Star, and of course, the POW Medal.

As might be expected of a returning fighter ace, Captain Plumb has many adventure stories to share, and he's been generous in doing so. My favorite is when he tells of enjoying a meal by himself in a Kansas City restaurant a decade after his return from a POW camp, a brief time after his retirement from the navy. Throughout the meal, he noticed a man almost staring at him from a table across the restaurant. Each time Charlie looked up, he would catch the man's eyes looking his way, seeming to examine him. About halfway through the meal, the man rose, walked to Charlie's table, and pointed a finger directly at him while stating, "You're Captain Plumb." Charlie indicated that indeed he was. The stranger continued to report a sequence of facts: "You served on the aircraft carrier *Kitty Hawk* in the Gulf of Tonkin near Vietnam, flew fighter jets, were shot down above enemy territory, parachuted out, were taken captive, and were held for nearly six years as a POW of the Viet Cong."

Captain Plumb readily agreed to all of these, but followed with questions of his own. "How do you know me?" and "Why is this part of my life of such interest to you?"

The man's reply was unexpected. "Because I'm the one who packed your parachute." Charlie indicated he'd thought about that parachute a great deal over the years, but he never thought he'd meet the man responsible for packing it. The man said he had just one question: "How well did your parachute work?" Charlie replied that not all of the panels opened, but he'd made it to the ground unharmed.

A typical T-10 parachute of that era was made of lightweight silk or nylon and consisted of up to twenty-four panels that, when inflated after deployment, formed a circular dome thirty-five feet in diameter. In the process, it utilized three hundred square feet of fabric. The combined design specification and automated manufacturing process had to be executed with great precision. That was only one of the two critical safety measures. The other was its manual packing procedure. A parachute must be carefully folded – referred to as *packing* – in a specific pattern. If a mistake is made, the chute may malfunction and fail to deploy properly. The men who pack parachutes are often called *riggers*, and they undergo a strict training and certification process before being assigned actual responsibility.

Now, years after the war ended, Captain Plumb was being introduced to his rigger for the first time. Charlie continued with his answer to the man's question, explaining that the man was not responsible for the unopened panels. Rather, it was his being forced to deploy at low altitude while still flying too fast. The man had done his job well. Charlie thanked the man profusely, further explaining that over the years he had reflected on the incident and was most grateful for the reliable handling of his parachute. Upon receiving this information, the man was satisfied, shook Charlie's hand, and took his leave. Charlie returned to his meal and continued thinking about their conversation.

That night, Charlie says he didn't sleep well. It wasn't the meal, and it wasn't, directly, the evening's surprising dialogue. It was something else, something he could not immediately identify that was bothering him. Before dawn, he successfully identified the reason his peace was disturbed.

Charlie had achieved the special status of jet pilot. Few men met the rigorous physical and mental qualifications. He did, and because he did, he was able to wear the brown leather flight jacket with the collar turned up in a cocky fashion. Even without the jacket, no one could deny he was handsome. At only college-age, Charlie had been entrusted by his government with the operation of high-tech, multimillion-dollar equipment. His F4-B Phantom jet carried a deadly mixed payload of ordnance including guns, cannons, bombs, and missiles. It was capable of performing interception, reconnaissance, bombing, or strike under his skillful hands. He routinely experienced the rare opportunity of flying in altitudes above 50,000 feet at supersonic speeds nearing Mach 2. He was cool and capable. The men looked up to him; some envied him. Charlie was like Tom Cruise in the film *Top Gun*.

By contrast, his parachute rigger – to whom, at the time, he never gave any thought – was laboring deep in the sweaty bowels of the ship. He was dressed in standard navy-issue bell-bottom trousers, with a back-bibbed shirt and a little round hat, just like every non-officer aboard. He was at sea, but only occasionally saw it. He was serving the sky pilots, while only occasionally seeing the sky, much less being up in it. His workday was spent below deck, where it was always hot, stationed at the long tables required for packing parachutes. He had to console himself that his job was important and take private pride in doing it consistently well. Few acknowledged him; no one thanked him. That sleepless night, Charlie belatedly became aware that his parachute rigger was one of those *no ones*. He had served aboard the *Kitty Hawk* with his rigger for about a year without ever greeting or meeting him. He hadn't shared a meal with the man, showed him his jet, or even thanked him for his diligent service – the service for which Charlie owed his life.

Let's expand our thinking by applying Captain Plumb's hard lesson to our lives. How many people have packed our parachutes over the course of our life? Who is still packing them today? Of course, they don't literally pack a parachute, but they do figuratively. Who is taking care of us quietly behind the scenes so that we can be a success and reach the sky? Who is faithfully doing so even though we've given them little consideration and have likely never even thanked them? These realizations may make us uncomfortable, but the resolutions can bring great peace to both parties.

The story could end here, but let's go further and invert the point of the series of questions above. Whose parachutes are we expected to be packing? Who is depending on us to perform, and to do so in a life-sustaining, quality manner? We need to examine and identify them so as not to let them down. They are counting on our performance so they won't crash and burn while relying on our being there for them.

Everyone is packing parachutes for others, and others are always packing our parachutes. We hope they are doing their jobs well, and they hope we are doing the same with their parachutes.

> *That he may know to refuse the evil and choose the good.*
> (Isaiah 7:15)

* * * *

Author's Note: Captain Plumb says that he shares his life story more than 100 times annually, estimating that he's told the story well over five thousand times since his release from the enemy prison camp in 1973. Charlie states that he intends to continue doing so as long as there's an audience. He titled his story "The Triumph of an Ordinary Man" and he titled his book *I'm No Hero*, because his appearance and background are that of an average man. He goes on to say, "What I've got to share is not really a war story; it's the story of a guy who had a big problem. As long as people have a problem, there'll always be an audience."[4] His motivation in sharing is to lift people into thinking better of themselves.

He says those six years of pain-filled confinement provided great personal training, but that the primary reason he was able to survive them is that he'd been exposed at several life junctures to people he calls *parachute packers*. He's not always referring to actual riggers; he also means people like his high school basketball coach, Francis Smith, or fellow sailor (another real parachute rigger) Doug Hegdahl. Plumb shares several subsequent lessons while confiding that they are rooted in having survived prison, and that having survived, he can't think now of a challenge in life he isn't able to overcome. He says, "I truly believe that if I could put each person through those years, they would come out with the self-confidence that I have." He emphasizes that each of us must struggle against life's adversities and inertia to emerge triumphant, improved, and successful, just as he had to do in Vietnam. That is, we must "learn to fight off 'prison thinking,' in which you think of yourself as a prisoner – you blame everybody else, you think you are the victim of circumstance and not the master."

In closing my story about Captain Plumb, I'll share three of his own brief story lessons from his life that I located on various Internet websites and substantiated by an article on his own website ("Bold and Spellbinding" by Bob Baker, *Los Angeles Times* staff writer at *speaker.charlieplumb.com/about-captain/triumph/*) Each lesson is largely rendered in Captain Plumb's words, as he is an accomplished storyteller and is best qualified to present them. His mini-stories contain points worth our contemplation. Also, I highly recommend his autobiography, *I'm No Hero*, and any of his several DVDs (all available on his website or at *Amazon.com*).

---

4   speaker.charlieplumb.com/about-captain/triumph/

Charlie's Story #1: "There was a crusty, old man named Francis Smith, my high school basketball coach in Overland Park, Kansas. It was his last year as a coach and we lost the last game. We were walking off the court and all I could think to say was, 'I'm sorry, Coach, I guess we're just a bunch of losers.'

Coach squeezed my shoulder and said:

'Son, whether you think you're a loser, or whether you think you're a winner, you're right!' I didn't understand what he meant! I asked him the next day at school and he said, 'Life is a choice, a choice between happiness and sadness, profit and loss, even life and death. Don't give away your choice by blaming others. I don't want you coming back in four or five years telling me the reason you flunked out of college was because you went to this school and didn't learn anything. I don't want you coming back in eight or ten years saying you got a job but you couldn't work with your mean ol' boss, and you couldn't agree with any of his philosophies, so you quit just to show him. I don't want you coming back here in twenty years telling me you married some gal and she was beautiful before you married her but after you married her, then she turned out bad and wouldn't support you with your family decisions, so you divorced her and that's the reason for your problems. The difference between happiness and sadness is not what's around you; it's the way you think about what's around you. And if you think you're a loser, or you think you're a winner ... you're right!'

Charlie's Story #2: "There was a kid named Doug Hegdahl, a navy seaman and parachute packer, who fell off his ship in a freak accident in the South China Sea and wound up a POW at the age of nineteen. He used to tell us, 'I wasn't captured, I was rescued!' In 1969, the North Vietnamese decided to release a few prisoners early, as a public relations gesture. The senior officer in my camp chose Hegdahl because he had managed to alphabetically memorize the names, ranks, next-of-kin, and phone numbers of about two hundred and fifty POWs. Here he comes home. He's got all this back pay in his pocket and he hasn't seen a woman in more than two years, and he's loose on the streets of San Diego. What would you do? Remember that in the navy, this kid was just a parachute packer. He started to travel. He went from north to south, east to west, contacting families, telling them that their prisoners were alive. Eventually, in person or by phone, Hegdahl spoke to a relative of every prisoner whose name he remembered."

Charlie's Story #3: He recalls telephoning home from the Philippines the day after his release and finding out that his wife had divorced him and was already engaged to another man. "I came back home and you wouldn't believe the *good advice* I was getting from the *professionals.* The lawyers were saying, 'We're gonna sue her and her boyfriend, we're gonna put her in jail for what she's done to you.' The psychologists had good advice too: 'Charles, you need to get mad about this. You need to get bitter. After all, if anybody has the right to be bitter, you do.' Well, I didn't learn much at the school of hard knocks over at the University of Hanoi, but I did learn this: Coach Smith was right! Life is a choice. Life is a choice in a prison camp in Vietnam just like life is a choice each day. Don't give away your choice by blaming somebody else for your problems. And I said to myself, 'Mister Lawyer, Mister Psychiatrist, I can sue everybody I can think of, I can feel sorry for myself, I can fall into a corner and atrophy and die. Or I can take Option Number 2. I can pick up the pieces of this jigsaw puzzle, put them back together as best I can, and put the energy in a positive direction. Thank you very much; I think that's what I'll do.' And I did."

The Parable of the Flat Earth

Everyone to the Starting Line

A time to plant. (Ecclesiastes 3:2)

F or the introduction, I borrowed a few lyrics dealing with time and change from a song by poet-singer-songwriter-musician Bob Dylan. It's titled *The Times They Are A-Changin'*: "The line it is drawn, the curse it is cast. The slow one now will later be fast. As the present now will later be past. The order is rapidly fadin'. And the first one now will later be last, for the times they are a-changin'."[5] Those are the closing lines from Dylan's eponymous 1963 ballad accurately predicting the outcome of that transitional decade's restlessness and upheaval. This isn't a statement indicating the changes were good or bad, but just that they happened with an otherwise unexpected vengeance and without any reversals to date.

This story is somewhat about the concept of time, but really it's more about the concept of change, even though the past, present, and future do play key roles. When I taught for the Indiana Department of Corrections, I attended a week-long course titled "Thinking for Change." In constructing this story, I was motivated by the close relationship between change and thinking in our lives – and, as so often is the case, personal choice may enter the equation as an influential factor. I determined that the best approach was to wrap the parable around an unusual word, *apriorism*, in order to enhance the related sticky-points. As a concept, it's found a lasting, special place somewhere in the back of my mind.

This word is apparently so underutilized that the Microsoft editing program marked it as a misspelling; I've subsequently added it to the internal dictionary. A formal Webster-like definition of *apriorism* is "belief in, or reliance upon, a priori reasoning, arguments, or principles." An informal, working definition is "hasty or faulty decision-making based on fallacious perceptions, generalizations, thinking, or concepts." In other words, it's when one depends on a preconception, which is to say, a deeply held conviction that's considered accurate regardless of circumstance, veracity, or fact. An apriorism can take the form of a judgment, concept, habit, or belief. Its conceptualization can be influenced by an experience, a mentor or teacher, an observation, a prejudice, a book, a doctrine, or a speech. It is generally resistant to modification, update, or discard.

In researching apriorisms, I found two websites that provided full and practical explanations under the general category of logic fallacies. One website offers the following: "Apriorism: *invincible ignorance,* closing one's eyes to evidence alleged against something one believes in … is frequently described as an attempt to deduce facts from principles, instead of inducing principles from facts."[6] The second website offers: "Apriorism: This fallacy consists in refusing to look at any evidence that might count against one's claim or assumption. An extension of this fallacy consists in being unwilling or unable to specify any conceivable evidence that might possibly count against one's claim."[7]

Beyond the fact that an apriorism may not be true or reliable, there is another serious inherent problem: change. Change is inevitable, and change may radically affect the accuracy of the apriorism. Change is not the problem per se. The problem is whether we update our thinking to reflect the change or whether we hold firm regardless. The danger is in the latter, not the former. Just because we sincerely believe something does not make it true; it just may mean we are sincerely wrong. Let's begin a closer examination with several broad historical situations and then move to a series of specific circumstances and people as proof-points.

In the early fifteenth century, everyone was absolutely convinced they were right about two things. Both were commonly accepted by nearly all of the population throughout the preceding centuries. The first conviction was that the earth was flat; the second was that the earth was fixed in the center of the universe, with the sun and planets orbiting around it. Both of these serve as large-as-life examples of apriorisms; however, we now know these to be incorrect. Today, science is more advanced, and we've replaced these old apriorisms with new, hopefully, accurate ones.

Are we certain that our current scientific *facts* are correct? Carl Sagan and his colleagues say the universe positively always was and always will be. In fact, they appropriated and then distorted the language of the Bible, which greatly preceded them. They go on to state that the universe itself resulted from the explosion of a super-compressed grain of pre-existent energy and that, thereafter, the diverse life found within the earth simply evolved from nothing more than a random, unknown batch of chemicals. Consequently, there's no god other than the universe itself, and that's a god with a very small g. There's no all-powerful, caring, eternal Creator God with a plan. Sagan has most of the population deceived into following along with his apriorisms. Perhaps his beliefs really are as foolish as, and more dangerous than, those fifteenth-century ones about the earth that now cause laughter.

We may never again confuse a spiracle earth with a flat one, but there are still plenty of other myths we accept as facts. Looking back again, consider, for example, the number of incorrect apriorisms the German people accepted during the decade leading up to World War II, all of which facilitated Hitler's rise to power and then left him in control far past the point of sanity. These included: Germans are a superior race; genocide and mercy killing are acceptable means to an end; Jews are responsible for all the trouble in the world; Polish and Slavic peoples are racially inferior; it's Germany's right to rule the world. A similar case can be made for the Japanese people during the same time frame. They only had slight variations in their apriorisms relating to national pride and practices, significantly beginning with their belief that the emperor was god and ending with a military-religious cult of *Kamikaze* suicide. In the first appendix to this book, I reference two disoriented mental conceits: *tunnel vision* and *drinking the Kool-Aid*. Twentieth-century German and Japanese thinking are two historical examples of these phenomena. If you're inclined to think that man has moved beyond false illusions of this nature, consider the sixty-plus radical Islamic nations with their billions of people today who hold similar beliefs to that of the Germans and Japanese, and who are presently acting on them to extreme degrees inclusive of murder, coercion, persecution, torture, genocide, subjugation, and conquest.

Let's reduce the scale our review a few notches through a detailed examination of a single commercial-industrial example. It holds a classic position in the world of marketing, and is known as the *Quartz Crisis* or the *Quartz Revolution*. In 1968, the Swiss manufacturers of mechanical watches held a comfortable 65 percent share of the worldwide watch market, with their share of revenue and profits varying from 80 to 90 percent. The Swiss had dominated the world watch market for centuries, but during WWII they gained hegemony in watchmaking. Their neutrality permitted them to almost solely and monopolistically continue manufacturing consumer timepieces while other nations were forced to undertake military applications.

The Swiss-manufactured products were beautiful and extraordinarily accurate, hand-assembled, jeweled-movement watches – truly works of art, the finest made anywhere. Their products were expensive, but worth the price, based on reliability and those highly sought-after intangibles of keen fashion sense and prestigious status. Beyond producing a product of high-caliber quality, the Swiss watch manufacturers were also great innovators, as evidenced by their many related inventions and numerous patents.

Twenty years after the war, the Swiss held only 10 percent of the industry's share and revenue. What happened? A change occurred, and the Swiss failed to move with it, either because they didn't recognize it or because they refused to accept it. Subsequently, they retained only a small, specialized segment of the market with most of their glory as manufacturing history. During that period, quartz-based electronic watches quickly gained in popularity and availability; they were suddenly dominating sales. Oddly, it was an employee of a major Swiss watch company who invented the electronic watch. However, when he showed it to his employer, it was deemed to be only interesting enough to exhibit at an upcoming technology exhibition for use as an attention-getting demo display.

The company didn't protect their invention with a patent because they thought it was too cheap and thus not able to engender sufficient interest to justify manufacturing it. Others, like United States-based Texas Instruments and Japan-based Seiko, saw it at the show and concluded different. Future purchasing demand quickly proved the new competitors right and the embedded Swiss wrong. Additional features were gradually added to the electronic watch: for example, alarms and full date (day and year) displays. In an effort to find niche markets, some even added non-time-related components like pagers and calculators. After a twenty year run, even these innovations could not fully insulate the general wristwatch market against eventual serious market erosion by unexpected new digital innovations. The wristwatch market suffered freefall when nearly everyone came to carry one or more Internet and wireless telephony-based productivity/communication devices like cell phones, PDAs, tablets, and MP3 players – all capable of flawlessly accurate time reporting, and – almost inconceivably – cameras, GPS, games, so much more.

One working explanation of an apriorism is how we view something; that is, our perception that things are best or right a certain, specific way and thus they are supposedly fixed, immutable, and universal. For an analogy, think of apriorisms as different pairs of glasses that we put on. Everything is seen through those lenses, and those lenses consistently influence our vision of the world. The view through those glasses affects judgment and decision-making by coloring, blocking-out, and distorting them in specific, set manners. The Swiss wore glasses that showed their dominant past continuing ad infinitum as they presumed consumers would continue to purchase only mechanical fashion watches.

For additional manufacturing examples, I'll review the time frame from 1876 to 1981, moving from oldest to most current. The following a series of brief vignettes showcasing famously unsustainable, know-it-all apriorisms. These examples, and multiple others, are available unattributed on many Internet sources. Although each opinion is proffered by a respected industry expert, all proved rapidly to be shortsighted and inaccurate – just like the Swiss watchmakers and the flat-earth centrists.

> 1876 – Western Union prevailed over the communications industry, but after studying the newly invented telephone, concluded it had "too many shortcomings to be seriously considered as a means of communication and therefore it has no value to our business."

> 1899 – Charles Duell, the commissioner of the United States Patent and Trademark Office, said, "Everything that can be invented has already been invented." He anticipated no longer being needed and perhaps becoming the last commissioner. Currently despite massive growth in employment, the patent office is so backlogged that,

depending on the category of the patent, the wait times are from one to fifteen years.

1911 – Marshal Ferdinand Foch, the French commander of all allied troops in WWI, said, "Airplanes are interesting toys, but of no military value." When a military conflict is undertaken today, no troops are sent in until airstrikes have been in play for the first thirty days. Air superiority and air support are together the most significant part of waging and winning war.

1932 – Albert Einstein, the famous physics theorist and one of the developers of the atomic bomb, said, "There is not the slightest indication that nuclear energy will ever be obtainable."

1946 – Darryl F. Zanuck, head of the movie company 20th Century Fox, said that "Television won't be able to hold on to any market because people will soon get tired of staring at a plywood box every night." Alternately, average daily viewing time is 171 minutes per capita and rising.

1947 – Howard Aiken, a pioneer in data processing systems, said that "Only six electronic digital computers will be required to satisfy the computing needs of the entire United States."

1962 – Decca Records rejected the Beatles by saying, "Groups using guitars are on the way out and have no future in the industry." At present, as has been the case for the past fifty years, nearly every band has a minimum foundation of three guitars, one each performing lead, rhythm, and bass lines.

1964 – United Artists rejected Ronald Reagan for a lead film role in *The Best Man* saying, "Reagan doesn't have that presidential look."

1965 – A Yale University professor of management advised his student, Fred Smith, the founder of thirty-billion-dollar FedEx: "Your concept for an overnight delivery service is interesting, but in order to earn a grade better than a C, it has to be feasible."

1967 – Dr. Lee DeForest, the inventor of both the vacuum tube and the radio, said that "Man will never reach the moon, regardless of all of his future scientific advances." Two years later, on July 20, 1969, Apollo 11 landed on the moon, where Neil Armstrong took his historic first step onto its surface.

1969 – A famous surgeon concluded his research by saying that "For most people, using tobacco is beneficial for their health." America is still desperately fighting to contain this deadly habit.

1977 – Kenneth Olsen, the founder and president of Digital Equipment Corporation (DEC), said, "There is no reason for anyone to have a computer in their home." Simultaneous to Mr. Olsen making that statement, I was entering the computer industry with an employment offer from Burroughs Computers (now Unisys). At the time, I held considerable admiration for this man and his company. Nevertheless, his apriorisms blindsided him and helped destroy the company. The personal computer prospered while the mainframe manufacturing industry went the way of Swiss watches, eventually even reducing the giant industry leader IBM down to its present far-more-modest size and significantly reoriented function.

1981 – Bill Gates, founder of Microsoft, is variously reported to have stated "640k of processing memory ought to be enough for anybody." Entry-level laptops currently have three to six gigabytes of RAM processing power (aka main memory), with the figure consistently moving higher. Six hundred and forty kilobytes would not be sufficient to operate a state-of-the-art calculator.

(In telling this story, I sometimes break the whole into two parts. The preceding, with its primarily impersonal perspective, as part one; and what follows with its primarily personal perspective, as part two.)

We all hold apriorisms about the world around us, and we also hold them about ourselves and how we fit into that world. We saw the belated humor in my previous historical examples in the areas of science, technology, and business. We are, however, all influenced by our deeply held apriorisms. Here are some that are fairly common for most young people, as well as for many adults:

- College is too expensive, so I'll never be able to afford to go.

- No boys will like me if I tell them no when they come on to me.

- Church is for old ladies and losers.

- I'm not smart enough to make the honor roll.

- That teacher just doesn't like me.

- I can run stop signs just like everyone else.

- I'm not pretty enough, or handsome enough, to get married to anyone really nice.

- Shoplifting is not a real crime; they build the losses into the price of the product.

- It's not fair; that's unfair.

- Marriage, sex, and family are any way you want to interpret them.

- No one cares about me; suicide seems like a good idea.

- I can control the drugs; a few times will be fun and it won't hurt me.

- I don't get along with my mom/dad because she/he never understands me.

- Cops are the real problem; they're the enemy.

- This is a boring town; nothing good ever goes on here, so there's nothing here for me.

- I'm not coordinated enough to join the team or to play a sport.

- I have to prove to him that I really love him by sleeping with him.

- It's okay to be in this country illegally; they probably stole our land anyway.

- I won't have any problem driving home after just a few beers.

- I practice safe recreational sex so I won't catch AIDS or any STDs.

- Mom and Dad will never find out; or, my spouse will never find out.

- Christianity is just one way to God; every other way is just as valid.

- The *man* is holding me down, or it's my skin color, or they're racist.

- Divorce is better for the kids than seeing us live unhappily together.

- I don't care.

- The police are prejudiced against my race.

- Everybody cheats during their marriage; what's the harm?

- I know that he beats me and the children, but he doesn't mean to; he really loves us.

- No one from my family has ever had a decent, well-paying job, so I won't either.

- Living off the government isn't a sin; they owe it to me.

- Abortions are no big deal; almost everyone has them.

- Why not grab all the entitlements I can even if I have to lie a little to get them?

- I'm handicapped, or, I have ADHD, or, I'm bipolar; so I can't help it or be held accountable for what I do; I'm a victim.

- I won't get pregnant if we're careful, or if it's the first time.

- White, male Europeans are to blame for everything that's wrong in the world.

- Who needs high school math and science? I'll never use them.

- I'm not fulfilled in my marriage, so I'll get a divorce.

- Cutting corners reporting my income is an acceptable way to provide better financially for my family.

- Jews – especially Israelis – are an inferior, trouble-making race.

- You can't get a really good job unless you know somebody on the inside.

- Cheating on exams is okay if you're having a hard time with that subject.

- Foul language and cursing are just words; they're no big deal.

- It's not my fault; or, I can't help it.

- Cutting classes, not doing homework, or sleeping in class won't make any difference.

These personal apriorisms are likely to be just as unreliable and will just as readily misfire as those industry ones held by Decca Records, Western Union, and the rest of those businesses and experts in the earlier examples. Our apriorisms are often incomplete, inaccurate, or completely messed up. Subsequently, we shouldn't be so quick to judge, label, or form rigid opinions about others and about ourselves. From our limited perspective, we almost never see the whole picture or have all the applicable information. We must keep watching and learning, and then be willing to change our thinking when it's clear that our beliefs are wrong.

In the last few decades of my life, I've seen much unexpected political and technological change: the fall of the USSR and the Berlin Wall; the rise of digital concepts and intelligence; the invention of products like the iPod, PC, cell phone, and fiber optics; a thousand channels of entertainment available where there was previously only three (NBC, ABC, and CBS); the divestiture of AT&T with hundreds of new telecom competitors; the demise of the former big three car manufacturers (Ford, GM, and Chrysler) due to dozens of new car lines manufactured in former emerging countries; the global resurgence of radical Islam and the rise of domestic terrorism; the sky-high climb of stock market indexes; China becoming a world-market competitor; major financial institutions collapsing in the market plunges; and traditional retirement plans replaced by previously unheard-of new personal investment strategies. Social change has been just as radical and unpredictable: selling of infant body parts, gay marriage, live-birth abortion, anti-Christian bigotry, promiscuous sex, dissolution of traditional marriage and family, sniping police officers, decay of civility, DNA and gene experimentation with production of modified foods, deliberate destruction of American exceptionalism, the rise of the dictatorial regulatory state, *dumbing-down* education, massive growth and acceptance of welfare lifestyles, radical-Islamic persecution of Christians and Jews, and so much more.

The following are eight specific maxims that are helpful in sharpening our judgment going forward. I'm willing to say that these are always true and are worth holding fast as unchanging truths. I state this with confidence, despite having just made presentations about constant change and the danger of apriorisms. I can confidently state this because eternal truths do exist, and truth never changes; it isn't relative, it's constant and permanent.

1. Apriorisms filter all our incoming data. In doing so, they cause us to miss and/or ignore anything that is new or doesn't fit neatly into our existing beliefs/mindsets.

2. Apriorisms must be kept open to change. The future requires us to be prepared to accept change, not reject or ignore it. Things change and people can change too; we are not hard-wired in a singular fashion. If we don't change, we risk a life of regrets filled with *shoulda-coulda-wouldas*.

3. The future is not a seamless extension of the past. We can't predict tomorrow based on what happened yesterday. Today is best lived for its unique merits and opportunities.

4. A successful past can inhibit our flexibility for the future if we get stuck in what-used-to-be and what-used-to-work. The creators and early adopters of new concepts are mostly outsiders who are not vested in the past and who have nothing to lose by adopting the new and departing from the old.

5. When a change occurs, most everything rolls back to zero – fresh thinking and new starts are required of every participant. All competitors are equal and back in line together at the starting block; no one has a lead. Linger too long with a head full of old thoughts and perceptions, and lose serious ground that may never be recovered.

6. Change may sound like it's all problem-prone on the front-end, but it's not, because later it creates as many or more opportunities as threats.

7. Our incorrect apriorisms can hold us back and cause us to think that we're victims or losers. When we operate under old or false precepts, we're stuck in position; when we're quick to accept new or accurate ones, we are free to move forward.

8. Seeming advantages can be disadvantages, and seeming disadvantages can be advantages.

From a purely physical perspective, I'll reinforce that final point by referencing the classic case of David and Goliath. David was inexperienced in warfare, was small, and had no body armor, spear, javelin, shield, sword, or armor-bearer. Goliath was an experienced warrior, was well equipped, had a singularly huge physique, and had an armor-bearer to assist him. On closer look, we know that giants have many health problems and shortcomings, not the least of which is poor eyesight, requiring them to engage in close combat. David stood afar off, where his small, unencumbered stature became an impossible target; yet still capable of the quick, free movements needed for using his unconventional and undervalued long-distance sling. Add to these natural pluses and minuses, the supernatural power invested in David by the God whom he trusted, and he becomes the surprise victor that has inspired so many over the centuries.

Change is natural; change is expected; change is part of God's plan. Consider nature itself, with its splendid display of changes such as the life cycles of the tadpole and the caterpillar, or in the cyclical unfolding of the four seasons and the revolving night sky.

The pharaoh of Egypt refused to accept change and clung tenaciously to his ancient apriorisms. He was stubbornly oblivious in the persistent face of Moses' many patient intonations about the soon-coming new direction. Multiple times his only action was stiffening his neck, while rivers turned to blood, frogs occupied the land, and lice plagued the people and livestock. Following in rapid sequence came flies and diseases, boils on men and beasts, crops devastated by hail with what little remained consumed by locusts, darkness during the day, and the death of every firstborn male throughout the land – even the eventual loss of his army, transportation, and weaponry in the waters of the Red Sea. Once the center of civilization, Egypt never again was a great leader nation. Over the following three thousand years, it became a third-world country subservient to a series of stronger nations, from ancient Greece to modern Britain,

From 1950 through 1969, it was commonly believed that the manufacturing label *Made in Japan* meant that Japanese products – like electronics and automobiles – were inferior. There were domestic bumper-stickers that read: "Made in Japan from old beer cans." From 1970 through 1989, the Japanese subsequently became good imitators as they observed and followed the Americans and Germans. In the States, however, we were not paying attention. Finally, from 1990 through 2009, the Japanese appeared fully transitioned into industry leaders with innovative features and lasting-build quality. Retaining the notion that we produced better products than the Japanese deprived the United States of its leadership position and market share in both multibillion-dollar industries.

What made the positive difference for Japan? An American by the name of W. Edwards Deming did. He had fresh, postwar engineering concepts which were rejected in Detroit and accepted in Tokyo. His ideas included TQM (total quality management), continuous improvement (*kaizen*), non-union labor forces, and close manufacturing tolerances. Deming was told reactionary statements such as "Let's get real," "Are you dreaming or what?" "That's not how we do it," "So you know better than all of us?" "That's impossible," "It's not that easy," and "You just don't understand." We've all heard iterations of these from time to time in our own lives. Sometimes we have failed ourselves by believing them and choosing not to act.

Each of us is just like those Japanese products. We often start out rough around the edges and flawed. With time, we develop into fairly good imitations as we observe our peers, select good heroes, make the right choices, and mature. With persistence and passion, however, we finally become excellent, quality originals (having acquired good character) that no one else is exactly like. These three developmental stages were true in my life (as I share further in the Epilogue). Most important, at the conclusion, we are able to finish well. The apostle Paul summarized it this way: *I have fought the good fight, I have finished the race, I have kept the faith* (2 Timothy 4:7). The greatest change possible in our life is that of being spiritually reborn into God's family. Take off the old, and put on the new, His eternal Spirit in place of our old dead one, the mind of Christ replacing our former carnal one. This is the biggest fresh start in life. Like the metamorphosis that yields a butterfly from a caterpillar, we can truly begin anew. We are offered the opportunity to finish well despite any and all earlier stumbles, false starts, sins, upsets, and failures. F. Scott Fitzgerald said there are no second chances in life; God says he was wrong.

I'll close on a light note with more lyrics borrowed from another classic Bob Dylan song, *My Back Pages*: "Yes, my guard stood hard when abstract threats too noble to neglect, deceived me into thinking I had something to protect. Good and bad, I define these terms, quite clear, no doubt, somehow. Ah, but I was so much older then, I'm younger than that now."[8]

And a time to pluck what is planted. (Ecclesiastes 3: 2)

* * * *

Author's Note: The sticky-points in my "Parable of the Four Farmers" and the sticky-points in my "Parable of the Flat Earth" may appear contradictory. The first is a caution about making changes, and the second is a caution about ignoring changes. The resolution is found in the following supporting statements: Avoid changes for the wrong purposes, such as greed, running from a problem, or dissatisfaction. Change may be generated by external circumstances, and thus forced on us; or change may be generated by our internal thought processes or personal choices, and thus be far more optional. When change is right or best, proceed – after prayerful consideration – in faith. Neither an attitude for nor against change is correct in every situation. We must be like the tribe of Issachar who read the times and knew what to do for their families and country.

My story concept on the relationship of preconceptions (apriorisms) and changes is not unique to me. The initial catalyst was a VHS training video I watched in the early 1980s during my first years in telecommunications. The video featured futurist Joel Barker and was titled *The Power of Vision*. The core concept stayed with me over the years, has been consistently expanded through personal experience and multiple complementary sources, and subsequently became one of my regular shared stories in retirement, as it was frequently customized to promote my immediate objectives. Its final iteration is this short story.

Stetson Kennedy

Killed Just for Shaking Hands

The battle is the LORD's. (1 Samuel 17:47)

With half a dozen Stetson Kennedys, we can transform our society into one of truth, grace, and beauty. The thing is, Stetson did what he set out to do" ~ Studs Terkel, historian

In 1916, Stetson (whose first name was William, but which he never used) was born into an aristocratic family in the Deep South city of Jacksonville, Florida. As his first name implies, he was related to John B. Stetson, the founder of both the iconic hat manufacturing company and Stetson University in DeLand, Florida. Stetson became a folklorist, environmentalist, labor activist, journalist, editor, human rights advocate, and the author of eight books: *Palmetto Country, The Florida Negro, Grits and Grunts: Folkloric Key West, South Florida Folk-Life, After Appomattox–How the South Won the War, Southern Exposure, Jim Crow Guide to the U.S.A.*, and perhaps most importantly *I Rode with the Ku Klux Klan* (later retitled *The Klan Unmasked*). The titles are illustrative of the adventurous and purposeful life he led.

The last four books listed are closely related in theme, and they are also the best known, most influential, and most enduring. Within them, Stetson dealt with the disreputable subjects of Southern racial segregation and the Ku Klux Klan (KKK). During the 1950s, Stetson's primary research and investigative actions helped to expose and cripple these twin evils. His tetralogy on these subjects was considered too inflammatory for any stateside publisher to print; subsequently, the famous French existentialist philosopher Jean-Paul Sartre identified with Stetson's cause and distributed them from abroad.

In the early years before his anti-Klan-related work and writings, Stetson was first a pioneering folklorist. He began his endeavors as a teenager gathering both black-race-related and white-race-related materials. His interest and output began while a student at the University of Florida. It continued after being commissioned by the WPA (Franklin D. Roosevelt's Works Progress Administration) to pursue, not just folklore, but oral history and ethnic studies as well.

While at the WPA, he adopted a bold working style, which was then prohibited in the South. Kennedy chose to partner in his field research with a black female novelist and anthropologist named Zora Neale Hurston. Prevailing ethics required them to travel separately, because dominant Southern apartheid prohibited them from any contact or attraction, whether personal or professional. These prohibitions were collectively known as the Jim Crow laws, and as Stetson said about them, they could frankly get you killed just for shaking hands – both colors, white and black. It may well have been his WPA experiences with Hurston that alerted him to the possibilities in the work he later came to fully adopt.

The Jim Crow laws were the post-Reconstruction Era racial segregation legislation that replaced the even more odious Reconstruction Era Black Codes after they were prohibited by the Northern-controlled federal government. Jim Crow acted as the open, pseudo-legal cover for the euphemistically titled *separate-but-equal* demands of Southern society that were in vogue from the Civil War Reconstruction Era to the Civil Rights Act. In practice, Jim Crow was a near-complete denial of civil rights perpetrated against the Negro race in the Southern states. Jim Crow laws were not enumerated as clearly against blacks as Nazi Germany's Nuremburg laws were against the Jews; there were, however, many similarities related to racial purity, nationalistic attributes, and white supremacy. They were also similar in application and practice – with Jim Crow arguably the more severe.

During Stetson's lifetime, the Klan's relationship to Jim Crow was as its covert, illegal strong arm – a combined and hasty lawman, judge, jury, and executioner. Segregation, white supremacy, and discrimination were enforced formally in the daylight by the police and sheriff's departments, and then secretly, often in the dark of night, by the fearmongering, violent KKK, with many of the same men participating in both groups.

The Klan that Stetson witnessed was the hate group's second reincarnation or phase. In 1866, the first phase of the Klan began in Pulaski, Tennessee, as pranks practiced by six Scotch-Irish white college students who'd recently returned from Confederate service. In ironic twists, one student's name was James Crowe and another's was John Kennedy (no relation to either Stetson or the president). Their nighttime activities involved riding horses while dressed in white bedsheets decorated with occult images. In a short time, the pranks turned into minor acts of terrorism against the large population of recently freed blacks. These acts continued to escalate in seriousness.

Soon the organizational structure formalized, membership increased, and secret rights of initiation were added. The notoriously brutal ex-Confederate Cavalry General Nathan Bedford Forrest accepted the top leadership position as its first Grand Wizard. This first phase ended after only a decade due to internal strife and opposing pressure from federal Reconstruction. The general resigned as the activities became too severe for his newly acquired peaceful sentiments.

The seed for the second phase of the Klan was planted with the 1915 release of D. W. Griffith's *Birth of a Nation,* a film based on Thomas Dixon's 1905 pro-KKK, obsessively racist novel *The Klansman.* Dixon intended, as he said, to "revolutionize northern sentiment by a presentation of history [that is, historic revisionism] that would transform every man in my audience into a good Democrat." The Klan would soon come to dominate the Southern Democratic Party, and greatly influence the national Democratic Party, for more than half of the twentieth century. Griffith's film was by far the biggest blockbuster of its time; it was viewed by a majority of the adult population. The storyline deliberately erred by depicting the Klan as protecting American morality against the depraved practices of free blacks.

Two-term Democratic Party President Woodrow Wilson and the first lady attended a premier showing of the film via a private screening at the White House; it was the first film ever shown at the White House. The film's already favorable reception was further enhanced through the assumed acceptance and indirect endorsement by the President. Prior to being elected, Wilson was a historian and an academic who used his influence to eliminate positive textbook references to blacks. Upon assuming the chief executive office, Wilson removed all blacks from federal service within the District of Columbia except one token black, the incumbent presidential valet. If Wilson was not a known member of the Klan, he was believed to have quietly approved of them.

Now with the promotional power of the film and the presidency at its back, the Klan was fully rebirthed through the efforts of disgraced Methodist minister William Simmons. In 1915, he initiated the renewed Klan by burning a cross above Stone Mountain, near Atlanta, and declaring himself the Imperial Wizard of the Invisible Empire. The regional Klan quickly roared back and membership soared. This Klan targeted new groups for harassment, which included Catholics, Jews, union organizers, civil rights workers, and immigrants, as well as blacks. Over one thousand white Americans, and countless black Americans, were eventually lynched. The Klan promoted itself outwardly as sustaining traditional biblical and American values, but in actuality it was more occult, un-Christian, and violent than ever.

The second phase continued for the next fifty years, with only slight disruptions by the anti-fascist feelings engendered during the Second World War. This phase had the longest tenure, became most entrenched, and was the most vicious. The Klan was able to infiltrate, and very often control, local and county governments and law enforcement agencies – often reaching both the state and federal levels. The famed Hoover FBI was unable, and sometimes unwilling, to bring down phase two of the Klan despite decades of on-and-off efforts to do so, with its own organizational structure having been penetrated by, or sympathetic to, the Klan. The secret internal nature of the Klan was its greatest protection, but it also benefited from overt membership numbers and wide, covert acceptance.

The Klan and Jim Crow dominated Southern society from Stetson's childhood through his middle age; their influences saturated every aspect of the social order. Many journalists, lawmen, ministers, businessmen, and politicians joined the Klan, and at the federal level, several long-serving Democrat senators and congressmen were members. The House Un-American Activities Committee protractedly neglected its charter mission and continued to declare the Klan to be an acceptable element of American heritage.

The Klan became so strong that at one point it took firm hold in some of the racially integrated Northern states, well beyond its Southern roots. In Indiana, D. C. Stephenson of Houston, Texas, established a base in Evansville. Through Stephenson's considerable sales and organization skills, membership reached 350,000, or nearly one out of every three men. The Indiana Klan controlled cities, counties, and even the governorship of Ed Jackson and other top state posts. They sustained control through membership, sympathy, threats, and bribe-based patronage. Stephenson accurately bragged, "I am the law in Indiana."

Stetson referred to the KKK as "home-grown fascists and racial terrorists." Beyond his experiences with the WPA, he had other good reasons for holding that view. When Stetson was a child, his family employed a black maid named Flo who was "almost like a mother" to him. After Flo was short-changed by a white bus driver, she attempted to recover the money due her. The penalty for this was a nighttime beating and serial rape by a KKK gang. Stetson had a disreputable uncle who'd achieved the high-ranking and amoral position of Grand Titan. Both of these circumstances left negative impressions on young Stetson.

Stetson accurately believed that the Germans and Japanese were also racists who utilized terror on an international scale. His peers had gone overseas and were doing their best to oppose them. Because Stetson was prevented from active service in the armed forces due to a childhood back injury, he was frustrated and disappointed that he was unable to be inducted into our military. (Additionally, he was the size of fictional Steve Rogers before morphing into Captain America – a popular comic book hero of the time.) Stetson resolved to perform his own voluntary, substitute patriotic duties; he would fight racist fascism on our home front instead.

Stetson determined to do so by taking on the Klan. He left Florida and temporarily moved to Georgia because, at the time, Atlanta was the headquarters for both the KKK and a related, Nazi-influenced youth group called the Columbians. Stetson decided to infiltrate both organizations. He did so by assuming a new identity, since his real name was already well known and hated by the Klan. Stetson went by the name of John S. Perkins, the fictitious nephew of his Grand Titan uncle, Brady Perkins. He took the Klan's blood oath, wore their hooded gown, burned crosses, and made hate speeches. This role-playing eventually earned him the position of Klavalier.

It was equivalent to an enforcer in the Mafia, so it was sometimes referred to as the *murder squad*. His time undercover was a dangerous double-edged sword: He could be mistaken by anti-Klan factions as a KKK collaborator, or revealed by the Klan as an informant.

Stetson collected and recorded solid information gleaned from these organizations while working undercover within them, with much of it suitable as legal evidence. The discovery data included secret code words and handshakes, decisions made during meetings, and the details of their rituals. Stetson would tip a trusted authority about the Klan's planned activities so they could intervene and prevent some of the potential violence. But event-by-event prevention amounted to a very small portion of the overall evil perpetrated. Action was needed on a larger scale. He determined it should be in the form of debunking the KKK as Christian patriots. He wanted to reveal their true nature as savage criminals.

The Klan had widespread support at many levels of society in the South and beyond, causing it to be difficult and risky for Stetson to know whom to trust with his information, as he could be double-crossed at any time. Subsequently, in 1947, he decided to bypass the usual authority channels and to feed the secret details he'd collected to Robert Maxwell, the producer of the exceptionally popular *Superman* nationwide radio program. Radio at the time was the single-most influential mass communications media. During the war, Superman – the greatest comic book superhero – had fought and defeated Hitler, Mussolini, and Hirohito; why not now take on the Klan? The anti-Klan series concept was accepted, and production consisted of four episodes a week for four weeks running under the title *Clan of the Fiery Cross*. These sixteen audio broadcasts are available today on the Internet and may be heard on YouTube.

Stetson's plan was effective because it stripped away the Klan's mystique, which was formerly its most tenacious strength. By trivializing and exposing the Klan's rituals and code words, he caused a negative impact on Klan recruiting and membership. In the radio episodes, Superman took on and defeated the evil Klan. Through Superman, Stetson made a foolish mockery of the Klan and it became a thing of ridicule, well known for the wickedness perpetrated in the dark, and under secret cover. Youth all across the nation began to accept that the KKK was an evil force and an enemy of our

American way of life. No decent father now wanted his child to know that he was a member of the Klan.

The reaction was immediate and substantive, as fathers and husbands formerly active in the Klan found their confidential positions reviled by their families and their best secrets open fodder for common disdain. Attendance at Klan meetings fell off, dues went unpaid, recruiting failed, and membership waned. The media initially helped create this phase of the Klan and the media subsequently helped destroy it.

Beyond the *Superman* episodes, and while the Klan was still reeling from the initial punch, Stetson and his co-conspirator informants continued their infiltration of the KKK and of other related white supremacist groups. They helped the authorities revoke the Klan's corporate charter; they testified against them in court; and they fed the names of prominent citizens who were Klan members to the famed muckraker, Drew Pearson, who revealed them nationally. Evidence recovered by Stetson from the wastebasket of the Klan's Grand Dragon was submitted to the IRS, resulting in yet another blow: a crippling financial tax burden of $685,000 in 1960 dollars.

Stetson quickly followed up the *Superman* series by introducing a second strategy based on an entirely different approach. He called it *Frown Power*, an effort to encourage people (one-on-one) to pointedly frown whenever they heard bigoted speech. This was intended to help ensure that prejudicial Klan-like behavior would have trouble gaining favor and becoming re-rooted.

Through Stetson's efforts, a terrorist movement that the FBI, the state National Guard units, Congress, and several attorney generals unsuccessfully opposed, or willfully tolerated, was eventually nearly eliminated by one brave man with creative ideas. What these agencies were unable or unwilling to do with power and prestige, Stetson did in a short time by personal courage and clever thinking. Stetson was the real superman who took on the KKK, but he used the comic-book hero Superman as his public cover.

Despite Stetson's good works and successes, he made many enemies. At one point, he stated that he was "the most hated man in Florida." The leadership of the KKK now turned their attention on the man who had brought them so much misery. Grand Dragon Sam Green announced a bounty on Stetson of $1,000 per pound of flesh. Even his family refused to associate with him. First, his dog was shot for menial punishment and as a warning. Shortly thereafter, his home in Fruit Cove (now a Jacksonville neighborhood) was sequentially broken into, attacked by armed men, and finally firebombed, which resulted in the destruction of much of his lifetime's research and writings. For a while, Stetson carried a shoulder-harnessed .32-caliber S&W automatic handgun and heavily armed his wife, his home, and his friendly neighbors to secure some measure of personal safety. When it became known that the KKK had begun dynamite bombing, he left Florida to live the next decade of his life in France. It was there, in 1954, that he wrote his most sensational exposé of the KKK, *I Rode With The Klan*. Eventually, Stetson returned to live once again in Jacksonville, Florida, at Beluthahatchee Park, where he reissued his books in 1990, including *The Klan Unmasked*.

Harassment of Stetson periodically renewed even into his old age. In 2011, the accuracy of his undercover writings were challenged by Ben Green, a writer who alleged that after months of studying Stetson's field notes, he could not substantiate some of the facts in *The Klan Unmasked*. Thus, concurrent with his death in 2011 at age ninety-four, he was no longer just fighting to preserve his physical life; Kennedy was fighting to salvage his reputation, protect the legacy of his work, and uphold historic truth. As a refutation of these accusations, and to help clear Stetson's reputation, David Pilgrim of the Jim Crow Museum at Ferris State University in Big Rapids, Michigan, had this to say in summary: "Infiltrating the Klan was an act of great courage, and the information in the books and on the radio shows led to the arrests of some Klansmen, the derailing of domestic terrorist acts, and the unpopularity of the Klan organization. That is good enough for me."[5]

Toward the end of his long life, Stetson stated: "Not everyone who devotes a life to a cause lives to see it come to fruition, and I consider myself lucky to have done so." Despite the obstacles placed in his path, Stetson remained active and productive until his end. His contributions were not limited to opposing the Klan; after its defeat, Stetson continued to devote his life to promoting social justice and human rights. Throughout his lifetime, Stetson frequently had to make difficult but significant choices: One was to find the best alternative way to serve his country; another was to exchange personal safety and popularity for improving the common good; and yet another was to expose and oppose evil rather than tolerate or contribute to it, as were the more popular and accepted choices of Stetson's neighbors. It would

---

5   en.wikipedia.org/wiki/Stetson_Kennedy#Beluthahatchee_Park

have been easy for Stetson to have compromised his beliefs and lifestyle to match those of his contemporaries, thus having a comfortable life filled with peace, friends, and security. Resisting peer pressure is indeed a step in the right direction, but a further step means openly opposing it. Stetson chose to walk in that direction and to take the extra step, which he summarized as: "To stand against a movement is painful, but to stand against one's people is even more so."

Our lives are full of unavoidable choices that we must make. Good and evil are consistently set before us. The choices we make determine the kind of person we become. Floating mindlessly along with the common, acceptable current is the same as making a choice. Practices are not right just because they are approved, accepted, or tolerated. They are right only if they are God-ordained and support His purposes. Other people, our personal physical and financial needs and wants, and a corrupt world all naturally tend to cause our actions to default toward the unprincipled, but we can promote righteousness by making the difficult choices. We may go the broad, selfish way of Nathan Bedford Forrest, D. W. Griffith, Woodrow Wilson, Thomas Dixon, William Simmons, D. C. Stephenson, and the majority population of Dixie-Democrats, who for two centuries serially supported slavery, the Confederacy, the KKK's racism/white supremacy, and finally Jim Crow segregation; or we may go the narrow way, demonstrating an overarching concern for others as did Stetson Kennedy. The choice is ours alone, and we cannot be forced against our will one way or the other. Stetson said, "Don't ask what's wrong with me [for choosing to oppose popular Jim Crow], but rather ask what's wrong with all the people who went along with it."

Any study of the KKK quickly reveals there's a life-and-death difference between claiming Christian status and actually acting and/or being Christian. Many people outwardly adopt a veneer of Christianity as a cover to disguise their real intentions while hoping to fool others. Others are not well anchored and are too easily fooled. Actions of this nature do a serious disservice to real Christianity. The acid test is simple enough, and it was revealed to us more than two thousand years ago: By what means do they act and what fruit do they bear? Both the means and the fruit must be virtuous in form. The truly Christian voice and position are nearly always a minority-position – often calling from the wilderness, often unpopular.

If there's broad agreement, it's likely time to step back and examine where the compromise crept in.

Stetson was raised among neighbors who were false Christians, dominated by loyalty to a political party, tradition bound, and white-supremacy educated, but his morals were rooted in a higher law than Jim Crow. He rejected a skin color-centric lifestyle that complacently yielded to the popular, bifurcated society that surrounded him. In regard to the dignity of human relationships, Stetson, like the great man Abraham Lincoln before him, conformed his will to those eternal and universal truths first revealed to mankind at Mount Sinai, that all are equal under God's Law and all are subject to it. To underscore this point, an aged Stetson summed up his own life by saying, "You can't embrace me without at the same time embracing fair play and equal opportunity."

Stetson's anti-Klan actions seriously crippled the violent terror network for a season, but they did not end the general practice of segregation in the South, nor completely eliminate every vestige of the KKK. Due to the ongoing practice of Jim Crow laws and the population's deeply held prejudices, the Southern Klan had fertile ground for a third and final reincarnation. This occurred after the effects of Stetson's successful opposition had sufficiently waned. The KKK thereafter reengaged as a reaction to the Civil Rights Movement of the sixties. It was, however, eventually dismantled by that same movement in roughly a decade, as increasingly publicized integration efforts received favorable nationwide support, and Southern apartheid became openly subject to international scorn. The Klan occasionally observed today is an emasculated, fringe group of neo-Nazi skinheads only remotely related to its previous phases.

Confronted as to why he'd reissued his books in the early 1990s long after de facto integration, Stetson compared their theme to the Nazis' Holocaust against the Jews, indicating it was a part of history that should never be forgotten, buried, revised, or untaught in the hope it would thus never be repeated. It's in that same spirit that I've included Stetson's life story. Reissuing his books was not an attempt to find cause where it had been satisfied and no longer existed. False acts of this nature are currently used far too often. They are appropriately called *race-baiting* and *playing the race card.* These insincere acts occur whenever a public posture is adopted that pretends to heal and restore race relations, but is actually furtively designed to sustain the open wound for selfish gains – outwardly champions of human dignity, but inwardly bigots. These bigots are worse than the alleged ones to whom they are pointing their fingers; they think they see a speck in their brother's eye, while ignoring the plank in their own. We have many active examples in American society today, several of them abusing the title of Reverend.

Stetson's comprehensive lifework on behalf of the American black is comparable to William Wilberforce's in nineteenth-century England when he secured a ban on slavery throughout the British Empire. If mankind had more men like these men who were dedicated to uncompromising humanitarian missions, it surely would have been possible to have alleviated and truncated the extended sufferings of the American Indian, as well as the considerable number of other oppressed races, nations, and religions around the globe and throughout history's timeline. Mankind has witnessed many defenders of a culture who were members of that same culture, such as Mahatma Gandhi, Nelson Mandela, William Wallace, and Martin Luther King Jr. Defenders of a culture who belonged to another culture are much more rare and all the more heroic. Such were, for example, the rescuers of the Jews during the Holocaust, men and women like Raoul Wallenberg and Irena Sendler (her story is included in this book). These outsiders dedicated and often gave their lives for the benefit of a non-native culture. They knew the answer to the question, "Am I my brother's keeper?"

When a young shepherd observed God's people submitting and cowering in a defeatist attitude before the advance of an enemy in possession of a degenerate lifestyle and brandishing malicious intent, he questioned his king, his brothers, and the whole Israelite army: *"Is there not a cause?"* (1 Samuel 17:29). This is an enduring question worthy of our continued and prolonged individual speculation. Stetson, who was both small of stature and an outsider, found and followed a noble cause on behalf of his *brother*. Like David, he used the humble means available to him and approached the giant challenge head-on without hesitation and with confidence in the right, not the might.

"And He will give you into our hands." (1 Samuel 17:47)

* * * *

Author's Note: Stetson Kennedy was first introduced to me via the book, *Freakonomics*, by Steven Levitt and Stephen J. Dubner. Thereafter, I had the opportunity over the course of writing *Stories of Uncommon Character* to spend several months respectively in Jacksonville and St. Augustine, Florida, while visiting and researching some of the places that Stetson Kennedy lived and labored, as well as leisurely reading several of his books at the local libraries. Both cities now present a much-changed environment than when he applied his charismatic, but unpopular, personality to their politics. Today, he would be pleased to witness the enlightened way his former locale has developed.

Ronald Reagan

America's Lifeguard, The World's Cowboy

The LORD has sought for Himself a man after His own heart.
(1 Samuel 13:14)

His life began the same year as Russia's Bolshevik Revolution and, fittingly, the final years of his life overlapped the demise of the Russian-led Soviet Union. There's so much of value in Ronald Wilson Reagan's epic legacy that many books, hundreds of pages each, have already been written. Many more continue to be written as additional detail is gleaned from newly opened archives, as others seek to commemorate him, and as the passing of time further underscores the significance of his contributions.

President Reagan is arguably the most influential and dominant world statesman in the latter half of the twentieth century, just as Winston Churchill (known as "Mr. England") was in the first half. Both men were decidedly cognizant of the monumental evil respectively represented by totalitarianism, and each knew how to lead figuratively and literally in opposition of them. The greater the challenges, the greater the men who rise to meet them. Their combination of motivational speech and intentional action brought relief to millions of hopelessly repressed people.

It's more than a passing curiosity to compare Reagan to another American president whose own messianic vision and mission led America through its most troubled time – a time when Americans fought each other and devastated much of the country. It was our Civil War; the man was Abraham Lincoln. Reagan and Lincoln have substantially more commonality in their backgrounds and personalities than a casual view reveals.

Both men had humble births and austere childhoods, fathers who provided little influence and with whom they had deficient relationships, and mothers who provided much and to whom they were close. Both lived as young men in small Illinois river towns, suffered many moves as children, and had modest educational backgrounds for the high rank to which they rose. Both were great orators, storytellers, and jokesters. Both knew many people while having few close friends, were generally thought of as loners, and married strong-willed women who were fairly unpopular. Both were exceptionally criticized and unfairly disrespected, called vile names by the press and by opponents, often referred to as ignorant while in truth they were brilliant, and sneered at by the career politicians of patrician background. Both liked reading and writing for relaxation, were athletic and rugged outdoorsmen in superior physical condition, held office during a time of war, and were able to change deeply held positions when the time was right to do so. Both were exceptionally active letter writers (extraordinarily skilled in the art), selected strong personalities for their cabinets, and were shot by handgun-carrying obsessed men. Both had warm personalities, were known for their honesty and personal generosity, were willing to stand alone, and were always close to their constituents. Both were elected to two terms, served little to no time in Congress, were strategic thinkers willing to compromise even when it angered their closest supporters and advisors, manifestly influenced their times and history into future generations, and openly displayed devout Christian faith with attending works.

The parameters for telling Reagan's life story are so daunting that forward from this point, I've settled on using a unique literary device as the best approach available to me. I'm presenting two series of compelling images, rather than attempting to put forth the countless further words necessary to convey the broad scope his life deserves.

The first series is the longest, but with the shortest images. They're offered in random sequence as follows:

- Romantic leading man starring in more than seventy films and twenty television programs

- California governor who broke the University of California, Berkley and City of Berkley protests

- Young lad nicknamed *Dutch*, rising from rags to riches in fulfillment of the American Dream in which he heartily believed

- Political mediator respected by friends on both sides of the aisle

- Attempted-assassination victim maintaining witty humor while fighting for his life

- Des Moines, Iowa, radio personality informing his audience with a pleasing voice

- Wise and tireless public servant toiling twenty years past the age when most men retire

- Sharing his spirited storytelling and savvy humor with the press and opponents during a debate

- Protestant leader bonding with Pope John Paul II to form the duo that defeated world Communism

- President joking with his Secret Service contingent who knew him fondly as *Rawhide*

- Youngster of eleven, accepting the Lord's salvation as he read an engaging Christian novel, not seeing the words as much with his poor-sighted physical eyes as with those of his heart

- Outlining the foundations of the modern conservative movement in his unceasing speeches delivered to every segment of society for a decade before even entering politics

- Collegian lettering in football and swimming

- Recovering, post-surgery patient waving from the hospital's ICU window to an assembled crowd of well-wishers

- Offering his favorite candy, jelly beans, to guests and visitors at the Oval Office as he munched on one himself

- Honoring the veterans gathered on a windswept Normandy Beach with a snappy salute, a warm handshake, and a proud smile

- Bighearted giver quietly writing an impromptu personal check to assist a needy individual or a worthy cause

- Commander-in-chief equally adept at employing military force and personal diplomacy

- Folksy-yet-urbane corporate spokesman for General Electric and Death Valley Days' 20-Mule Team Borax appearing regularly on prime-time television

- Broad-shouldered rancher easily manning barbed-wire fencing and a chainsaw

- Smiling and waving to the press corps as he departs or arrives via the presidential helicopter

- Devout Christian unashamedly praying in public and sharing one of Jesus' parables at the Moscow Summit

- Revitalizing the Republican Party with well-delivered convention speeches from 1964 to 1992, beginning with "A Time for Choosing"

- Gentleman overtly conscious of his assumed role to model only the best example at all times

- Tax-cutting nemesis of big government and the welfare state

- Corresponding late into the night from his White House desk, like Lincoln before him – touching people, not reading surveys

- Legally blind army captain helping win WWII on the home front by producing four hundred training films and promoting war bonds

- Advocate and implementer of the practical economic theories collectively known as "Reaganomics"

- Gravely wounded chief executive surrounded by Secret Service agents pushing him into a waiting limo

- Influential global titan teamed with Britain's Thatcher and Israel's Begin

- Labeling the *evil empire* instead of following State Department politically correct compromised speech – the very personification of anti-Communism

- Archetype for every well-meaning politico who followed him

- Chairman of the Screen Actors Guild (SAG) who, ironically, later reined in the Professional Air Traffic Controllers Organization (PATCO) as president

- Nuclear summit arms-reduction negotiator with steely resolve staring down a series of Soviet dictators, and walking away from Mr. Gorbachev's SDI ultimatum at Reykjavik

- Fatigued fighter, fondly called *The Gipper,* offering a friendly wave and a blank grin as he resists the encroaching loneliness of life with Alzheimer's disease

- Nancy's beloved spouse and her dedicated husband

- Noble statesman of proven integrity and tested character

- At rest in the Washington National Cathedral while receiving homage by five living presidents and numerous dignitaries from around the globe

A further honing of those many general images of Reagan resulted in seven more that provide a salient picture of his motivations and goals. Frequently, when a word or picture image of our fortieth president is invoked, it's messianic in nature. Not messianic in the ultimate and eternal sense of Jesus as Messiah, but rather, messianic in the moderate and temporal sense of one who has offered a significant portion of his life to saving a substantial number of others from troubling and unfortunate circumstances, and has subsequently achieved laudable success in the effort.

The second series is shorter, containing only seven select messianic images. They are slightly more detailed and are presented chronologically:

- Embarrassed small boy who, once again finding his father

passed-out drunk in the snow-covered yard, half pulls and half carries the man to the safety and privacy of their home

- Robust teen lifeguard stationed on a riverbank overlooking the threatening currents while maintaining a watchful eye on others who are depending on him

- Big screen actor – occasionally performing his own stunts – film-after-film rehearsing his character studies so that he's mentally prepared to perform his many roles as heroic leading or supporting man, the one who stops the bad guy, makes the winning play, or rescues the damsel in distress

- Hollywood-handsome cowboy, physically capable of taming the land and animals at his expansive Western ranch, arrayed in characteristically appropriate white hat while mounted on a sturdy horse

- Hospital patient, recovering from near-deadly wounds, having some unusual free time to contemplate the reasons his life was sovereignly spared from an assassin's bullets fired at close range

- Stylishly suited chief executive of our nation standing boldly at the Berlin Wall, inspiring the world with his soaring rhetoric and a renewed sense of urgency to complete his ordained mission to end the Cold War by eclipsing Communism and its biggest proponent, the USSR

- Leader of the free world – with a keen appreciation and understanding of biblical history and prophetic end-time events – successfully pressuring Gorbachev to release the USSR's Jewish population who were denied emigration while being force-fed the mandatory national religion of atheism, thus triggering a second exodus from captivity to the safety of the Promised Land as more than one million Jews rapidly responded to the opportunity by making *aliyah* south to their eternal homeland, Israel

There are additional messianic images available to us from his life, such as the college sports victories and Screen Actors Guild battles, but the ones emphasized above most appropriately illustrate the many phases and major themes of Reagan's life. A person who had just one of these experiences would be justified in assuming a messianic perspective. The combination of these seven images prefigure a person, like the mythical Phoenix, who could potentially rise out of the ashes of the country's decay and capitulation and apply himself to restoring America to its former glory. Reagan was certainly en route to climactic accomplishments in the arenas of peace, prosperity, freedom, and goodwill. His lifetime record is like the man himself: epic in scope and so comprehensive and dynamic that if it were fiction, it wouldn't be credible.

The messianic images are of greatest interest because they capture the experiences that best reveal Reagan's closely held motivations and objectives, thereby helping us to understand why he chose the path he did. Within these seven, is there a key that acted as a catalyst for many of the images – especially the messianic ones? Reagan said, "There is sin and evil in the world and we're enjoined by Scripture and the Lord Jesus to oppose it with all our might." Without a doubt, Reagan is expressing messianic language and is prepared to pursue a complementary role.

Having recognized this, it's natural to ask subsequent questions like the following in regard to his overtly messianic nature and its established legacy: Where did he learn to do this? What was the source of his vision? How did he have the confidence to proceed so single-mindedly, with so much assurance? What did he so powerfully believe about his purpose in life? How was he able to stay on the charted course? What was planted in his psyche at an impressionable age, and how did it get there? In short, we're in pursuit of the small story that's not so obvious and not so well covered, yet it's the driver behind his larger story that is already so well known and accepted.

His redemptive spirit was first hinted at, then revealed, and finally confirmed at a riverside park during his teen years. Lowell Park, situated on the Rock River, is the pride of Dixon, Illinois. It was named after James Russell Lowell, who wrote one of his best poems there, "The Washers of the Shroud," and whose family later donated the land. Its three hundred acres of natural scenic beauty were enhanced by three famous designers, including Frederick Law Olmsted of New York City's preeminent Central Park. The city was only twenty years old and had a population of about five thousand during the 1920s, when the Reagan family made it their home. Dixon is located roughly at the midpoint on the Rock River's three-hundred-mile-long course.

The City of Dixon's website offers this description of naturally wooded Lowell Park:

> Until you have walked through this nature wonderland, you will not appreciate this wonderful gift that was presented to the City of Dixon near the turn of the 19th century.... It has stood through all these years as a place whereby people could relax and enjoy recreation to its fullest.... We hope you will enjoy the picturesque scenery and that someday you'll visit this magnificent park on the National Register of Historic Places. The scenic overlook from the park has been an artists' delight for nearly a century. You can view the scenery for miles and observe the river meandering along its course.

The Rock River begins in Wisconsin, north of Horicon National Wildlife Refuge, and flows in a gradually southwestward direction to the Mississippi River. Its watery neighbors are Lake Michigan and the Wisconsin River. During its course, it connects the states of Wisconsin, Illinois, and Missouri. The river's flow is enhanced by several tributaries as it pursues its winding southwestern route through a number of cities, the largest of which is Rockford, Illinois.

Central Illinois summers are just as hot and sticky as the more publicized ones in the Deep South. Thus, before the days of widely available public and private swimming pools – and well before air-conditioning was efficient and affordable – people of all ages gathered regularly at the Rock River in Lowell Park to dip, exercise, play, and cool off. This was a common practice, despite the facts that the vast majority of the population was unable to swim and the river possessed dangerous currents.

Young Reagan was a natural athlete, well built, with a strong interest in the sports of swimming and diving. Later, he swam at the varsity level for nearby Eureka College, where he captained the team. At fifteen, he took lifesaving lessons at the YMCA. Soon after, he pursued and won a summer job at the park as its primary lifeguard. In the years just preceding Reagan's hiring, several people had died while swimming at the park location. He held his position through high school and college, for seven straight summers. Even though the bathing area was near his favorite fishing spot (later renamed Dutch Landing after his boyhood nickname), it was all business now. Jobs were difficult to obtain, and he sorely needed the income to help support his family and to pay his tuition. Reagan worked at his lifesaving station twelve hours a day, seven days a week in the warm summer months. When he was eighteen year old, he was offered a position at an Olympic swim-training camp; Reagan turned it down, stating that his family needed the income afforded by his continuing as a lifeguard.

During his seven-year tenure as the primary park lifeguard, Reagan had ample opportunity to earn his fifteen-dollar-a-week paycheck, as the river had a strong, hidden undertow. Bathers who moved along the steep bottom beyond their comfort zone or who were swept off their footing by the current always promptly received the lifeguard's attention – all too often involving life-and-death circumstances. After each of these desperate situations was redeemed and the survivor safely recovered, Reagan would place a notch in a large tree trunk. He said any rescue he could walk to wasn't a real rescue, and so it didn't receive a notch; that is, only the deep rescues where he was personally at risk received a commemorative mark. He called it the difference between his *housekeeping duties* and the *real emergencies*. When his tenure at the river concluded and he was ready to move on, witnesses counted seventy-seven notches. There was never a life lost while he was on duty. His own life was often on the line as panicked swimmers – many larger than him – could easily have choked or drowned him. Drawing a parallel with the young George Washington story herein, God sovereignly preserved Reagan's life because He had greater purposes for him later, and He knew Reagan to be a man He could trust to perform them.

Reports in the area newspapers corroborate Reagan's personal accounting and later recollections. His situations often made the pages of the local paper and, occasionally, the headlines. This was especially true of one after-dark rescue when another lifeguard had given up the effort. Reagan was reported to have tossed off the thick glasses he required on shore and dove in, as he says, half-blind due to poor eyesight combined with the dark. Another article reported young Reagan setting a record time in a swim competition held regularly on a stretch of the river.

Think of it! How many twenty-one-year-olds can substantiate that they single-handedly, one individual at a time, over a period equivalent to a third of their life, snatched seventy-seven lives from near death? Perhaps there is none other. That kind of perfect success ratio combined with that degree of challenge and that kind of high purpose could not fail to make a deep and lasting impression on Reagan. Perhaps it was not just a single impression, but a range of unforgettable impressions including those of possibility, of mission, of special purpose, of unique selection, of confidence, or of universal human need. In his autobiography, *An American Life*, Reagan said that lifeguarding offered him "one of the best vantage points in the world to learn about people." His personal memory of these events has left us, but the notched log still stands as a silent witness to his deeds, along with the testimonies of witnesses and survivors. Each river rescue was a type of re-baptism and a precursor to his ultimate ministry.

Reagan's lifeguard experiences surely became the collective gateway experience to his greater callings at the Berlin Wall, Normandy Beach, Reykjavik, Warsaw, Moscow, Washington, D.C., Sacramento, and the various Republican Convention locations. Lifesaving enabled all those other wonderful iconic images outlined earlier to come to pass. When Reagan became president in 1980, he pledged himself to restore "the great, confident roar of American progress, growth, and optimism." The assassination attempt and associated near-death experience early in his presidency, in tandem with his subsequent miraculous recovery, served to reconfirm his messianic purpose and give him fresh resolve to complete it urgently. Reagan said, "All of us have to have a place we go back to. Dixon is that place for me. There was the life that has shaped my body and mind for all the years to come." He fondly recalled the time when he was recovering from the assassination attempt and he opened an especially meaningful card. The man offered get-well greetings and a prayer, but the correspondent also mentioned that he was one of those whose life was saved by Reagan many years ago in Lowell Park.

In his book *Ronald Reagan: Fate, Freedom and the Making of History*, John Patrick Diggins wrote: "From his earliest teen years as a lifeguard when he pulled ashore drowning swimmers, to his last presidential days in office when he sought to obtain the release of hostages in Lebanon, Reagan saw himself as a rescuer; the romantic hero who saves lives from the treacheries of nature and politics…. Reagan would in turn be a rescuer in the arenas of politics and diplomacy, saving people as he saw it from the dangerous currents of the liberal state and the evil empire."

What he learned on the Rock River led Ronald Reagan to become America's lifeguard. The image of the young lifeguard eventually morphed into one perhaps even more uniquely American. It's that of the cowboy with a horse, a ten-gallon white hat, and a pair of big-barreled six-shooters strapped to his hip. It was an understandable and easy transition for observers to make, and one fully justifiable, given his movie roles and Western rancher's lifestyle. The iconic cowboy became even larger, and far more public, than the lifeguard image. The self-reliant Western cowboy traveling a wild and lawless land is how the rest of the world symbolizes America. So as Reagan's messianic leadership gradually extended beyond our shores, it was an easy transition for foreign nations to visualize Reagan not as a lifeguard, but as the Western cowboy.

Reagan as the world's cowboy came to pass because Western Europe needed rescuing from near death under socialism and its impotent military, while Eastern Europe and the Asian satellite nations needed rescuing after being militarily subdued in every measurable way. These many nations were literally held captive within the suffocating prison walls of imposed atheistic Communism. On their behalf, Reagan strategically outmaneuvered the Soviets while decreasing intercontinental nuclear threats, immediately resulting in a better world for all of them. His bold rhetorical challenge at the Wall between East and West Berlin, "Tear down this wall," when combined with his other actions, resulted in hundreds of millions in formerly captive populations being set free. Many other figurative walls went down along with the brick and concrete one. As president, he was able to issue that admonition and make it stand, because the world knew it was backed up by a ready military, a strong economy, a consistent record opposing Communism, and his overwhelming popularity. Even more than these, he understood it was based on a righteous position. Reagan said essentially that the "struggle between freedom and totalitarianism today is a test of faith and spirit." He carefully chose when and how to play his strong hand.

Reagan the lifeguard first saved America from going under. Reagan the cowboy then utilized that newfound personal and national strength to rescue much of the captive world from its long peril. He became known as *the man who won the Cold War*. Britain's "Iron Lady," Prime Minister Margaret Thatcher, said, "He won the Cold War without firing a shot, he did it by turning enemies into friends."

Let it never be said of Reagan's successes – especially the domestic ones – that he simply continued the policies of the man he followed in office.

Little, if any, of what he inherited deserved to be retained. The nation was in the malaise of economic depression, gas shortages, and autocratic price controls on retail sales. There were historic record-high levels of inflation and unemployment, our military was out of date and rudderless, and entitlements and budgets were out of control. Additionally, Iranian radicals were holding Americans hostage and burning our embassy, home-grown radicals were controlling our college campuses, and auto manufacturing and electronics quality was a decade behind the Japanese front runner. Capital and jobs were traveling abroad, major cities had gone bankrupt, and a permeating and embedded attitude of post-Vietnam quagmire-related defeatism imbued society. We'd become a distant runner-up to the Soviet Union, no longer the leader God intended.

Offering a brief analogy in place of a longer description, our nation was, at the time of Carter's presidency, a larger version of what Detroit is today. Reagan led us out and into the *city on a shining hill* that he alone envisioned America was intended to be and was still capable of becoming. There is great potential power inherent in ideas, beliefs, and personal vision. Just as surely as men like Hitler demonstrate that in a negative way, men like Reagan demonstrate it in a positive way. Somehow, despite seemingly being surrounded by everything contrary to the American Dream, he was able to cling confidently to his faith in it – a faith that put God first, and subsequently, he was able to see God's hand still at work in America. Reagan summed it up thusly: "Live simply, love generously, care deeply, speak kindly, leave the rest to God." With that strategy, he engineered a prosperity that lasted twenty years and five presidential terms beyond his time in office. It was indeed the *Reagan Era*.

This transition for America from the height of its liberalism to the opposite height of its conservatism – what Reagan called the *New Morning* – can be lyrically recapped by employing Dickens' introduction to *A Tale of Two Cities*: "It was the best of times, it was the worst of times, it was the age of wisdom, it was the age of foolishness, it was the epoch of belief, it was the epoch of incredulity, it was the season of Light, it was the season of Darkness, it was the spring of hope, it was the winter of despair, we had everything before us, we had nothing before us, we were all going direct to Heaven, we were all going direct the other way–in short, the period was so far like the present period...."

The measure of a man's influence can be seen in the ferocity and tenaciousness of his enemies – those who will commit any lie in an attempt to defraud. They fabricate and tell untruths because they know there's no negative truth available to use for their false purposes. During his lifetime, and especially regarding everything related to his presidency, Reagan was severely criticized – most of it unjustly and just plain incorrectly. For example, Reagan stopped publicly attending a formal church shortly after being elected president. This was presented as either evidence of his hypocrisy or as proof he wasn't a Christian. The truth was far more practical; he did not want to disrupt the worship service by having the focus be on himself and subjecting the congregation to the security measures necessary for any president, especially one who had just survived an assassination attempt that eventually killed one and severely wounded several of those in the crowd near him.

As of this writing, approximately thirty years after Reagan's presidency – ten years after his death and one hundred years after his birth – some hate-filled perjurers are still engaged in an enduring effort to diminish the man and his record. One radical homosexual activist consistently accuses Reagan of cutting funding to AIDS research during his terms as president. Fact-checking informs otherwise, as the disease was first *discovered* during his presidency and he was the first to advocate funding federal AIDS research. Some sufferers are said to have received unheralded handwritten letters of sympathy and encouragement from the president, occasionally with a personal check enclosed. The people who attack in such manners do not really oppose Reagan the man, as he was especially likeable; they oppose the Christian values he represented and their Author. The bottom line is always the same: It's God they're after, it's God they hate. Their bitterness is usually founded in some false personal grievance from their past or from hidden sin in their present. As they lose face or political position, they rage more as they lose more. The dark always attempts to diminish the light, but the light overcomes; that was the solid promise firmly held within Reagan's well-selected *new morning* and *shining hill* analogies.

We needed rescuing in many fiscal and moral ways, thus adding credence to Reagan as America's lifeguard. Applying the most concise phrases possible, here's a recap of the extensive legacy Reagan endowed to America: economic recovery, a sound economy with decades of prosperity; the defeat of our classic enemy, the evil empire of the USSR; a renewed American spirit and lasting sense of optimism; a practical Christian perspective on political leadership; a strong military; a sound conservative template; and a worthy paradigm of what a moral man and an honest politician should be (along with Lincoln), the best the nation had witnessed since George Washington first demonstrated the criteria in the realms of military, politics, citizenship, and faith.

Hear again Reagan's messianic speech, "A Time For Choosing" (note the echoes of Churchill) and marvel at its scope, mark its sincerity, and embrace its promise: "You and I have a rendezvous with destiny. We'll preserve for our children this, the last best hope of man on earth, or we will sentence them to take the first step into a thousand years of darkness. If we fail, at least let our children and our children's children say of us that we justified our brief moment here. We did all that could be done." America may yet experience another "rendezvous with destiny," but to qualify, we will need another Josiah-like president (2 Kings 22-23) to lead the necessary values revival, one such as we were granted in Ronald Reagan.

I close with words borrowed from Margaret Thatcher's eulogy of President Reagan at the National Cathedral: "We have lost a great president, a great American, a great man, and I have lost a dear friend."

And the LORD has commanded him to be commander over His people. (1 Samuel 13:14)

* * * *

Author's Note: Some years after completing my story, I happened upon the book *My Father at 100: A Memoir*, written in 2011 by Ron Reagan, son of President Ronald Reagan and First Lady Nancy Reagan (their biological and younger son, who – unlike his adopted and older son Michael – unwisely chose rebellion rather than follow his father's righteous ways). In it, Ron dedicated an entire chapter to his thoughts and research about his dad's time in Dixon, Illinois, as a lifeguard, specifically chapter 6, titled "Local Hero." Ron has done an excellent job and in doing so delivered it with a fine writing style I can't hope to duplicate. There's even a wonderful story about a sixty-year-old California Governor Reagan rescuing seven-year-old Alicia Berry at a pool party, while fully clothed in business-casual attire, and without a log to notch. Instead of competing with Ron, I recommend a reading of his book, as I didn't revise my story to incorporate his writings. Prior to finding Ron's book, information about President Reagan's time as a lifeguard was difficult to acquire. For the reader's convenience, I share a quotation from the book that helps cement my core point: "… my father had come to value order in all things. Someone drowning at his beach, on his watch, would have brought chaos to his moral universe, casting a dark cloud over his beloved Dixon and calling into question his own capabilities. By hurling himself into the river to save the lives of drowning strangers, he was not only proving his worth, <u>he was setting the world aright</u>" (emphasis added).

Richard and Sabina Wurmbrand

Remove This Disgrace

Blessed are those who are persecuted for righteousness' sake.
(Matthew 5:10)

S ince the fall from Eden, when a shadow fell over our spirits, mankind
has sought to determine the purpose of life. Many have vainly searched
for it in wealth, power, sensuality, ritual observance, fame, athletics, politics, and intellectual pursuits. I believe Sabina and Richard Wurmbrand
accurately identified, and then wholeheartedly pursued, mankind's highest purpose. Through the example of their lives, we are able to discern the
highest purpose of life, as well as to better understand how to pursue it.

In Richard and Sabina's lifetime, first the Nazis and their minions in the
Iron Cross subjugated their Romanian homeland; then the Communists
followed suit. (See the related story on Eva Mozes Kor.) Both regimes imprisoned, deprived, and tortured the Wurmbrands, largely on the basis of their
Jewish roots. The Wurmbrands managed to evade the German death camps,
but most of their family did not. They utilized their blessing of freedom
to rescue Jewish children from the ghettos, preach in bomb shelters, and
evangelize soldiers – despite constant opposition. Scheduled for execution
near the end of World War II, Richard and Sabina were spared by God's
sovereign care and intervention.

Their ministry activities were illegal, and severe state penalties accompanied them if uncovered. Sabina expressed the Wurmbrands' contrary perspective when she stated: "We have a duty to mislead those whose sole aim is to destroy." The Wurmbrands and Dietrich Bonhoeffer were contemporaries who spoke similar messages of encouragement to the church – Dietrich in Germany and the Wurmbrands in Romania. Each held firmly to their shared belief that it is the fundamental duty of government, as ordained by God, to uphold laws for the well-being of its citizens; if it does not do so, then it has no claim on the compliance of its citizens. Each backed up this belief with active outreaches to those oppressed by corrupt authority. In many countries today, resolving any nuances related to this question of submission to ungodly authority is of immediate concern; soon it will be in America and other Western countries as well – working out our salvation with fear and trembling.

With Germany's military collapse, the Wurmbrands had only a brief reprieve before the repressions of life under Communism took full root. They used the time to clandestinely witness to large numbers of the one million Russian troops stationed in Romania. As former atheists, Richard and Sabina understood the deepest needs of these soldiers who were raised in a culture that denied God's existence. The young men had known only a godless society since birth, and they hungered for the hope and love-filled literature, words, and Bibles offered by the Wurmbrands. Following Romania's false liberation by Russia, the same ill treatment the Jews received under the Germans began under the hand of its new oppressor. The Wurmbrands were soon destined to disappear into Aleksandr Solzhenitsyn's bottomless *Gulag Archipelago*, a chain of unidentified, secret prisons spread across the vast USSR frontier. It was the same gulag that swallowed, and never released, the young Swedish rescuer of Jews, Raoul Wallenberg, at the conclusion of WWII, as well as countless other innocents during the unrelenting purge-filled regimes of Lenin, Stalin, and Khrushchev.

In the prewar decade, Richard and Sabina led a pleasure-filled good life as hedonistic atheists and wealthy stockbrokers. Their lives changed shortly before Romania lost its independence to the Nazis. This change experience came by way of a divine appointment; specifically, it arrived in the form of an aged carpenter. The old man had prayed many years for the opportunity to lead a Jew to the Lord's salvation, before he was to die. But there were no

Jews in his rural village; that is, not until Richard, who was convalescing from a serious case of tuberculosis at a nearby sanatorium, felt compelled to go for a walk. He was led that day to a wood shop in just the right village out of twelve thousand others in Romania. Little did that carpenter know what great and terrible events he'd set in motion. It was in his shop that Richard's spirit was renewed and his life direction changed. Later on, Sabina, although at first shocked and reticent, also chose this path, the way of the cross. Thereafter, the Wurmbrands no longer missed past pleasures, as they had freely yielded to another cause before the German Nazis and the Soviet Communists engendered sufficient strength to mandate their perverted precepts to the established churches in their Central and Eastern Europe satellite nations.

The Wurmbrands' new life, with its incumbent years of incarceration, torture, and hard labor, was a distant one from their former, easy lifestyle. Under the Russian domination of Romania, they experienced a rapid transition. Richard and Sabina overtly marked themselves early as so-called enemies of the state while attending a Soviet-sponsored Congress of Cults in 1945. It was held in the capital city of Bucharest, but broadcast live to all satellite nations. A stream of quisling-type presentations by various national religious leaders distorted the eternal gospel message in order to match the Communist party line, hoping to gain favor or acting out of fear. This prompted Sabina to encourage Richard to stand before the four thousand assembled multi-faith clergy to "remove this disgrace from the body of Christ." Knowing the cost, he did so without hesitation, and in an uncompromising voice. Richard declared that only God was sovereign, not Stalin or any transitory earthly power. The minister of cults retaliated, saying his right to speak was withdrawn, to which Richard replied he had a right from God, and he continued until his microphone was shut off. Richard's words encouraged many, and he received hearty applause, but the words sealed his fate for years, as he understood they would. The direction of the Wurmbrands' lives changed forever from this pivotal point forward.

Having openly challenged the authority usurped by the state, the Wurmbrands would never again be permitted to live freely in any society within the vast USSR evil empire. During their years in prison, they were sustained not by any earthly provisions, but by the promise of John 16:33: *"In the world you will have tribulation; but be of good cheer, I have overcome the world.*" More than anything else during this time, they learned to love God better through loving His enemies. They realized their persecutors were the true sufferers, with lives defined by only meaningless, empty existence and floating hostility toward a God they claimed didn't exist.

Richard experienced fourteen years of confinement under the Communist dictatorship of Romania, with three of those years in solitary lockdown. This time it was less on the basis of his Jewishness, and more owing to his unyielding commitment to Christianity. Never was a word of encouragement permitted to penetrate his subterranean prison walls; and all news of Sabina and his son, Mihai, was withheld. Perhaps it was for the better that he did not know their difficult fates. Barely managing to stay alive, they too suffered mightily and faced frequent threats of death, ranging from starvation to execution. Under the Communists, Sabina was arrested in the dark of night, told that Richard was dead, and assigned to a series of harsh labor camps, where she slaved under relentlessly cruel and perverted taskmasters. Surviving on the barest of rations, she was forced to perform hard physical labor out of doors from before sunrise to after sunset, wearing only the barest of rags in severe cold and acute heat, even when seriously ill and with broken bones still not mended.

The deprivations suffered by the Wurmbrands under Communism are too many for enumeration here, but they're detailed in Sabina's moving book *The Pastor's Wife,* and in Richard's influential first book, *Tortured for Christ* (translated into forty languages and one of eighteen books he authored). Eight-year-old Mihai was virtually on his own at this time, denied life's basic needs as a consequence of his unrepentant *criminal* parents. Their crime against the unholy dictatorships that were sequentially tyrannizing their homeland was simply an unyielding faith in another humble Man. Like the Wurmbrands, this innocent Jewish man suffered similarly from wrongful beatings, false trials, and torture that concluded with His brutal murder in Jerusalem two millennia earlier.

Richard came to be known throughout the gulag by both guards and fellow captives as *prisoner number one.* To defray pressures caused by his rising reputation, the government continually perpetuated the falsehood that he was dead. Eventually, both Wurmbrands obtained their releases through subterfuges created by a combination of influential former enemies to whom they had witnessed while imprisoned, and through the faithful activities of intervening friends. After their releases, they were encouraged to emigrate from Romania to avoid reincarceration. The Wurmbrands accepted the advice, and the necessary papers were purchased with substantial cash ransoms provided by supporters. A typical passport cost under $2,000; Richard's price was $10,000 (1964 value). The Wurmbrands first moved to England and then to America. There they could – without restriction – declare to their sleeping brothers and sisters in the West a message about the suffering Christians who'd been abandoned. A third of the world lay ignored or unknown behind an invisible *iron curtain* – so named by a prescient Winston Churchill, a man who understood early the inherent evil in both Nazism and Communism.

Their inaugural outreach was in Berkley, California, where Richard stood boldly before a massive rally of pro-Communists on university property. This situation was eerily similar to his experience at the Congress of Cults. The positive difference was afforded by the liberty then still available in America, contrasted with the demagoguery of the 1930–1940s German Third Reich and the 1940–1960s Soviet Union. After hearing lie upon lie, Richard wrested control of the microphone and removed his shirt to display a badly damaged body with eighteen deep wounds just in his torso; this physical witness surpassed that of his words. The wounds were barely healed, thus revealing the truth in his bold statements warning of the dangers of godless Communism, or, as Richard labeled it, *militant atheism*. As with Thomas upon Jesus' appearance in the Upper Room, the doubters could see and touch the piercings, some of them sufficiently deep to place a finger inside. Upon hearing Richard Wurmbrand on this occasion, one reporter wrote: "He stood in the midst of lions, but they could not devour him." Another wrote: "Here is a new John the Baptist ... another voice crying in the wilderness." Eventually, pursuing this course of action led Richard to stand before Congress and testify in the same manner against ongoing Communist repression. What Giovanni Grazzini said of Solzhenitsyn, who was another victim of the Communist Inquisition, might well be said of Richard: "... among the most powerful voices of the tradition that regards it as the writer's duty to insist on consistency between the work and the man, to believe in what he says, and to bear on his flesh the bruises of his ideas.... He crossed frontiers and ideologies, affirming the dignity of man" and of God.

The Wurmbrands traveled unceasingly for the remainder of their lives, throughout their adopted country and the world, proclaiming a plaintive, but powerful message: "We, your brothers and sisters, are being sorely persecuted for our faith. Please do not forget us…. Every church service that does not remember the martyrs and offer them prayer is not fully valid before our God." These are strong, convicting words from a couple who not only had lived the message, but had also become the message. Fluent in fourteen languages, it's estimated the Wurmbrands delivered a million presentations in eighty countries. Testimonies to God's love were thoroughly integrated into their beings. They continued faithfully sharing the truth in the face of massive indifference, ignorance, and opposition, smuggling the Bible into lands where it was forbidden. They displayed through their lives the truth of the Bible from Romans 5:3-5: *But we also glory in tribulations, knowing that tribulation produces perseverance; and perseverance, <u>character</u>; and <u>character</u>, hope. Now hope does not disappoint, because the love of God has been poured out in our hearts by the Holy Spirit who was given to us.* (emphasis added)

Perhaps their most significant lesson came at the greatest personal cost: Love your enemies, even those who had persecuted them without mercy. They were quick to forgive their torturers and share the love of Jesus with them while undergoing unthinkable mental and physical provocations. Whether they were familiar with the words of their contemporary, Viktor Frankl, I can't confirm, but they nevertheless embodied his words: "When we are no longer able to change a situation, we are challenged to change ourselves."

Longtime Communist puppet and dictator of Romania, Nicolae Ceauşescu, was deposed in December 1989, shortly after the fall of the Berlin Wall. Hearing the news, Richard and Sabina quickly returned to their homeland after an absence in exile of twenty-five years. They were received as returning national heroes, and the city officials of Bucharest made them a stunning offer. In the former palace of Ceausescu – the very basement of which Richard was once held in solitary confinement and underwent torture – they were permitted to open a printing shop and bookstore for their ministry. Their son, Mihai, also survived Communism, escaped to freedom in the West, and continues in a ministry similar to that of his parents. Jews like the Wurmbrand family are also known by the term *Hebrews*, which has been variously translated as "those who crossed over" and "back from the dead." Both translations are befitting of the Wurmbrands who had, indeed, crossed back into life from their physical burials in the gulag.

The Wurmbrands' faith was messianic, meaning simply those of Jewish birth who recognize Jesus as both Israel's and the world's Messiah. They were early representatives of the biblical *one new man* – the blend of Jewish Old Testament believer with Christian New Testament believer. Bible prophecy indicates this movement will grow mighty in the final days before the Second Coming. As messianic believers, they dedicated themselves to supporting all underground, imprisoned, and persecuted believers around the globe for half a century. Before departing us, they left an international organization in place to continue their mission, Voice of the Martyrs, headquartered in Bartlesville, Oklahoma. The legacies of the Wurmbrands and VOM are inseparable. (I'm pleased to be associated with a publisher, Aneko Press, who also prints titles authored by the Wurmbrands and distributed by VOM.) VOM's organizational mission statement is an extension of this couples' lifework: "Serving persecuted Christians through practical and spiritual assistance and leading other members of the Body of Christ into fellowship with them."

Richard and Sabina died a few months apart at the turn of the new millennia, 2000–2001. Richard was variously eulogized as *Voice of the Underground Church*, *Father of the Messianic Church*, and *Father of the Persecuted or Martyred Church*. He has also been referred to periodically as *Iron Curtain St. Paul*, as there were many similarities in Richard's and Paul's personalities and missions. What greater affirmation could a man receive?

The real heroes of the church – yea, of the world – have always been its martyrs, whose uncompromised stories are a testimony of eternal principles lived on behalf of God and mankind. The number of Christians awakened to the suffering church has grown since the Wurmbrands' time on earth, but so has the number of hostile areas and peoples. The need has not diminished. Our continuing challenge and opportunity is to be that voice.

The true God, whom the Wurmbrands served, has never left His throne, no matter the amount of evil perpetrated by fallen men and demons. All times and seasons are within His pleasure. The love of God overcomes evil, and His Spirit is always with His people to give sufficient peace, hope, and healing. This is the primary point of Richard and Sabina's story. Also here is the answer to our opening question. Since our fall from grace, the purpose of life is to learn how to love God and how to love others – including our enemies, those that despitefully persecute us – so we're prepared for eternal life with Him in heaven, where these two pursuits are manifestly displayed. In doing so, we are frequently admonished to fear not and to wait on the Lord. Thank you, Richard and Sabina, for your ample contributions, for VOM, and for the answer to life's greatest question.

> *For theirs is the kingdom of heaven.* (Matthew 5:10, the last beatitude)

* * *

Author's Note: In Romania today, despite the absence of Richard and Sabina, the same life message of liberation and love is still shared by Voice of the Martyrs with the victims of their re-aroused ancient enemy, the Muslims. Before the Nazis and communists, portions of Romania were brutalized under Muslim rule for four hundred years by the repressive Ottoman Turkish Empire. Many of its neighboring countries were beleaguered even earlier by Islam, beginning in the seventh century A.D. Recently, Romania was nominally reclaimed by a resuscitated international Islamic caliphate as their permanent property, based on their supposition of *once Muslim, always Muslim.* Islam seeks to again dominate and enslave Romania and much of Eastern Europe, the countries adjacent to the Mediterranean, the Iberian Peninsula, the Levant (including Israel), and so much more in a manner not unlike – in recent history – that of the Nazis and the communists. Their Islamic religious-political system already prevails over the lives of a quarter of the world's population through a combination of sharia law and jihadist coercion.

Islam is accurately labeled *a politically motivated repressive movement, or -ism, with a façade of holiness.* When they speak of a caliphate, they mean a single, enormous Islamic state where all facets of life are controlled by one supreme religious despot – operating out of a Mideastern capital like Mecca – who censoriously forces his extreme will on the entire population. The English word *caliphate* comes from the Arabic word *khalifat*, which means "something that has been replaced or exchanged." They intend to replace Judeo-Christian law, religion, and ethics by ultimately exchanging the one true God for their false surrogate god. They will not stop after reoccupying and controlling only previously conquered Arab and non-Arab lands; they'll continue to press for worldwide domination similar to their subsequent successes throughout Africa and Southeast Asia. Political appeasement by the West will not prevent Muslim aggression any better than it did Hitler's or Hirohito's. The *Chrislam* religious movement, which blends elements of Christianity with that of Islam, will only weaken Christianity and promote the ascendancy of Islam.

The translated definition for *Islam* is "submission"; it refers, in part, to their core belief in the forced domination of all peoples and lands to its idols and tenets. Where Islam has gained strength and taken root, adherents of other religions are offered four choices: convert, become slaves, flee, or die; and their internally sanctioned means of enforcement is beheading. The Muslim world knows that jihadist Islam is based on the Koran and on the life of Muhammad; they consider it the purest form of their religion. These violent followers are not doing anything that Muhammad himself didn't do. They use the same bullying tactics that he did in order to conquer, assemble, and maintain his large, suppressed, religious empire. These have been accepted Islamic practices from then to now. The much falsely maligned Crusades were a reaction to aggressive Islamic seizes and subjugations.

Islamization is performed on edifices as well as on people and lands. Muslims have a longstanding practice of forcefully acquiring the buildings, locations, and symbols of other religions, then converting their appearance and functions to match Islam, and thereafter claiming they had precedence (their religion permits them to lie to an *infidel*; that is, any non-Muslim). This is exactly what they did, for example, in the seventh century A.D. when they built and then rebuilt the first of their two mosques, Al-Aqsa, on the site of Solomon's Jewish temple, despite the fact that Solomon's temple had previously occupied that space one thousand years before the birth of Jesus, and sixteen hundred years before Muhammad. They've made many similar moves with Christian and Jewish sites in Israel and Europe, and wherever else they conquer. This Islamic practice began with Muhammad when he literally constructed his false, replacement religion on the far-more-ancient Judeo-Christian foundations, attempting to variously supplant or usurp our traditions. The Muslim purpose was, and remains, to undermine the legitimacy of the two older, legitimate monotheistic religions, Judaism and Christianity.

Aggressive Islamic physical actions are made all the more despicable when they call upon the name of Jewish prophets and the personage of our Judeo-Christian monotheistic God to justify their perverse behaviors. It's a weak and an evil god who relies on his followers to make and retain adherents by means of violent measures and deceptive precepts. They call America and Israel the big and little Satan, respectively; in doing so they are like the Pharisees who accused Jesus of having a demon while they were the ones operating under demonic influence or possession.

The majority of the ongoing ministry at the Wurmbrands' VOM is to imprisoned, enslaved, and persecuted people within Islamic nations. As a singular but typical example, Monica (not her real name) was forced to watch terrorists murder her husband, and then she was partially beheaded and left to slowly die. Voice of the Martyrs contacts obtained, and then financed, her lifesaving medical treatments; later, they placed her in a safe house and equipped her with a sewing machine as a means of income. Initially, the ministry focus was on victims of communism; today, it is on victims of Islamism.

Voice of the Martyrs meets the Islamic enemy directly; not in kind, but with prayer, love, and the Word of God. In his lifetime, Richard Wurmbrand regularly advised us to hate communism but love the communists; if he were alive today, he'd advise us to hate Islam but love the Muslims. After a long and terrible run, communism peacefully fell in Romania and its neighbors in 1989 without physical warfare. Our hope now is for the same to occur with regard to Islamism. It hardly seems fair; Muslims don't stand a chance. It's either accept God's grace and mercy now, or reject it and receive His justice later in eternity without the seventy-two dark-eyed virgins. Paraphrasing what Jeanne Kirkpatrick said abut Americans: Muslims need to face the truth about Christianity, no matter how pleasant it is.

The one true God draws us through love, and shows us the way to purity of thought and action. Voice of the Martyrs expresses God's love to His persecuted body in locations anywhere in the world. They call these nations *closed* and they number sixty, as of this writing, including a few non-Islamic, communist countries. From one perspective, *closed* means that Christians and Jews are not permitted to exit the country and are often deprived, imprisoned, tortured, and killed; or they may not practice their religion and/or are forced to practice a false one. From the other perspective, *closed* means that the Bible, humanitarian assistance (food, medicine, clothing, funds), and missionaries are not permitted to enter.

Voice of the Martyrs has five main purposes, which are based on Hebrews 13:3. They are:

1. Encourage and empower Christians to fulfill the Great Commission in areas of the world where they are persecuted for sharing the gospel of Jesus Christ.

2. Provide practical relief and spiritual support to the families of Christian martyrs.

3. Equip persecuted Christians to love and win to Jesus those who are opposed to the gospel in their part of the world.

4. Undertake projects of encouragement, helping believers rebuild their lives and witness in countries where they have formerly suffered oppression.

5. Promote the fellowship of all believers by informing the world of the faith and courage of persecuted Christians, thereby inspiring believers to a deeper level of commitment to Jesus and involvement in His Great Commission.

Gregory Jessner

Can't Help But Worry

The tree of life was also in the midst of the garden. (Genesis 2:9)

O ne December morning in 2002, after many weeks of secret planning, armed officers known as U.S. marshals appeared nearly simultaneously and in large numbers at high-security prisons in Pelican Bay, California; Concord, New Hampshire; Sacramento, California; Florence, Colorado; Folsom, California; Leavenworth, Kansas; Chino, California; and San Quentin, California. Marshals operate as the enforcement arm of the U.S. Justice Department, which is managed by the executive branch of the federal government. They have a 220-year history of law enforcement, older than the Old West and older than any other existing national or state enforcement agency. The marshals were created in 1789 by none other than President George Washington.

The goal of this massive raid in 2002 was the rapid and unannounced roundup of forty criminals: twenty-nine inmates, five women on the outside, three released ex-cons, one former prison guard, and two unidentified individuals. Those targeted were all members of an infamous prison gang formerly known as the *A.B.* for *Aryan Brotherhood*, but now renamed *The Brand*. The gang took its latest name from its distinctive tattoo, a shamrock surrounded by a swastika with *666* superimposed across it. The shamrock reflected The Brand's roots as an Irish biker gang. All twenty-nine inmate members were shackled and loaded onto a single Boeing 727 (yes, just like in the Nicolas Cage movie *Con Air*) whose final destination was a Los Angeles courtroom, where they stood trial, accused of ten felonies wrapped within a charge of criminal conspiracy. Unlike the movie, these cons did not escape; they were successfully delivered to the intended location.

These gang members were directly responsible for as many as 100 murders committed not on the streets, but inside prison walls. Prison system officials estimate that while only one-tenth of 1 percent of inmates belong to The Brand, it is responsible for 25 percent of all in-system murders. They were also indirectly responsible for additional crimes and murders committed by others who were implementing their orders on the outside. The twenty-nine men were the most dangerous in our prison system – men feared by fellow inmates and by their guards; men feared on the inside and the outside; men with nicknames like *The Beast,* who stabbed another inmate seventy-one times because he was accidentally shoved during a basketball game; or *The Baron*, who beheaded an inmate thought to have disrespected him. The extreme security prisons known as *supermaxes* were conceptualized as a means to control The Brand – albeit unsuccessfully.

Authorities describe The Brand as a Mafia-like criminal organization whose membership consists of convicted felons, mostly murderers. The gang was born in a single prison and is now present in all of them. It controls most of the drugs, prostitution, alcohol, extortion, protection, hits, alcohol distribution, and gambling that occurs therein. Membership is gained by performing random, unprovoked murder of inmates and guards. Thereafter the initiate is tattooed with the unique shamrock while reciting a blood oath.

Most of the gang members are *lifers,* beyond parole with nothing left to lose. The Brand has operated almost invisibly and with impunity for decades. Rarely did anyone challenge their motto of *Blood In, Blood Out*. No member will ever publicly admit to membership or even admit the gang's existence, and every member is required to perjure himself about the gang when questioned about it. They kill for hire, they kill for free, they kill for fun, and they kill for revenge. They kill inside prison walls and outside on the street. And they kill as openly as possible in order to intimidate and gain power. They kill.

Prison officials were desperate because they were unable to control the gang. The best they could do was move the members to different prisons, but that just spread the infection all the faster and farther. Even placing the members in isolation cells did not help. The criminal justice system needed a critical break. That break came in the form of a courageous, young assistant United States attorney in Los Angeles, Gregory Jessner. Gregory was born at about the same location and time as The Brand, near San Quentin State Prison in the mid-1960s. Unlike his bulky, mustachioed, shaven-headed gang nemeses, however, Gregory was slight, clean-faced, and boyishly handsome with trim, neatly parted hair.

It was Jessner's investigative probing that led to the 2002 raid and to the subsequent trials. It began in 1992, a decade earlier. It concluded with thirteen boxes of documentation and ten years of preparation just to bring the first Brand member to trial. Jessner's real goal was to take down the entire gang, not just deliver a handful of murderers to justice. (A goal similar to Stetson Kennedy's against the KKK – please refer to the associated story.) These men were already serving life sentences for murder. His chosen strategy was to use a combination of the Racketeer Influenced and Corrupt Organizations Act, known as the RICO statutes, and the federal death penalty introduced under the Clinton administration. The former was passed for use against the Mafia; the latter, to provide an extreme penalty when required in federal crimes. These enabled him to legally attack the entire hierarchy of the criminal organization rather than just a few targeted members. To be successful, he needed the sentences to be death penalties. He wanted these to send a strong message back into the prisons to discourage any new gangs from replacing The Brand if and when he took them down. He wanted that message to be: "You cannot kill with impunity. You will answer for it."

When the press asked Jessner during the trials to describe the gang, he replied, "This is a homicidal organization. That's what they do. They kill people." Asked if he feared for his life, Jessner said, "You can't help but worry. But I also believe that just because you rob a convenience store or cheat on your taxes, you shouldn't receive a death sentence." By that comment he meant that anyone entering prison for any reason or length of stay was prey to The Brand and could be randomly killed by those evil men just for sport or for promotion within their ranks.

The good news is that all twenty-nine inmate gang members were found guilty on all charges. The bad news is that the lenient California juries – practicing their religion of destructive moral relativism – could not find the internal strength and conviction to deliver death sentences. Consequently, each of the convicted murderers returned to prison, where they continue managing their illegal gang activities, as well as performing the random killings that give them the power to ignore laws and human decency.

The Brand is really no different today than how Hitler's Nazi Brownshirts and S.S. Death Troopers were yesterday. Their techniques of power grabbing and the subsequent abuses are the same. Much of their trappings are identical: nearly the same tattoos, symbols, names, secrets, words, unfounded hatred, and senseless killings. Required reading includes *Mein Kampf.* The Aryan name may have been dropped, but not the random, unprovoked, consistent violence that membership demands.

There are some positive takeaways in this story. For certain, Gregory Jessner is a heroic man of principles. The most vital takeaway was negatively demonstrated by the juries. They let their sentimentality overcome a true, clear, and righteous sense of justice. They could not, or would not, find the inner strength and uncommon wisdom to do their whole duty for society. They failed the prison system, they failed Gregory Jessner, they failed the courts, they failed the justice system, and they failed us all. Finally, they failed God, who unambiguously instituted the death penalty for our benefit and left its application to us. Organized crime and the countless, violent deaths of innocent people continue and multiply as a result of the jury not making the sober choice in favor of capital punishment.

People try to assign moral equivalency to capital punishment by saying, for example, that if you oppose abortion, then you must oppose the death penalty; otherwise you're not consistently prolife and thus are hypocritical. Don't accept that false position and negative label, and do not back away from these two issues. They are not the same. The distinctions are clear, simple, and significant. One is the death of innocent babies without guilt, without civil rights, without trial, and without the force of God's Law. The other is the death of the guilty with the full force of God's and man's law. Even then, judgment never transpires until the perpetrator has been indulged with every imaginable legal right and delay tactic. The situation is black and white, not the gray that the world would try to repaint it as being. Being pro-abortion and anti-capital punishment is the real hypocritical position, because that combination of beliefs applies the death penalty to babies, and grants life to murderers (who have taken innocent life from others, and who may continue to do so whether in prison or out).

Gregory left his seventeen-year career in prosecution after receiving the disappointing final verdicts, knowing The Brand had been given society's backhanded endorsement to continue its perverse lifestyle. He opened his own law practice in the heart of urban Los Angeles, Phillips Jessner LLP. Is his current specialty criminal law? No, it's family law. Who could fault him for the change?

And the tree of the knowledge of good and evil. (Genesis 2:9)

* * * *

Author's Note: In some ways, researching The Brand disturbed me more than my studies on Hitler, Islam, Communism, and the KKK. All in all, doing so increased my admiration for the brave, young attorney who elected to mire himself in the depths of its filth for a decade of his life. One area that bothered me was realizing that it could have and should have had a much more positive ending. The blame is society's, not Mr. Jessner's. The cons did not forcefully escape like in the movie; in real life they were released as the result of faulty moral equivalency, and thus permitted to continue propagating their evil. It's upsetting that there's an element in America who will always take advantage of the goodness, freedoms, and privileges we collectively enjoy and openly extend to others, and to know that they will eventually misuse these against us, abusing them to our hurt. The offense may come from a terrorist, a multi-generation welfare lifer, an illegal immigrant, a race-card player, or – as in the story – an incarcerated criminal. Their crimes against specific persons, or against society in general, share the same root. More upsetting yet is knowing there's another element in America that appears to perversely take pride in assisting the few at great cost to the many. In psychology, what feel-good humanists do on behalf of the undeserving is known as enabling, and it is America's current failed – but politically correct – methodology. It's a permissive attitude toward sinful lifestyles that masquerades as an excessive appreciation for, and application of, liberty and charity. What it really is at its most fundamental level is a refusal to honor the covenant that our country's founders established with

God; and left unchecked, it will continue to destroy our nation from the inside out. On the matter of dishonoring covenants, 2 Chronicles 36:15-16 cautions: *And the* Lord *God of their fathers [i.e., ancestors or founders] sent warnings to them by His messengers, rising up early and sending them, because He had compassion on His people and on His dwelling place. But they mocked the messengers of God, despised His words, and scoffed at His prophets, until the wrath of the* Lord *arose against His people, till there was no remedy.* (emphasis added) In circumstances like those in the story, the tough-love process takes on wholesome and practical application as the superior, proven approach. It's a successful approach to rebellious teens, and the potential positive yield for individuals, society, and country is far broader and deeper.

Haym Salomon

Saving the Fourth of July

And as I have purposed. (Isaiah 24:14)

I s there a Fourth of July in Great Britain? I often begin a school day by presenting the class with a brainteaser to get their attention and move them into thinking mode. One involves framing up the time of the war for America's independence against the British Empire. Then I follow through by asking the question with which I opened this story. The most frequent response is something akin to "No, we won the war and celebrate the victory on the fourth of July, but they lost, so they have nothing to celebrate. It's an American holiday." My wrap-up is that the correct answer is, "Yes, they do because England uses the same calendar as we do and therefore they have a third and a fifth of July with a fourth always coming in between."

There was a time when a positive outcome to the Revolutionary War was far from certain for the North American colonies. For seven of the eight conflict years, it looked like the Fourth of July would become a British holiday celebrating the retention of their subservient thirteen colonies. Many patriots contributed their best to bring about the reality of our sovereign and free outcome. Possibly more great men and women of high ideals were in motion at that time than before or since in the history of the world. The story at hand focuses on just one of these men, a man largely overlooked by history, yet one who helped save our Fourth of July as a day to annually celebrate independence and national birth. This was a new nation with a beginning and a purpose like none other except for our recent ally, and God's own chosen land, Israel, in 1948.

As an aid to fully appreciating the first portion of the story, it would be helpful to locate a one-dollar bill in United States currency, then keep it handy as the story unfolds. That Federal Reserve Note is our smallest printed denomination, but it represents a substantial amount of history, incorporates a timely message for today, and contains a hidden testimony to a hero within its intricate design.

In 1776, the First Continental Congress requested that Benjamin Franklin head a small group of men tasked with designing an official governmental seal. Due in part to the disruptions related to war, the project took four years to finish and another two to gain approval; thus, it was completed about the time of the war's end, in 1782.

On the back of the dollar bill are two circles. Each circle represents one side of the double-sided Great Seal of the United States as designed under Franklin; together, the circles comprise the whole seal. On the left circle – the back of the Great Seal – there's a pyramid. The front is lighted, but the western side on the pyramid's left is dark. This illustrates that the country was just beginning and the vast West had not yet been explored. The pyramid was left uncapped to further signify that the work of building the new nation wasn't finished. Inside the capstone, floating above the pyramid, is an all-seeing eye representing a watchful and all-abiding God. It was Franklin's belief that man couldn't finish the job of building a new nation without God's help, so he placed the eye at the top of the seal. Stated in Latin above the pyramid is *ANNUIT COEPTIS*, which translates, "God is favoring our work." In Latin below the pyramid is *NOVUS ORDO SECLORUM*, which means "Something new has begun." At the pyramid's base is the Roman numeral equivalent for 1776 (MDCCLXXVI).

In the center of the bill, displayed between the two halves of the Great Seal and helping to link them, is the familiar statement, "IN GOD WE TRUST." On the right circle, which is the front of the Great Seal, there's a design that has come to be known as the presidential seal whenever it is used alone. It continues to be used in an identical format in many formal governmental locations and circumstances.

One reason the bald eagle was selected as our nation's symbol is that it is said to wear no crown of tufted feathers on its head. This was a reminder that we had broken away from the king of England, the crowned head of the worldwide empire. The flag shield in front of the eagle is unsupported, signifying that this new country could now stand on its own. In the eagle's beak is the familiar Latin phrase *E PLURIBUS UNUM*, meaning "Out of many, one." The eagle holds an olive branch in one talon and arrows in the other. The image is intended to promote the message that the new country wants peace, but it will never be afraid to fight to preserve and protect that peace. The eagle prefers to face the olive branch on its left, but in times of war, his gaze will turn toward the arrows on its right. The arrows, of course, symbolize war.

Please note the prominent use of the number thirteen and its numerous appearances. There are symbols arranged in nine groupings, all of which contain a quantity of thirteen elements. The number thirteen corresponds to the number of colonies whose representatives signed the Declaration of Independence, participated in the war, and signed the Constitution along with its Bill of Rights. The quantity thirteen appears consistently on the dollar bill in all of the following images: the stars located above the eagle, the arrows in the eagle's talon, the stripes in the shield, the letters in the phrase *Annuit Coeptis*, the rows in the pyramid, the letters in the phrase *E Pluribus Unum*, the fruit encircling the unique star cluster, and finally, both the leaves and the berries in the olive branch in the eagle's talon. Several of these groupings of thirteen may be coincidental, but certainly most are deliberate placements.

Returning to the thirteen stars located above the eagle, we'll focus on the mystery behind their exact arrangement. When more closely examined, the stars are seen as placed in an exact design known as the Star of David (aka the Shield of David, Magen Da'vid, and the Jewish Star). The star was specially ordered by George Washington as an honor and remembrance for a hero of the Revolutionary War. This unique design leads to the second portion of the story.

The man whom Washington wanted to honor was Haym Salomon (sometimes spelled Hyim Solomon). He was a Jew of successful means living in Philadelphia during most of the war years. He had the ability to create substantial wealth somewhat comparable in methods to Warren Buffett, and he invested it as political capital, making him the Koch Brother or H. L. Hunt of his generation. When Washington asked Haym what he'd like as a reward for his services on behalf of the new nation, Haym said he wanted nothing for himself. Haym expressed that, as an alternative, he would appreciate something commemorative on behalf of his people, the Jews. The two patriots settled on placing the Star of David on the Great Seal. After nearly two millennia, some Jews began to find peace and acceptance in the newly established United States. The Jewish people had no homeland at this time, having been cast out of ancient Israel in a forced dispersal to wander the globe for two thousand years before the re-establishment of modern Israel.

In the pantheon of America's heroes and Founding Fathers, Haym Salomon (1740–1785) has legendary status. His life was a brief and tumultuous forty-five years, but his lasting impact on America is substantial. The shame is that most modern Americans aren't familiar with him, when we should know his story as well as that of Jefferson, Adams, Franklin, Hancock, Hamilton, and the rest of our country's forebears.

Haym was not always forgotten. He was last remembered in a special way in the 1970s, when the U.S. Postal Service issued a stamp series titled *Contributors to the Cause* – the cause being America's movement for independence. One of the stamps hailed a man as the financial hero of America's founding; the man was Haym Salomon. Interestingly, this stamp, like the others in the series, was uniquely printed on both the front and the back sides. The glue side of the stamp actually contained the following words printed in pale green ink: "Businessman and broker Haym Salomon was responsible for raising most of the money needed to finance the American Revolution and later to save the new nation from collapse." The front of the stamp read simply: "Financial Hero."

Haym was an immigrant to our country, arriving only a few years before the war. He was born in Lissa, Poland, in 1740, to an Ashkenazi (Northern European/Germanic) Jewish family. His ancestors moved there generations earlier to escape the bloody Catholic Church Inquisitions in Spain and Portugal. Haym spent his first thirty-two years moving around Western Europe, where he developed fluencies in several languages and gained a wide range of experience in finance. He also came to hold a strong belief that America would be a temporary safe haven for the Jews. Such a haven was sorely needed after centuries of persecution and forced migration. As a the son of a Jewish rabbi, he also believed in the Torah (aka the Old Testament), which promised that one day in the future, Jerusalem would rise from the dust, the Jews would return to their ancient homeland, and Israel and Jerusalem would once again be the international home and capital city of the Jewish people, who would no longer have to wander and suffer Gentile discrimination and denial. Salomon determined to do all that he could to finance the Revolution so that America could survive until the time when those promises would become reality. (His dream – the dream of every Jew – was fulfilled in 1948 with the reestablishment of the Jewish national homeland of Israel, with Jerusalem as its capital.)

In 1772, Haym immigrated to New York City and quickly established himself as a successful merchant and broker of foreign securities. Striking up a close acquaintance with the famous Sons of Liberty, Haym became an active patriot in the emerging cause for liberty. When war broke out only three years after his arrival (1775), Haym won a contract as his part in the war effort. He was to provide supplies to the American troops in New York. One year into the war (1776), he married Rachel Franks, whose brother, Isaac, was a colonel on George Washington's staff. The marriage was the beginning of a close relationship with Isaac, leading soon to another relationship directly with Washington. (See the related story on young Colonel Washington.)

In the third year of the war, British occupation forces set fire to New York (1777) and arrested Haym as a spy. He was tortured aboard a naval ship and then imprisoned for more than a year. They released him (1778) because the British wanted to use his language skills to communicate with the German Hessian mercenaries whom they'd hired. Haym had other ideas and covertly encouraged the Hessians to desert instead. He was rearrested (still 1778), but this time his property was confiscated and a British military court condemned him to death by hanging. He escaped with the help of the Sons of Liberty and fled, penniless, to the American capital city, Philadelphia, where his family was able to rejoin him for the first time in two years.

Once in Philadelphia, Haym rebuilt his business and resumed his trade. Just a few years (1781) after his arrival in the capital, he had, again, advanced from penniless fugitive to respected businessman, philanthropist, and defender of both his peoples – the Americans and the Jews. He risked his fortune, pledged his good name and his credit on behalf of the Revolution, and defended religious liberty for Jews.

In 1781, Congress established its first Office of Finance in an effort to try to save the war and the United States from fiscal ruin. Haym began interfacing with the appointed superintendent of finance, William Morris, and soon became the most effective man in America in meeting federal government and military expenses. He was responsible for raising most of the money needed to finance the American Revolution, as well as those funds that were later required to save the newly independent nation from collapse.

The Congressional Record of March 25, 1975, reads, "When Morris was appointed Superintendent of Finance, he turned to Salomon for help in raising the money needed to carry on the war and later to save the emerging nation from financial collapse. Salomon advanced direct loans to the government and also gave generously of his own resources to pay the salaries of government officials and army officers." Incredibly, Haym was able to maintain a thriving private business; perform many official duties for the United States, France, Holland, and Spain; give interest-free personal loans to James Madison, Thomas Jefferson, and General von Steuben; and fund both the Continental Army and the Continental Congress.

Later that year (in August of 1781), a unit of the Continental Army trapped British General Cornwallis in the Virginia coastal city of Yorktown, between the York and James rivers. Washington and his main army – along with General Rochambeau of the allied French army – wanted to march from Hudson Heights, New York, to Yorktown in an effort to combine all forces and deliver a heavy blow in the hopes of ending the nearly decade-long war. Unfortunately, Washington's war funds were completely depleted and Congress was broke as well. He needed at least $20,000 (value circa $55 million today) to finance the campaign. When told there were no funds and no credit available, Washington unhesitatingly issued one simple order: "Get me Haym Salomon." Haym came through by raising the money and by funneling it to the cause.

Washington conducted the Yorktown campaign, which proved to be the final battle of the long eight years of war. The Revolutionary War formally ended on September 3, 1783, with the signing of the Treaty of Paris, but this did not end the financial problems of the newly established nation. It was Haym Salomon who still managed, time after time, to raise the money needed to bail out the debt-ridden government and thus, hold it together.

Haym had to manage these successes despite operating within the context of a society and an age that mistakenly considered all Jews as wicked shylocks and selfish moneygrubbers. He and his Jewish people were regularly socially discriminated against and even physically harassed. He died at age forty-five in 1785, a mere two years after the war. Haym left behind a wife and four young children with debts larger than his estate. All his wealth and property had either been destroyed by the British or given to the Americans.

Private individuals like Jefferson and the federal government owed him a total of eight hundred thousand dollars, about forty-two billion dollars in today's (2015) purchasing power. Although Haym never asked for repayment of these loans, his son petitioned Congress to recover some of the money owed to the family and much needed by it. Various petty government committees refused to recognize the family's claims and never made good on any of the loans, many times "losing" the necessary documentation regularly provided as authentication of the obligations owed Haym's family. To this day, the Salomon family has received no repayment; the debt is fully outstanding and mention of it is rarely endeavored.

Despite personal setbacks, Haym Salomon's name is forever linked to the idealism and success of the American Revolution, as well as to the substantial history of contributions made by the Jewish people to the cause of freedom worldwide. (There were other Jews aligned with him, including the Rothchilds, Franks, and Sassons.) Few people today know it was Haym Salomon who saved the financial well-being of several Founding Fathers, the Continental Army, and the nation through his generous contributions; fewer still know that he died broken in both health and finance because of those selfless and patriotic acts.

Ever wonder how the United States and Israel became such close allies? There are many good and sound historical reasons, but one of the earliest is Haym Salomon's legacy. It was a precursor to the bond that has held for over two centuries between the United States and the Jewish people and, more recently, since 1948, between our country and the modern State of Israel. Some wonder whether it is fact or fiction that the Jews are God's chosen people and Israel His chosen land. This story, and so much more history, offers proof that these are both fact.

As Haym Salomon hoped and believed and worked toward, America did immediately become the safe haven for the Jewish people, and, 170 years later, the country of Israel was reborn as well, with Jerusalem as its capital. Haym was buried in Philadelphia's Mikveh Israel Cemetery, in a grave that is sadly, but typically unmarked. Since we don't know which grave is his, we cannot pay our respects or erect a memorial marker at his graveside. Nevertheless, as Americans we can remember and honor him for the debt we owe by standing firm in our support and prayer for a strong and secure Israel, as well as an undivided Jerusalem, under the rule of Haym Salomon's spiritual descendants, the Israeli people.

In downtown Chicago, at the intersection of Wabash and Wacker, stands a statue of three men: Washington, Morris, and Salomon. Its plaque reads: "Haym Salomon – Gentleman, Scholar, Patriot. A banker whose only interest was the interest of his Country." Historians who have studied Haym's life all agree that without his contributions to the cause, there would be no America today and hence, no Independence Day to celebrate. That's how and why a Jewish immigrant from Poland saved our Fourth of July holiday celebration.

So it shall stand. (Isaiah 14:24)

✻ ✻ ✻ ✻

Author's Note: Occasionally the supporting details of a story are seen as true or false based on the writer's, or the reader's, perspective. The story of Haym Salomon illustrates this potential in that the iconography of the dollar bill has been ostensibly proven to be both wholly Masonic on the one hand, and wholly Christian on the other, regarding its origin and intent. The balance is found in understanding that there actually was an alliance at that time in history between the two; one which is now largely antithetical to our modern, bifurcated, and fixed viewpoints. George Washington's personality, for example, was clearly an amalgamation of both Christian and Masonic influences and activities.

I encourage the reader to utilize solid fact-checking before relying wholly on a story for any purpose beyond which the story was intended. Haym's story, as well as the others, is primarily intended as a vehicle for demonstrating his heroic character. I further encourage the reader to find complementary readings and supplemental research beyond my simple story outlines. There is so much more to uncover about the lives and contributions of these interesting people. Motivating the reader to undertake further educational pursuit is an intentional objective of *Uncommon Character*.

Charles Norris and Alexander Gettler

Body of Knowledge

Men will seek death and will not find it; (Revelation 9:6)

In the first decades of the twentieth century, America saw a distressing mix of influenza epidemics, Prohibition and bootlegging, political corruption, technological war horrors, transportation revolution, industry monopolies, and Depression economies. The world had changed quickly, and perhaps nowhere did the outcome appear more out of control than in the largest metropolitan area of the country, New York City.

More than anything else, this was the age of the rise of chemistry. World War I was labeled the *chemical war*, as each major national participant developed and produced its unique selection of poisons. Germany had mustard gas and chlorine gas; France, phosgene and tear gas; and America, lewisite (a chlorine and arsenic mix). After the war, these military poisons were controlled and banned, but poisonous household chemicals were not. The average home and typical business were a poisoner's unrestricted pharmacy with a periodic table of death containing lethal chemicals such as arsenic, thallium, radium, cyanide, and morphine. All were widely manufactured, easy to acquire, and frequently used in mundane personal care and general cleaning, as well as in many conventional industry applications. These represented the legitimate face of commonplace poisonous chemicals, but there was also its darker, criminal side.

These poisons have a special place in criminology because early efforts to detect them – especially arsenic – in the human body were the foundation for the modern science of forensic toxicology. A practical way to understand forensics is to accept it as the point where the legal system, chemistry, biology, and laboratory science all intersect. Since the mid-1990s, there have been a number of television series loosely based on forensic science. These series combine an ultra-competent crime scene investigator with technical lab processes, both real and imagined. The genre is represented by such successful shows as *CSI: Crime Scene Investigation*, *Forensic Files*, and *Bones*. These programs are viewed by their idiosyncratic audiences with interest sometimes bordering on the fanatical, the kind usually reserved for *Star Trek*. Not having had a TV for the past thirty-five years, I'm not intimately familiar with the shows, nor am I endorsing them. My goal is to breathe some truth and background understanding into this popular subject by revealing the two crusaders who dedicated their lives to establish and perfect the craft. They did so in pursuit of several noble causes; prurient entertainment was decidedly never intended as one of them. In researching and revealing their achievements, I've gained a unique tale that can easily be woven into chemistry and biology classes as well as the general sciences. But don't lose sight that this is intended as a story, not a science lesson.

The story is centered on two professional scientists who collaborated in their medical specialties; the result was the development of a new science. Its credibility was established to the point where it literally withstood examination in a court of law, while often being the key to determining crime or accident, guilt or innocence. Their shared purposes were to diminish crime and sickness in New York City, which was then the nation's most prominent metropolitan area and the world's largest city. As a by-product of succeeding in their primary missions, these men also contributed previously unavailable and sorely needed working models and reference databases. Their contributions greatly assisted the proliferation of professional criminology practices throughout the United States and beyond. Their legacy is the widespread application of forensic toxicology by professionals for the public good, leading ultimately to acceptance by the legal community as well as to the founding of the federal Food and Drug Administration (FDA).

One scientist was Dr. Charles Norris, who was the first appointment to the post of chief medical examiner for New York City. The newly created position was forced upon the mayor by the governor as a reaction to massively embarrassing scandals associated with the former city coroner. Prior to Dr. Norris, deaths were certified by the politically appointed coroners, who were both thoroughly corrupt and woefully unqualified. Dr. Norris was eminently accomplished, having graduated from Yale and then from Harvard. He was the son of well-to-do parents with deep family pockets generated on both sides by banking fortunes. This is not a trivial fact, given that the bitter and corrupt Mayor Hylan, whom he served under, spitefully withheld the necessary monies to properly fund even the department's most basic operations. Thus, a conscientious Dr. Norris was forced to pay for much of the equipment, transportation, and salaries from his personal finances in order to run the department in a competent manner.

The other scientist was Alexander Gettler, whom Norris knew professionally from having worked with him at the famous Bellevue Hospital of New York City. The two men could not have been more different in physique and family background. Dr. Gettler earned both of his graduate-level degrees from Columbia. He was small in stature, poor, and Jewish, compared to Norris, who was over six feet tall, wealthy, and a WASP (white Anglo-Saxon Protestant). By age, Gettler could have been the son Norris never had. A Polish immigrant, he paid his way through school with a job on the midnight ferry while also teaching chemistry – the latter being his focus and his love. He reported to Dr. Norris and acted as his specialist in chemical applications, which was a valuable and necessary skill in toxicology work. What the two men shared most was dedication to their work and brilliance in performing it. To apply the overused moniker that they acquired, they were indeed to become a *dynamic duo* when they combined efforts to concentrate their attention on the high volume of deaths by poison – over a thousand annually in New York City alone.

Theirs is a very large story, which, by necessity, I've encapsulated. If there's continued interest in their story, you're encouraged to pursue it further, although I've observed that related information is not easy to acquire. It can also be very dark drama, which I've labored to keep light. Ironically, in contrast to the popularity of crime shows mentioned earlier and the overlapping explosion of reality shows, late in their careers Norris and Gettler were asked to star in radio and television shows based on their pioneering endeavors and compelling experiences. They modestly refused to do so, like so many other true heroes. They respected the dignity and sobriety of their profession. Shortly before his retirement in 1959, and considerably after Norris had passed away, Gettler finally did become the unwilling subject of a *Harper's* magazine profile titled "The Man Who Reads Corpses."

The position's inherent responsibility is evident in a statement by Gettler's son, Joseph. A capable organic chemist and university professor, he said he'd decided early on not to pursue his father's career because of all the lives and deaths that would be on his conscience, just as they had been on his father's. He wanted to avoid the cumulative effect of Alexander Norris's years of researching data that often determined the fate of so many others. Occasionally, the team's mission was described as a deadly game of cat and mouse with poison murderers. The Industrial Revolution multiplied the tools of the poisoner's trade, but the scientific knowledge to detect them lagged behind; that is, until the innovative partnership of Norris and Gettler, which lasted for almost two decades. Gettler consistently committed the results of their research to book form; many of the books are still referenced regularly today.

Poison has a long, devious, and inglorious history. Recall fifteenth-century Italy, when Lucrezia and Cesare Borgia practiced combining arsenic with politics, or when Socrates was forced to drink hemlock from his own hand after being falsely condemned for heresy. The use of poison precedes forensics by millennia, but its all-too-common use led ultimately to the foundation of that modern science of criminal investigation. Poison was the personal murder instrument of choice for centuries because it is difficult to detect. Even if its use was known or suspected, the poisoner generally remained difficult to connect to the crime, thus being virtually impossible to identify or convict with surety. The use of poison has been an exceptionally successful means to accomplish unpunished murder. Its discreet application was used so frequently to eliminate heirs to thrones or fortunes that poison has historically been referred to as the *inheritance drug*. Often a poison can imitate a natural sickness or disease sufficiently well to avoid even being apparent or suspect. For two or more millennia, if you contemplated premeditated murder, a poison was the best choice.

Until the middle of the twentieth century, the bathroom and kitchen cabinets of the average household contained a plethora of legitimately obtained poisons. Poisons were easily available because they are basically simple chemicals having a variety of helpful purposes. Regardless of such evil-sounding names as arsenic, chloroform, strychnine, and cyanide, they all served common practical functions and were present in the not-too-distant past as primary components in paints, pest controls, cleaners, and cosmetics. Most poisons are one of two basic types: either strong alkaloid (metallic straight elements) or complex compound elements. When poisoners practice their trade against humanity, it's basically the science of chemistry meeting that of biology. "The dose makes the poison" is an old saying in toxicology. It means that with proper, knowledgeable application, there's usually no harm in poison, and the intended positive results are obtainable; but with too aggressive an application, it becomes lethal.

What makes the use of poison against a person so loathsome are the calculated intent of the criminal and the insidious nature of the crime – a particularly frightful combination. A poison victim who survived would find it challenging to trust anyone, especially those most intimate and close, as they have convenient access. After surviving being victimized by a poisoner, how could one ever again trust anything set before them to eat or drink? It's often a person physically and emotionally close to the victim who is the poisoner. The person applying poisoned doses is not acting emotionally, grasping for any available weapon in the heat of the moment. It's malice aforethought, with a willingness to repeat the act as many times as necessary, and the patience to wait through the victim's lingering suffering for the anticipated result, which is death.

When Norris and Gettler assumed office, death by poison was still all too common, not just in their realm of New York City, but across the nation and the world. Its use was common as a means of murder, but its use was also common in terms of accidental or unintended death. In 1922, 101 New Yorkers hanged themselves, 444 died in car accidents, 20 were crushed in elevators, 271 were fatally shot or stabbed, but 997 died by poison.

For greater clarity and accuracy, these poisoning deaths may be placed into three broad civilian categories. The first category is criminal in nature due to deliberated murder. However, many poison-induced deaths were not even suspected as murders; when they were, the poisoners were rarely caught, and, if caught, were even more rarely convicted. Accurate methods of detecting and identifying poisons in the human body were badly needed. Early twentieth-century America is replete with highly publicized poison-saturated histories, horrors, and mysteries: Jean Crones of the University Club, the Postal Lunch eatery and Shelburne Restaurant mass poisonings, the Bradicich and Depuy manslaughter trials, and sordid family murderers Mary Frances Creighton and Everett Applegate.

The second category is accidental and would be considered manslaughter at worst. Victims frequently became ill or died as the uncalculated by-product of legitimate and practical use of a poison by themselves or by another, often associated with a commercial-industrial application or employment. There was simply a broad lack of understanding about the deadly effects of many commonly used industrial chemicals. What was needed for prevention was detailed lab research and subsequent safety-based regulation. Some employment-related deaths straddled a gray line between accidental and deliberate. Most commonly, this murky relationship existed when neither the employer nor the employee initially knew of the danger. When the danger became highly suspect by both, it was calculatedly denied and/or covered up by the employer, who persisted in the dangerous practice for financial gain.

On frequent occasions, it was the consumer who suffered the ill effects and became the businesses' unwitting victim. By the 1930s, circumstances of this nature were so common that muckrakers Arthur Kallet and F. J. Schlink wrote a book titled *100,000,000 Guinea Pigs: Dangers in Everyday Foods, Drugs, and Cosmetics*. They presented the facts leading to their belief that the consumer population was unknowingly acting as experimental guinea pigs for American product manufacturers. The truth was often far more flagrant, because even when the harmful effects to the human guinea pigs were well known, product sales continued unchanged and unabated.

The egregious practices of U.S. Radium Corporation and their radium girls, and Standard Oil refinery with their looney factory both fall into this gray area, as do many other business-related cases. Corporate actions of this deadly nature were legal in the sense that there were no specific laws yet prohibiting or punishing these activities, but they were never moral. The federal government purposely straddled this same gray line throughout the decade of Prohibition by ordering various known poisons to be added to commercial alcohols in unsuccessful experiments intended to discourage bootlegging. This became known as the *Chemists' War,* as illegal bootleggers employed capable chemists on their staffs to maintain their defiance by detecting, identifying, and counteracting the government's additives.

We can relate to a more recent example of the same type of industry *gray.* The changes in tobacco promotion, use, and regulation have similar circumstances. Until the mid-twentieth century, some doctors were still recommending tobacco's use for its presumed health benefits – this despite nicotine's being one of the most lethal compounds on the planet (a potent alkaloid found in the nightshade plant family that includes the tobacco and deadly belladonna plants).

After the discovery of radium by Marie and Pierre Curie, it was wildly promoted for decades as a health additive and a miracle cure. This in itself was not unusual, as many poisons were misunderstood and first introduced as health tonics. Men consumed radium-based drinks for energy as we presently do Gatorade and coffee; women applied it in facial creams and eyeliners; and children ate it as an ingredient in candy and soda. It was thought to be a new wonder drug – able to restore bones, tissues, and organs. We now know the opposite to be true.

The third category is suicidal death – intentional and all too easily performed with clear access to numerous poisons. There's another non-civilian category: military – as in the WWI applications. This was generally beyond the scope of the medical examiner's office, with the exception of exposed soldiers who'd returned to civilian lifestyles while unknowingly suffering ill effects from a military-grade poison. The Norris-Gettler team worked on cases involving all four categories. Before issuing a death certificate, they had to determine to which category it would be attributed. Was the cause of death by poison? If so, which poison? Was it murder, accident, suicide, or military exposure? This was their regular focus and never-ending challenge. The following brief case studies exemplify the nature of their occupation in general, as well as present detailed case examples of the first two poisoning categories.

Irishman Mike Malloy was frequently so drunk that many nights he simply passed out on the bar of his favorite Bronx speakeasy. He was in that sad condition the night the owner, Tony Marino, and three other regular patrons decided to purchase insurance policies on Mike and name themselves as beneficiaries since he had no permanent address, regular employer, or known relatives. In exchange for an unlimited supply of free drinks and bar snacks, Mike easily endorsed the policies. Mike was old and in poor health, and was a physical wreck after a lifetime of heavy drinking. The conspirators, however, determined to speed up Mike's earthly departure. This act would immediately provide the sorely needed Depression-era cash settlements that they intended to share equally.

Their first action in a series of unsuccessful attempts was to greatly increase Mike's intake of risky Prohibition-era booze. The next unsuccessful action was still more drinks, but those were deliberately made with poisonous methyl alcohol as a hopefully lethal substitute for good booze. Frustrated by his refusal to die, they laced Mike's food with rotten ingredients, metal shavings, and ground glass. Still Mike survived and may have even prospered some, seeming to gain weight. Thereafter, they dragged an unconscious Mike outside in the freezing temperature and doused him with cold water – again, a no-go. Next, a cab driver was hired to run him down and leave the body unattended. A week after suffering the accident, Mike unexpectedly returned to the club for his free drinks and food. He'd been taken to the hospital by a Good Samaritan, where he was treated for a fractured skull and several broken bones. Mike had no idea how he'd arrived at this condition, but he was coming to be known as *Mike the Durable*. Frustrated but committed to their plan, the conspirators rented a simple gaslit hotel room, put the once-again-unconscious Mike to bed, and ran a tube from the lighting fixture into Mike's throat until he finally, but surely, died.

The conspirators paid an undertaker to quickly bury Mike. It was "officially" stated that Mike had died slowly by his own hands from alcohol poisoning, and the death certificate was fixed to read the same. The insurance money was subsequently collected and distributed. All was well until a suspicious rumor reached the police, and the unembalmed body was exhumed and tested by Norris and Gettler. After considerable groundbreaking research, it was concluded that Mike had died from an unnaturally high concentration of carbon dioxide. By virtue of the toxicology data, all of Mike's killers were found guilty of murder in the first degree and sentenced to die in Sing Sing Prison's electric chair. Had they embalmed the hurriedly buried body, the tests would have proven inconclusive and one more murder by poison would have gone unsolved. Mike's death was a clear example of death-by-poison category one: murder.

Meanwhile, in the industrial city of Orange, New Jersey, across the border from New York, a strange and unidentified illness began to infect otherwise healthy young female factory workers. Their bones shattered, their teeth fell out, their jaws rotted away like lepers, and sores randomly appeared across their bodies. Within a few years of incalculable suffering, they died while still in their twenties. The only thing they had in common was employment at U.S. Radium Corporation. The business of U.S.R.C. was a glow-in-the-dark paint, which the workers applied to a number of clocks and other devices. The company determined that the girls had simply worked themselves into a state of exhaustion and developed anemia – supposed proof that the weaker sex was not intended for employment beyond domestic.

Harrison Martland, the local medical examiner, suspected otherwise. It was openly known that the luminous, light green paint contained a radium-based mixture. Could this widely used and much-heralded miracle drug be hurting them instead of helping them? Even French scientist Marie Curie, the discoverer of radium, did not fear for her safety throughout her years of closely handling the element while conducting groundbreaking research. Martland needed to find the cause, so he requested the help of the better-equipped and more-experienced lab team at Bellevue across the state line. The bodies of the victims were exhumed; their bones were removed and sent to Norris for exploratory tests. Meanwhile, he conducted his own research on those girls still alive. He soon found that they exhaled radon gas, and some of them even glowed in the dark. The factory girls had been encouraged to keep the tips of their small paintbrushes sharp in order to maintain a good edge and close pattern. To do so, they licked the tips or placed them in their mouths, thereby swallowing a significant amount of radium. Some even decorated their nails and faces with the paint for fun and glamour.

The bone research at Bellevue determined that the radium in the paint, as well as the radium in the dust scattered throughout the factory, were acting together on the workers' bodies in a manner reasonably similar to calcium. Both calcium and radium are alkaloid metals easily absorbed by the human body, with most going quickly into the bones. Unlike calcium, however, radium is always in a state of breaking down and casting off particles. Once in the bones, this decay process included breaking the workers down as well; they were being eaten alive from the inside out.

Norris's research results and his conclusions were sufficiently strong evidence for a suit against U.S.R.C. Eventually, a suit was brought with only five of the many affected girls as plaintiffs. Most were afraid of losing their jobs; others did not have the funds to pursue legal action; many had already died; and for some, the statute of limitations had expired. The suit was greatly prolonged by the corporation, who denied its responsibility. The girls finally won the suit as the court heartily agreed with the scientific findings, but settlement awards were consistently minimal. The girls' deaths were clear examples of death-by-poison category two: accidental through dangerous industrial employment.

As in these two detailed examples, case by case over the years, Norris and Gettler converted the mundane and distasteful labors of the pathology lab into respected and effective science. In the process, the criminal justice system was revolutionized; innocent people recovered their lives and victims received satisfaction; corporations were held liable for their products, their consumers, and their employees; the double-edged nature of chemicals came to be better understood; textbooks were written that are still in use today; chemistry advanced from wet to dry applications; public safety gained institutionalized government advocates for product testing and ingredients listing; a generation of *Gettler boys* replaced political cronies; the use of chemicals became regulated; the new science of forensics was invented, with pathology recognized as one of the champions of modern health care; and, taking its history back to the starting point, poison fell from use as a common means of murder. Homicidal poisoning all but disappeared after Norris and Gettler. The two did not begin with a determination to change the world, but in consistently performing a distinctly nonglamorous job with integrity and competence, they did it. Their century closed on an entirely different note than it had opened in regard to both crime and chemistry.

An appropriate inscription remains partially visible on the autopsy room wall of the now-abandoned Pilgrim State Hospital in Brentwood on Long Island, a brief drive from Bellevue Hospital. It reads: "Let conversation cease. Let laughter flee. This is the place where death delights to help the living." It's the English translation of a Latin quote by Giovanni Morgagni, the eighteenth-century Italian physician known as the father of anatomical pathology. Norris and Gettler labored surrounded by a surreal array of flasks, test tubes, Bunsen burners, beakers of formaldehyde, and distiller arrays. Their postmortem labors in the morgue, autopsy room, and research laboratory of Bellevue Hospital at first exposure seem wholly macabre, but as a body yielded its secrets to them, Morgagni's statement was fulfilled.

The data teased by chemistry to the forefront from a corpse helped determine guilt or innocence; whether accidental, suspicious, or natural; the specifics of time, cause, or place; and perhaps most positively, a better understanding of related prevention and cure. The gains for the legal system are enumerated in qualitative and quantitative terms. For survivors coping with the outcomes of crime, loss, sickness, and accident, the benefit is informed decision-making for going forward with their lives. For them especially, death has become the servant of the living.

And search for it more than for hidden treasures. (Job 3:21)

* * * *

Author's Note: Three fundamental, non-exclusive, sources contributed inspiration, fact-checking, and basic information in the preparation of "Body of Knowledge." These were: PBS's documentary film *The Poisoner's Handbook* and its related website (*www.pbs.org/wgbh/americanexperience/features/teachers-resources/poisoners-guide/*); Deborah Blum's book *The Poisoner's Handbook: Murder and the Birth of Forensic Medicine in Jazz Age New York* and two Wikipedia websites (e.g., *en.wikipedia.org/wiki/Alexander_Gettler* and *en.wikipedia.org/ wiki/Charles_Norris*). The reader is encouraged to peruse these and other resources for additional information on the subject.

Pasquale de Nisco

The Priest Who Adopted a Town

If the foundations are destroyed. (Psalm 11:3)

Two physicians met in 1961 for a casual dinner in a small Pocono Mountains town an hour east of Wilkes Barre, Pennsylvania. One man was a country general practitioner by the name of Benjamin Falcone; the other, Stewart Wolf, a recognized specialist employed at the University of Oklahoma. Neither suspected their casual conversation had the potential to improve the lives of all who heard its eventual outcome. The small town was Roseto, Pennsylvania. It had taken its name from Roseto Valfortore, a medieval village located in a similar environment in the Apennine Mountains outside of Rome, Italy.

Life in Roseto Valfortore, Italy, hadn't changed much over two millennia. It was a consistently poor village where the men either worked in the mountains as stone cutters, or in the valleys as farmers. Not many families ever came or left; that is, until 1871, when a former resident – after becoming a Jesuit priest – was transferred to America for his first assignment. His letters home encouraged a small group of eleven Rosetans to emigrate, with several of them finding employment in the Poconos' slate quarry pits.

Initially, the Italian authorities considered the act of leaving the country to be unpatriotic, and they discouraged the citizens from pursuing it.

Sometime thereafter, however, the unceasingly poor economic conditions of Southern Italy caused them to relent. The enhanced flow of enthusiastic letters home influenced more and more families to purchase the inexpensive ship passage and depart for America in hopes of realizing the promised greater economic opportunity. Within a decade, Roseto Valfortore almost ceased to exist; it had essentially been relocated to the New World. A majority of its population, about twelve hundred, immigrated to Pennsylvania, where they settled together and named their new town Roseto – dropping *Valfortore*.

Quarry work in the mountains was hard, dangerous, and didn't pay well. It was plentiful, however, because the previous settlers – mostly English and Welsh – disdained this risky, unskilled labor. The Rosetans were not accepted by their neighbors because they performed the low-tier work, didn't speak English, and continued their seemingly backward Old World customs and practices. The shunning left them with no alternative but to remain close to each other in an essentially closed and isolated ethnic geographic community. Their life remained much like the one they'd recently left in the Italian province of Foggia.

Their new town was soon found to be an unexpected challenge, if not an outright disappointment. Wages were insufficient; Sicilian-style knife-fighting and drunkenness were common; the town rested on ground stripped bare of foliage by rapacious lumber companies; they were forced to shop at company stores that charged exorbitant fees; and perhaps worst of all, in their perspective, they didn't even have a Catholic church with a local priest. The new Roseto was clearly in turmoil; that is, until a dynamic young priest by the name of Pasquale de Nisco arrived.

The priest quickly assumed leadership of the community, and their situation began to steadily improve. It did so to a level so unusual that the outcome gripped the attention of Dr. Wolf more than a half-century later. Father Pasquale has been described as educated, cultured, organized, dedicated, and energetic; the first three traits were sorely missing in early Roseto. He was capable of assisting the Rosetans in economic, political, social, family, and spiritual matters. This made him something of a modern Renaissance man. Such a description would seem to be either flattery or fictionalized overstatement, except for the proven, sizable record he soon compiled and its enduring positive legacy. In his book, *The Power of Clan: The Influence of Human Relationships on Heart Disease*, Dr. Wolf states that "Father de Nisco's persistent exhortations, coupled with his personal generosity, encouragement, and practical assistance, shaped the community and its people into a close-knit ... town."

He instituted a comprehensive civic plan of his own design that, in addition to establishing the greatly needed and wanted local Catholic parish, included assisting the Rosetans with obtaining citizenship, learning the English language, gaining formal schooling for the children, voting and participating in politics, introducing social clubs, provisioning sports fields, instituting laws, incorporating the township, and beginning a circulating public library. Souls were given attention through the development of four separate Christian mutual-aid societies dedicated to promoting healthy spiritual living and morals – one each for adult working men, wives and mothers, boys, and girls. He was hands-on in demonstrably reducing crime and knife-fighting; his methods sometimes included permanently running troublemakers out of town.

Father de Nisco's physical church went far beyond the construction of a building for worship services. It was an entire plaza, with the church at the center of twenty-eight city lots. He personally financed and purchased all of it. Initially included in the original plaza were a park, school, hospital, well, and cemetery; later, a post office, convent, and newspaper were added. After completing the plaza, he actively administered across the whole of Roseto by encouraging and teaching the residents to plant trees, flowers, landscaping, and gardens – even purchasing the seeds himself and distributing them to all who did the soil preparation. Along with beautification came the necessary sanitation measures. He supervised the regular removal of garbage and trash and assisted in matters of public health, even employing quarantines and curfews as his tools. Within a few years, land and housing values doubled and continued to rise for years thereafter.

De Nisco's next major project was to begin improving the income of the families. The quarry managers were mistreating the Rosetan men by employing them in only the most dangerous jobs, while paying substandard wages on an infrequent basis and, subsequently, coercing them to shop exclusively at uncompetitive company-owned stores. When personal requests and negotiation with management failed, he alternately established a union, led a strike, and won badly needed concessions for the workers.

He also encouraged the young, unmarried girls to earn wages in the shirt factory in nearby Bangor. With their demonstrated success, he subsequently was able to convince a group of wealthy local businessmen to build a shirt factory in Roseto. This reduced travel time and expense for the girls, and they were now paid on a piecework basis. Shares of stock in the new company were open to purchase by both the employees and all Roseto citizens. The plan was successful and everyone profited by it.

All this was accomplished while not neglecting his personal spiritual habits and his substantial regular corporate duties, such as church worship services, marriages, funerals, sacraments, celebratory festivals, and family counseling. In 1906, de Nisco was offered a promotion by his archbishop, which he turned down, replying that he "would rather die with his boots on in Roseto." Some have described Father Pasquale's role in Roseto as its de facto lifetime mayor, building inspector, social worker, police chief, labor board, and health department. The initial derision by Roseto's neighbors toward the city eventually turned to admiration – in no small part due to the unrelenting care of the priest who essentially adopted the town.

Roseto continued well into the twentieth century in a manner reflecting its unique dual heritage; that is, its birth from an Italian province and its refined nature inherited from the priest's vigilant care. It retained the character of a well-operated, attractive, neo-Italian village secluded in the forested mountainside. Regardless of these admirable strengths, it continued to fly well below the national radar, with few outside visitors and rarely any new residents. Roseto never made the news because it had no serious crime and never suffered a murder. The city was virtually unknown for seventy years, and would have remained so, except for a visiting physician.

Dr. Wolf came to Roseto for a conference, ending his day by dining with one of the local general practitioners, Dr. Falcone. During their meal conversation, the local doctor mentioned that during his seventeen years of practice, he'd never treated a single case of heart disease in Roseto, although he had done so in the surrounding communities. In fact, he thought he'd observed that the Rosetans generally enjoyed a higher level of general health than his non-Roseto patients.

At that time in America, heart disease – especially myocardial infarction (heart attack) – was the number one medical cause of death for people under the age of sixty-five. Heart disease killed more people than the total of the next three leading causes of death. Finding a way to reduce its deadly effects ranked as high then, as doing so with cancer does now.

Dr. Wolf prolonged his stay and called in John Bruhn, a sociologist experienced in statistical research, to assist him. Together they committed to determine why Rosetans had fewer heart attacks than people in nearby communities. The answer would benefit all of humanity, as well as bring professional acknowledgment to the team and international recognition to Roseto.

Thus began a fifteen-year study drawing on collected medical histories, physical examinations, and laboratory tests. Large samples of these criteria were compared and contrasted between inhabitants of Roseto and inhabitants of two similar neighboring communities. Next, the medical research was followed by a sociological study of the three communities. There was a real mystery to be solved in determining the secret to the Rosetans' health.

Was it diet? They cooked with lard, and 40 percent of their diet consisted of calories from fat. They loved sausage, pepperoni, salami, eggs, and baked goods. This criterion did not seem cogent, and after due consideration was eliminated by the resulting research conclusions.

Was it exercise? They were obese well beyond the national average and more overweight than other Italian communities. They smoked heavily as well. This criterion did not seem cogent, and after due consideration was eliminated by the resulting research conclusions.

Was it genetics? Something in their biological makeup, within their DNA? Their relatives in America and in similar Old World villages were studied. They were suffering heart disease at the average rates. This criterion did not seem cogent, and after due consideration was also eliminated by the resulting research conclusions.

Was it geographic location? Two nearby rural Pennsylvania cities were studied: German-settled Nazareth and Welsh/English-settled Bangor. This criterion yielded no insights and was also eliminated as a possible cause.

If their health secret was not diet, exercise, genes, or location, then what was it?

The secret was confirmed as something which came to be labeled *community*. Roseto possessed an exceptionally high degree of it due to the combination of what had transferred from the original Roseto and what had been added to it by the dynamic young priest. For Roseto, this was further defined as a common spiritual heritage and practices centered on church, God, and worship. This spiritual core was further supplemented by twenty-two supporting civic organizations in a town with a population of slightly over one thousand. Father Pasquale de Nisco had preserved, and then enhanced, the social structure of the Rosetans, thereby helping to further create an even more powerful, protective community. This community was certifiably capable of insulating them from the pressures of the modern world. The study of people living in Roseto conclusively determined that their uniquely close family relationships, spiritual practices, and community-wide societal support gave them a healthier general lifestyle overall, while specifically lessening their chance of a fatal heart attack. Their health was generally better than that experienced in villages in Italy, as well as in other predominately Italian towns in America.

For clarity, I'll break out and restate each positive factor individually. They are: cohesive ethnic background, shared societal values and traditions, exceptional bonding developed due to shunning by the ethnically different residents in nearby cities, insulated rural location somewhat distant from modernity, active Christian religious practices, close family ties (clans), a persistent habit of mutual support, and a substantial number of complementary and sustaining civic contributions gifted to them by Father de Nisco. Although not likely a critical or even significant factor, the Rosetans, interestingly, also had a tradition of storytelling. Through all these factors, the Rosetans developed an exceptionally high degree of community. Regardless of circumstances, they could depend on immediate family. They could also depend on other citizens, both directly within their neighborhood and indirectly through mutual-aid organizations such as church and the many social clubs. A sampling of these societies includes the Marconi Social Club, Columbia Fire Company, Holy Name Society, and American Legion.

The good news continues. There were health benefits beyond heart disease, such as reduced incidence of syphilis, brain disorders, depression, psychoses, and senility. The village also enjoyed confirmed benefits in the following societal areas: fewer divorces, illegitimate pregnancies, and adolescent rebellions; less alcoholism, drug addiction, and suicides; and never a case of murder, including abortion. As Dr. Wolf nicely concluded: "Roseto emerged as a buoyant, fun-loving community that was more enterprising, more self-sufficient, more optimistic, and more prosperous than its neighbors."

The Baltimore Sun newspaper articulates a worthwhile analysis to serve as a recap: "The lesson the Roseto experience offers Americans is that the thwarting of their biological need for social cohesion, community, and emotional security is doing them tremendous harm–and that they need, urgently, to find distinctly American ways to share their lives with one another in warm, supporting communities."

A number of well-documented studies involving infants help to substantiate the Roseto postulation and the newspaper's conclusion. Newborn infants who received substantial warm human contact prospered; infants who received little or none were unhealthy, with many withering to the point of expiration. It's long been accepted that human relationships, together with impressions from our environment, powerfully shape a person both behaviorally and cognitively; now we can confidently add medically as well. If we are consistently sustained and nourished emotionally, we can anticipate minimized health risks while enjoying an enhanced overall sense of well-being; it's a double win.

After the 1970s, Roseto again served as proof of the newspaper's statement regarding the thwarting of biological needs for community. When it began acquiring conditions characteristic of most other American cities, Roseto started losing its unique, shared, and cohesive community-building/sustaining factors. With those losses came the gradual erosion of its precious advantages in physical health and societal well-being. Roseto underwent many changes; and change itself is sufficiently stress inducing to increase vulnerability to disease – think of shingles and hives as modest examples, or heart attack and stroke as more severe examples. Later generations of Rosetans expressed declining interest in traditional social values, the core family, and the community-building institutions; instead, they aspired to the same materialism and lifestyles commonly seen in the media. Many insiders moved out, while newcomers from the outside moved in. Today, Roseto is medically indistinguishable from the rest of America. Having lost its protective and unique insulations, it also lost its health benefits. (For more information regarding the nature of change, refer to the "Parable of the Four Farmers" story.)

Can we recapture family where it's been substituted by the individual or eroded by government incursion? Can we replace competition with cooperation and common purpose? Can we reestablish the centrality of the church and the primacy of Christianity where they've been denigrated by state and secularism? Probably not entirely. However, inasmuch as we can make small restitution in these areas of community, we will pay ourselves dividends in health and happiness. If we had more spiritually well-grounded pastoral leaders working in the so-called roles of community organizers or community activists, they could at least point the socio/racial/ethnic groups in the proper direction – and act as much-needed good examples – as opposed to the puffed-up reverends (e.g., Jackson, Sharpton, Wright) and galvanizing mullahs who deliberately cause self-serving division instead of committing their lives to truly helping their people; they are the wolves who devour the sheep. Words of shame, hatred, and blame can never produce harmony. Pastor Pasquale de Nisco has undeniably shown them, and all of us, the more righteous way to comprehensive healing and health for our fellow man.

What can the righteous do? (Psalm 11:3)

* * * *

Author's Note: An expression of gratitude and acknowledgment is due Malcolm Gladwell. As an author whose sociological studies I enjoy, he was the first to introduce me to Pasquale de Nisco (as well as to the towns of Roseto) in his book on success, *Outliers*. Additionally, the concept of framing questions related to the exploration of the Roseto health advantage was first established in *Outliers*; that is, was their superior health due to diet, exercise, genetics, or location? My subsequent story development utilized multiple research sources, but Mr. Gladwell's writing was the initial catalyst.

Jesus Christ

"Who Do You Say That I Am?"

Having loved His own who were in the world. (John 13:1)

Part 1 – Jesus as the Son of Man

Our Western (Gregorian) calendar marks the year of this Man's birth. He was conceived contrary to the ordinary laws governing natural life. His birthplace was a barn, He grew up in an obscure rural village, and His parents were plain-living peasants. Their ancestry was fully Jewish – known as God's chosen people, but hated by the world. They possessed neither wealth nor influence; they were just an ordinary, poor couple lacking any formal education or stature.

Yet His arrival was announced by angels and caused panic in the heart of a king. As a baby, He was prophesied over twice by strangers at the temple during His dedication. As a toddler, He was visited by three accomplished foreign scholars who traveled and searched for months in order to locate Him. As a teenager, His wisdom already impressed, engaged, and surpassed religious professionals and highly placed lawyers. As a young man, He apprenticed quietly in his father's carpentry shop until He was thirty, after which He worked for the next three years as a traveling preacher without a church building and without a congregation to support Him.

In the three final years of His unnaturally short life, He belatedly demonstrated the fullness of His nature by walking on water, commanding violent storms to be at peace, converting water into fine wine, healing the sick, raising the dead, and multiplying a handful of fish and loaves sufficient for the satisfaction of thousands of His hungry companions.

He never ran for nor held an elected office, and He never had nor accepted a title, yet the multitudes wanted to proclaim Him their king and were prepared to forsake all other appointed and inherited rulers in exchange for just this one Man. He never owned a home, never married nor had children, never attended college, and never gained any formal credentials or positions. As an adult, He never lived in a big city or even traveled more than a hundred miles from the place where He was born. He had nothing in this world except the simple clothes He wore.

He never wrote a book, and yet all the libraries in the world contain books written about Him. He never wrote a song, but hundreds of thousands of songs have been written about Him with more being added daily. He never painted, sculpted, nor drew, yet the greatest artists in the history of mankind have consistently sought to honor Him by selecting Him as the subject of their masterpieces. He never founded a college nor earned a degree, but all the schools in the world cannot claim as many students. He never commanded troops, drafted a soldier, planned a troop movement, won a war, or fired a gun, and yet no other leader has ever had more volunteers and followers – most of whom are prepared to die for Him.

He never practiced psychiatry nor studied pharmaceuticals; still, He has healed more broken hearts than all the doctors of the world. He cured countless desperately afflicted multitudes without medicine – even raising several from the dead. He turned no one away while they were suffering, never acted inconvenienced, and never charged for His services. His only incentive was the benefit another would receive.

He certainly was no movie or rock star, and He played no professional sports. He never appeared on television nor spoke on the radio, He never blogged or tweeted, yet His words are broadcast worldwide on a daily basis. He never did any of the things contemporary society considers an indication of greatness or importance. He was a true hero and His life remains worthy of imitation by every generation.

Despite all the good He did, He was criticized for befriending society's outcasts. His words and deeds were forcefully opposed by the ruling elites. His family doubted His motives, and at times thought Him mentally unstable. The tide of popular opinion turned against Him while He was still young. Many were jealous of Him and many others hated Him. Friends deserted Him, one denied Him multiple times, and another bitterly betrayed Him to His enemies. He was arrested by His adversaries, and suffered the harassment and lies of a mock trial. Although wholly innocent, He was pronounced guilty, whipped, spat on, beaten, pierced, and sentenced to a criminal's public death in a painful, bloody manner. He was nailed to wooden cross-beams, set high between thieves, then speared, ridiculed, and cursed. As He was dying, the executioners gambled for His only possession, a simple robe. His last words were those of forgiveness and love for the very men who persecuted Him.

For His burial, He was to be laid in a borrowed tomb donated through the pity of a stranger. Upon His death, the earth shook violently and split open, the skies thundered, the sun disappeared, and graves yielded their dead who walked the streets – all bearing witness to His innocence and to the promise of mightier things to come. Although His enemies had tried, they couldn't destroy Him because even the grave was soon proven unable to hold Him.

Had there been time for an obituary, it would have read similar to this:

Jesus Christ, aged 33, of Nazareth, died late Friday in Jerusalem on Mount Calvary, also known as Golgotha, the Place of the Skull. Sentenced to death for crimes against the Roman state and Jewish religion, Jesus was crucified along with two other criminals by order of Roman Prefect Pontius Pilate with the approval of King Herod Agrippa. Causes of death were extreme exhaustion, severe torture, and profuse bleeding. Jesus was a descendant of Abraham, and a member of the royal Jewish House of David. He was the firstborn son of the late Joseph Ben David, a village carpenter. His place of birth was Bethlehem of Judea, but he grew up in Nazareth of Galilee. He is survived by His mother, Mary, three brothers and two sisters, twelve apostles, and numerous disciples. He was self-educated and spent most of His adult life working as a pastor, teacher, community organizer, and social worker.

The body was buried prior to the Sabbath in a hillside grave
previously owned by family benefactor Joseph of Arimathea.
In lieu of flowers, the family has requested that everyone honor
the deceased by following His teachings. Donations will be for-
warded to charities supporting the poor and the sick.

However, there was no time or need for an obituary, because three days thereafter, He was resurrected and back even stronger; teaching, speaking, preaching to His friends and family in full view of the public. He departed soon thereafter on His own terms and in His own timing. As He left, He promised an imminent return while leaving His immortal Word and providing a great, new Gift intended to comfort us in the interim.

Soon the world discovered that all the armies that ever marched, all the navies that ever sailed, all the governments that ever were established, all the kings who ever reigned, and all the presidents who ever held office have not affected history as powerfully or as positively as this one Man's life. Although twenty centuries have now come and gone since His brief time on earth, He's continuously been the centerpiece of the human race, its greatest source of guidance and divine inspiration. Many times every week the world over, countless multitudes gather to study His teachings and to show their respect for Him.

The modern world still has difficulty understanding Him. Schools are reluctant to teach about Him. Leaders can't succeed if they ignore Him. Historical revisionists have tried but can't erase Him. Scientists remain baffled by Him. Communism and atheism can't silence Him. New Agers and Muslims can't replace Him. The proud can't accept Him. Religion can't sanitize or convolute Him. And none of the commercial commentators on TV or radio are able to explain His continuing popularity and influence.

Time itself recognizes His earthly presence by its division between that which came before and that which came after His birth. Today when we celebrate the date of His arrival on earth as both a holy day and a holiday, His enemies dispute incessantly against the mere mention of His name, and they oppose any display of the plain symbols relating to His humble birth. They harass public officials and school boards, they wear out the courts with endless mean-spirited petitions, and they disrupt the celebrations enjoyed by a majority of the population. His birth is not their issue; their real issue is the Man Himself: His heavenly ancestry, His incarnate birth, His Jewish heritage, His pure life, His selfless death, His church on earth, His eternal and unchanging Word, His renewing resurrection, His claim of being God, His universal authority, His kingdom of saints, His eternal judgment, His second messianic coming, and His everlasting presence.

The names of the eminent statesmen and thinkers of ancient Greece and Rome have come and gone. The names of past scientists, philosophers, and theologians have also come and gone. But the name of this Jewish man multiplies more and more with every season that passes. His life, His works, His words are continually studied in minute detail from every possible perspective: historically, educationally, doctrinally, practically, comparatively, medically, critically, devotionally, prophetically, and analytically, and there is always enough to satisfy everyone while keeping them hungry for more. Even though more than two thousand years lie between our generation and His time on the earth, His name still lives on – JESUS.

Part 2 – Jesus as the Son of God

He is the First and the Last, the Beginning and the End, and the Alpha and Omega. He is the Creator and the Covenant Maker. He always was, is now, and evermore shall be. He is the Great I Am.

He was bruised by us and for us, yet He brings healing. He was killed by us and for us, yet He brings life and eternity. We enjoy peace, wisdom, and joy simply by being in His presence.

He is our Light, Lover, Liberty, Logos, Lamb, Lord, and Life. He is Goodness, Kindness, and Gentleness. He is Holy, Righteous, Powerful, Merciful, and Pure. His ways are always right. His Word is eternal and true. His will is perfect and unchanging. His wisdom is beyond measure and far above that of all others.

He is our Redeemer, Savior, Guide, Counselor, Friend, Hope, King, Judge, Lawgiver, and Advocate.

His eternal names, written in the heavens, are Adonai, Lion of the Tribe of Judah, Jehovah, Majestic One, Messiah, Dayspring Who Has Visited Us from on High, Emmanuel, Dear Desire of Every Nation, Fairest of Ten Thousand, Lily of the Valley, Propitiation of All Sins, the Only Mediator Between God and Man, Ruler of All Nations and of All Nature, Ancient of Days, Faithful One, and Israel's Strength and Consolation.

He provides the blood that cleanses whiter than snow, every blessing we need, answers to our prayers, living water so that we will never again thirst, bread for our spiritual hunger, healing balm of Gilead for our pain, and jewels for our crown of life.

He has revealed Himself to us as a Bridegroom, a Brother in Time of Need, a Branch to Abide In, a Banner Over Us, the Bright and Morning Star, the Builder of Our Soul, the Bridge to Eternal Life, and Our Blood Covenant.

He's the greatest phenomenon that has ever crossed the horizon of this world. He's God's Son, the sinner's Savior, and the centerpiece of civilization. He chose to be born a Jew, He's a Jew today, and He will be a Jew for all eternity. He's unique, unparalleled, and unprecedented. He is the loftiest idea in literature, the highest personality in philosophy, and the supreme problem in higher criticism. He's the foundation of all true theology, doctrine, beliefs, and religion.

He strengthens, supplies, and sustains the weak, and He provides victory for those who are tired, tempted, tested, and undergoing trials. He cleanses lepers, forgives sinners, discharges debts, delivers the captives, defends widows and orphans, and serves and forgives all who ask, because that's His divine pleasure and nature.

He has given us the mind of Christ, a new spirit, eyes that truly see and ears that truly hear, a heart of flesh in exchange for one of stone, and an eternal home in glory. He has created us in His own image; commissioned us with dominion over all the earth; made us nearly equal to the angels; given us new life filled with resurrection power; equipped us with the gifts and fruits of the Holy Spirit; set our feet on solid, high ground; defeated our satanic enemies; and given us the banner of victory over death, hell, sickness, and the grave.

He cannot be minimized, marginalized, or ignored. He is the deciding factor in whether we live or die, prosper or perish. God the Father raised Him from the dead and seated Him at His right hand in the heavenly places, far above all principalities, powers, might, dominion, and every name that is named – not only in this age but also in that which is to come. He will come again to judge the nations, establish equity and justice, and rule forever with unerring truth and righteousness. He stands forth upon the highest pinnacle of heavenly glory, proclaimed of God, acknowledged by angels, adored by saints, and feared by devils as the risen, personal Christ, our Lord and Savior. *Jesus* is the name given to Him by the Father before the beginning of time.

Man was not created to go it alone; all attempts to do so have ended in tragedy. When nothing's real in your life, when you've reached bottom, when your marriage is sinking, when you can't hold on any longer, when you're all used up, when you're all alone, when you have no more resources, when you've run out of excuses, when you need a fresh start, when you feel you can't be forgiven nor can even forgive yourself, when you are flat broke, when no one is there to help you, when you're not certain why you are even here, when you need a fix or a drink, when your pain or shame seems to be more than you can bear, when you don't know what direction to turn, when you feel like a failure, when you want to quit, when your health is gone, when you need a lover, when you're ready to run way, then I Am is the All-Sufficient One and He is offering Himself to you right now, just as you are.

Part 3 – Jesus as the Living and Incarnate Word

The Bible – regardless of translation – offers a content of more than two hundred names, titles, and character references for Jesus. These reflect His nature, His position in the triune Godhead, His earthly ministry on our behalf, and His relationship to us. The names given to those who appear throughout the Bible – Old or New Testament – have specific meaning and reveal life purpose; for example, Adam means "earth" and Jacob means "deceiver." This concept is also true for Jesus, whose name means "God saves." If we want to know someone better, we need to know their traits, their nature, and their character. To have a closer relationship with Jesus, we need to know as many of His names, titles, and character inferences as possible. He has chosen to reveal much of His nature to us so we may come to know Him best.

The Lord our Strength and Song who has become our Salvation; Creator and Possessor of the Heavens and the Earth; the One whose likeness we bear, having been made in His image and granted free will; our Shield and our Exceeding Great Reward; God Most High Who Walks Before Us; Everlasting God and Maker of the Eternal Covenant; Angel of the Lord who has redeemed me from all evil; God the Holy One of the Nation and the People of Israel; the Almighty Who Blesses; I Am Who I Am; the Lord God

Who Heals Thee (*Raphe*), Whose Banner Over Us Is Love and Victory (*Nissi*), Who Sanctifies (*Makadesh*), Who Provides (*Yireh*), and Who Sees (*Roi*).

The Lord God Merciful and Gracious, Long-Suffering, and Abounding in Goodness and Truth; who keeps mercy and forgives iniquity, transgression, and sin; Lord of Hosts; the Mighty One and the Light of Israel; the One Who Sits Between the Cherubim; a Tabernacle for Shade in the Daytime from the Heat; a Place of Refuge, a Shelter from the Storm, a Hiding Place from the Wind, and a Cover from the Tempest; as Rivers of Water in a Dry Place and as a Shadow of a Great Rock in a Weary Land; Wonderful, Counselor, Mighty God, Everlasting Father, Prince of Peace; One Who Sits Upon the Throne from Everlasting to Everlasting; He Who Opens and No Man Shuts, Who Shuts and No Man Opens; Zion's Rock, a Tried Stone, a Precious Cornerstone, a Sure Foundation, and a Stumbling Stone for the Nations; the Lord Our Judge, Our Lawgiver, and Our King.

In the Beginning was the Word, and the Word was with God, and the Word was God, all things were made through Him, and without Him nothing was made that was made, in Him was Light, the Light was the Light of Men, the Light Shines in the Darkness, it is the True Light that gives light to every man who comes into the world, a Great Light That Shines in the Darkness, the Only Begotten Son Who is in the Bosom of the Father and has declared God, His Name shall be called Jesus, which means "God Saves," for He Saves His People from Their Sins, He shall be known as Immanuel, which means "God with Us," God has highly exalted Him and given Him a Name that is above every name, that at the Name of Jesus every knee shall bow and every tongue confess that Jesus Christ is Lord to the Glory of God, His Father; King of the Jews, the Shepherd and Ruler of My People Israel – in Greek, the Christ; in English, the Anointed One; and in Hebrew, the Messiah.

Lord of the Harvest who sends out laborers, He is the Coming One who demonstrates His Power when the blind receive their sight, the lame walk, the lepers are cleansed, the deaf hear, the dead are raised up, and the poor have the Gospel preached to them; Lord of the Sabbath who gives an invitation to those who labor to come into His rest, to take up His yoke for it is light, to learn from Him because He is Gentle and Lowly in Heart, to give rest for our souls and a light burden; the Temple to be raised up in three days greater than any earthly temple, He is the Resurrected One, the

One Greater than Jonah, Elijah, Abraham, and Moses; He holds the keys to death, hell, and the grave and has taken captivity captive; My Servant whom I have chosen, My Beloved Son in whom I am well pleased and have put My Spirit so that He will declare justice to the nations and in His name they will trust.

In the parables, we know Him as the Sower of the Good Seed, the Pearl of Great Price, the Hidden Treasure, the Owner of the Vineyard and the Vinedresser, the Seeker of the Lost Coin, and the Light of the World.

He is the One Who Commands even the waves and the wind; the Son of Man, sitting at the right hand of the Father in power and coming on the clouds of heaven; whose death tore the veil of the Temple from top to bottom, split rocks, caused the earth to open, the skies to darken, and the earth to give up its dead when they found New Life and walked again in the streets of Jerusalem; the Reason for our Peace, our Joy, and our Hope; He walked the Sea of Galilee and called us out of darkness to become fishers of men; He taught with authority as One knowing the Father on hillsides, in the synagogues, on the streets, and from boats at sea; He commissioned us to share the Good News of the Son of Man to whom all power and authority has been given and to baptize them in His Name; whom even the demons call Jesus, Son of the Most High God; who comforts us in all our tribulation that we might be able to comfort those who are in any trouble; the Son of God who was preached among you was not yes and no, but in Him was yes, for all the promises of God in Him are yes and in Him Amen to the Glory of God.

He Who Establishes Us has anointed us and also has sealed us and given us the Spirit in our hearts as a Seal and as a Witness and as a Guarantee; He who supplies Seed to the sower, and Bread for food and increases the Fruits of our Righteousness; who calls those things which are not as though they were and they come into existence; He is the Image of the Invisible God, the Firstborn Over All Creation and He Is Before All Things and in Him All Things Exist; He is the Head of the Body and the Church, the Beginning and the Firstborn from the Dead that in all things He may have the preeminence, for in Him dwells the fullness of the Godhead bodily, that is Christ in you the Hope of Glory and a Mystery Hidden From the Ages; the Root of Jesse and Offspring of David; the Bright and Morning Star, the Dayspring who has visited us from on High, the Son of Righteousness who rises with healing in His wings; the Alpha and the Omega, Beginning and the End, the First and the Last who was and is and is to come.

He has reconciled us to Himself and has then given us the ministry of reconciliation, for He who knew no sin has become sin for us and has become our Passover and our First Fruits; a Prophet dishonored in His Own country, among His Own relatives, and in His Own house; who says to us, "Be of good cheer, do not be afraid, only believe, go in peace, your sins are forgiven, be healed of all your afflictions for above all I desire that you prosper and be in good health for I am not willing that any should perish but that all shall be saved and enter into eternal life."

Part 4 – Jesus in the Old Testament

Jesus said, *You search the Scriptures, for in them you think you have eternal life; and these are they which testify of Me* (John 5:39); and to some of His disciples on the Emmaus road He said, *"O foolish ones, and slow of heart to believe in all that the prophets have spoken!" And beginning at Moses and all the Prophets, He expounded to them in all the Scriptures the things concerning Himself.* (Luke 24:25, 27).

In the book of Genesis, Jesus visited in the garden of Eden and walked with Adam in the cool of the evening, later working with him to create Eve, and still later banished both from the garden; met and talked with Abraham as Melchizedek; appeared twice as the Angel of the Lord to comfort Hagar, the mother of Abraham's son Ishmael; dined with Abraham and foretold Sarah's birth of Isaac; announced the coming destruction of Sodom and Gomorrah; appeared on Mount Moriah to prevent the sacrifice of Isaac and to provide a sacrificial lamb; introduced Himself to Jacob and advised returning to the land of his birth; and wrestled with Jacob, changing his name.

In Exodus, Jesus appeared again as the Angel of the Lord when He gave Moses instructions for leading the nation of Israel out of their bondage to Egypt; met Moses at the burning bush; saved Israel and destroyed the first-born of her enemies on the night of Passover; and descended as a cloud to pass by Moses while showing him His glory.

In Numbers, the Angel of the Lord cautioned Balaam, spoke through Balaam's donkey, and then revealed Himself standing in the way and holding a sword.

In Kings, Jesus strengthened Elijah when he was fleeing from Jezebel and He destroyed 185,000 soldiers of Sennacherib's army.

In Judges, Jesus chastised Israel for not doing as commanded; met with Gideon face to face and commissioned him for service; delivered the Israelites from the nation of Midian; and appeared to Manoah and his wife to announce the coming birth of Samson.

In Samuel, King David approached the Lord near Araunah, the Jebusites' threshing floor, so that he could repent.

In Daniel, Jesus was the Fourth Man to appear in the fiery furnace with the three Hebrew youths who refused to worship King Nebuchadnezzar.

In Psalms, Isaiah, Hosea, Zechariah, and Ecclesiastes, Jesus makes additional appearances as the Angel of God.

Part 5 – Jesus' Miraculous Works

The Bible records thirty-seven miracles performed by Jesus as witnessed by the four gospel writers. These were loving acts beyond natural means and explanation, and are given as evidence of who He is. Some of them include:

- Delivering the demon-possessed man in Capernaum

- Healing Peter's mother-in-law

- Cleansing a Galilean leper

- Turning water into wine at Cana

- Commanding the paralytic to rise and walk

- Making whole the withered hand

- Healing a nobleman's son in Cana and a centurion's son

- Restoring from death the widow's son in Nain

- Calming the stormy sea

- Delivering the Gadarene demoniac

- Healing the paralytic at Bethesda

- Curing the woman afflicted with hemorrhaging for twelve years

- Raising Jairus's daughter

- Returning the sight of two blind men in Capernaum

- Healing a demon-possessed mute

- Feeding the five thousand and the four thousand

- Walking on the waters of Galilee

- Healing the Syro-Phoenician woman's daughter

- Restoring the sight of the blind man of Bethsaida

- Withering the fig tree

- Healing the man born blind

- Straightening the woman stooped over

- Healing a man who had dropsy

- Cleansing the ten lepers

- Healing blind Bartimaeus

- Restoring the servant's ear

- Raising Lazarus from the dead

As the evangelist John wrote: *There are also many other things that Jesus did, which if they were written one by one, I suppose that even the world itself could not contain the books that would be written* (John 21:25). The greatest of God's miracles performed through Jesus was His resurrection and ascension after He defeated death, hell, and the grave, and set the captives free.

Part 6 – Jesus as Savior and Lord

Who, then, is Jesus? In Bethsaida, Israel, Jesus asked His disciples, *"Who do men say that I, the Son of Man, am?" So they said, "Some say John the Baptist, some say Elijah, others Jeremiah or one of the prophets." He said to them, "But who do you say that I am?" Simon Peter answered and said, "You are the Christ, the Son of the living God."* Jesus' question remains valid today. Many men presently say Jesus was a profound teacher and rabbi, a good example, a prophet, a wise philosopher, a faith healer, an itinerant storyteller, and an exorcist, or perhaps, just a really nice or charismatic guy. Is He fully and wholly what and who He said He is, as presented in the five sections above – Son of Man, Son of God, Living and Incarnate Word, Eternal God of the Old Testament, and Miracle Worker? If one does not accept Him for all

He said He is and all that He revealed about Himself to us, then one must reasonably conclude that He is a joker, that He is crazy, or that He is a liar. Jesus said He was *the way, the truth, and the life* (John 14:6).

If one cannot believe all the wondrous things that Jesus' apostles, evangelists, preachers, teachers, and disciples have spoken and written about Him, then do as Richard Wurmbrand sagely advised: Believe His powerful and worldly enemies. The Pharisees said, *"Teacher, we know that You are true, and teach the way of God in truth; nor do you care about anyone, for You do not regard the person of men."* Judas said, *"I have sinned by betraying innocent blood."* Pilate said, *"Behold the Man!" "I am innocent of the blood of this just Person,"* and *"Behold your King!"* The captain of the Roman guard at Golgotha said, *"Truly this was the Son of God!"*

If one demands to see proof that Jesus is God, as His enemies often did, one must be willing to sincerely ask Him in faith for it, and then be teachable and open to receive and to act on whatever Jesus chooses to reveal directly into our spirit and/or into our life. Once presented with the truth, we are responsible for what we do with it. Jesus called Himself the Truth. He cannot simply be ignored; a decision must be made on who He is. The decision is a personal one, a mandatory one, and an eternal one. Once we have been informed, we are responsible for what we've heard and we cannot claim ignorance. Jesus admonished us thus: "It is written, have you not heard? Have you not read?" We're encouraged to choose well from what is set before us. Is He Savior and Lord? Who do *You* say Jesus is?

He loved them to the end. (John 13:1)

* * * *

Author's Note: The general inspirational seed for "Who Do You Say That I Am?" was "One Solitary Life," a brief essay credited to Dr. James Allan Francis. Part 1 contains several brief paraphrases from that essay. Dr. S. M. Lockridge delivered a famous sermon in 1976 titled "That's my King" which provided additional inspiration. A direct reading of his classic is recommended. Scripture phrasings utilized in Parts 2 through 6 are from the New King James Version (NKJV) of the Bible. The concept of an obituary for Jesus was found uncredited on numerous Internet sources; the version presented is mine.

Epilogue

Each of us is composing a nonfiction story; although most may never commit it to book form, it's our life story. Others read our story when they witness how we live. When that occurs, we are all teachers sharing our story, knowingly and willingly or not. I've read that the average life is observed by twelve to eighteen people; but for Christians, that number is multiplied by a factor of seven to ten. As our story unfolds, it's merged into the larger story, God's story. *You are our epistle written in our hearts, known and read by all men; you are manifestly an epistle of Christ, ministered by us, written not with ink but by the Spirit of the living God, not on tables of stone but on tablets of flesh, that is, on the heart* (2 Corinthians 3:2-3).

The promotional description for Scott McClellan's book *Tell Me a Story: Finding God (and Ourselves) Through Narrative*, adds a further dimension to our calling as story writer, that of storyteller: "Jesus called His followers witnesses. We are, in fact, witnesses to His unfolding story. This story is not only our calling – it's the next generation's best chance of identifying with the Church and changing the world. As we become storytellers, we learn to see the world in terms of stories being lived and told. We discover deeper insights into God, ourselves, and others."

As worthwhile as such an effort could be, I am not challenging us to commit our stories to writing – that is, composing our autobiographies or memoirs – but, in *How to Tell a Story*, professional writer Donald Miller does recommend something closely approaching that discipline. He justifies writing it as a worthwhile exercise for everyone: "We are all on a journey, of course. We all want things for ourselves and our families and those desires launch us into stories. And stories are filled with risk and fear and joy and pain. In each of our stories, friends and guides have passed through and those friends have taught us things." Miller continues this line of thought by adding some personal reflection:

> The point of any story is always character transformation. I am so grateful to have studied story if for no other reason than it has helped me realize how much I've changed over the years as a human being. Story has given beauty and meaning to my life because it's no longer passing by without me reflecting on it and noting its positive and negative turns and what those turns have done to me to make me a better person. I believe it's true every person should write their memoir if for no other reason than it helps them understand who they are, what's happened to them, and who it is their lives have caused them to become. A person who understands themselves is easier to connect with, more settled, and, most importantly, can see how their story interconnects with the stories of others.

Writing for the *grammarly.com* blog, Allison VanNest expresses a similar sentiment to Miller's. Stated more succinctly, she says, "The most valuable thing you have to offer is the story only you can tell." By this, she seems to be expressing two convictions: that each life is a story possessing unique meaning and purpose, and thus it is worthwhile sharing; and that those who are creative storytellers with tales of fiction or nonfiction inside should seek either verbal or written expression of them.

I have some suggestions to help each of our personal stories, written or not, to be good ones. I may not have the track perfectly aligned, but I know I'm close and I believe it has lasting expediency. I don't say that with a cavalier attitude, because it took me a lifetime to even get this close. First, invite God in to assume His rightful place. You do that by committing your life to Him, asking for His help with important decisions, and continually seeking His guidance. Second, determine what you like to do, what you are good at doing, and what you believe in; that is, assess your talents and passions. God made you with certain unique preferences and equipped you with the specialized skills and the enabling anointing required for your particular calling. There's no reason to feel guilty because you are enjoying the pursuit; and conversely, just because it may be difficult does not mean it's wrong. Third, keep your eyes open for opportunities along the way. As Vince Lombardi said, "Run to daylight." God will open certain doors and close others. If you stay in touch with Him, you will be able to tell the difference between the two, and when you make a mistake, He'll be quick to help you realign. Sometimes you require dreams, prophecies, or visions to jerk your chain and re-center you when you're far off course. When you're walking closely with God on a daily basis, the more spiritually extreme actions aren't required to get your attention. It's probably a good sign if you aren't moving from one spiritual goose-bump experience to another. Fourth, and last, be prepared to candidly share your life stories to encourage others; this is called testifying, as in being an open and ready witness to what God has done in your life. This fourth step is paying forward the fruit reaped during the first three. *For he* [man] *will not dwell unduly on the days of his life, because God keeps him busy with the joy of his heart* (Ecclesiastes 5:20).

This plan may not always be easy to execute, but conceptually it's that simple. In his cartoon series *Pogo* (a favorite of mine during middle school), political satirist Walt Kelly stated the plan humorously: "We are confronted with insurmountable opportunities." By the grace of God, it's easier to write a successful personal story in America today than it has been throughout previous centuries and in any other country. Dinesh D'Souza said that what is uniquely American is our access to equal rights, self-determination, and wealth creation. America has many haters internally and externally, but he shares that America is not the problem – America is the answer. Dinesh means an America characterized by the capital Cs: Christian, Conservative, Constitutional, and Capitalistic. He is not saying America is God, but that God has blessed America because it honored His biblical and covenantal principles. He knows God is the ultimate explanation. God made America a refuge for the world, especially for the Jewish people. Within that refuge, by God's goodness, are great opportunities so that we, in turn, may fund the gospel throughout the world and participate in its propagation. That's the big story. We just need to figure out where our personal page fits into it.

It is more than okay to wholeheartedly pursue the planning steps I suggested; it's what He intends us to do. When we do what we were purposed to do and enjoy what we do, we are more creative, satisfied, and productive, and we are all the more effective witnesses to His story. As He demonstrated during the six days when He conceived the universe, creativity and productivity are traits of God. Satisfaction is also His, as further demonstrated on the seventh day when He said, "It is good," and then rested. God encourages us to rest one designated day each week; adopt this practice and do so without guilt, as it similarly yields productivity and creativity for us during the other six days.

The first third of my adulthood I got what I've proposed above close to entirely wrong; then in the middle third, I got it about half right; and finally in the last third, I got it spot-on. I can tell the difference; others probably can too. My story was a journey from naïve and unconcerned to autopilot liberal to oblivious fence-sitter to sincere but unfocused seeker to conservative and committed Christian.

I understand there are times when life preparations or our occupations are not fun. We have to guard against confusing *worthwhile* with *easy*. We aren't able to select or to know our story's ending, but we can strive to stay in the race and to finish well no matter the mistakes and regrets along the way. Sometimes we are offered a do-over along the way; sometimes we aren't. What we can control is whether we squander the time and opportunity we're allotted and whether we add to our burden through bad choices. We are exhorted to work out our own salvation with fear and trembling. Applying that statement broadly to the entire course of our lives, I think it simply means we have been assigned a uniquely personal mission, one that is only ours. In pursuit of it, we'll have to keep checking with our Creator and Master for the necessary adjustments to our story until we finish and hear Him say, "Well done, good and faithful servant; enter into the rest that is prepared for you."

Editor, writer, and publisher Po Bronson wrote in *What Should I Do With My Life*: "If we are the victim of an injustice, it is up to us to find a meaningful way to channel our anger. If we suffer a terrible crisis, only we can transform this suffering into a launching pad for a new life. These are the turning points from which we get to construct our own story, if we choose to do so. It won't be easy, and it won't be quick. Finding what we should do [that is, writing our own story] is one of life's great dramas."

President Reagan's biological and younger son, Ron – unlike his adopted and older son, Michael – unwisely chose rebellion rather than follow his father's righteous ways. He does, however, provide us with a fine supporting comment: "Virtually everyone creates a mental album of memories and anecdotes that, ultimately, passes for our version of a life story. We are all the protagonists of our own narratives, of course – the indispensable main character; on a good day, the hero." Each of our stories is vital and worthwhile. Write your life story with chapters where you go for the gold, make the right choice, climb the mountain, enjoy the big adventure, find the love of your life, finish the race, and act the hero.

Upon examining their progression from ordinary to extraordinary, the people in this book emerge as role models and mentors; and although our life story may not yet compare to theirs, the long-term plan is to embrace the apostle Paul's admonishment: *Forgetting those things which are behind and reaching forward to those things which are ahead, I press toward the goal for the prize of the upward call of God in Christ Jesus* (Philippians 3:13-14). The end of the journey – the conclusion of our life story – is of more exemplary and eternal consequence than how we started, or about the ups and downs along the way. Strive to finish well!

Appendices

Appendix One

An Anatomy of the Character Stories

The allure and grip of a great story isn't found in its grammar, facts, composition, length, format, language, or style; it's in the measured revelation of truths that are too cosmic or too personal to be ignored. Stories are our culture's intellectual, emotional, educational, and spiritual DNA, because as they are transferred from person to person and generation to generation, they affect how we live and grow – yes, even the type of person we become.

The short stories in this collection were originally presented to audiences orally, but now they are captured for inspirational reading. Each was developed from experience and refined while teaching in elementary schools and high schools, in prisons and recovery centers, in small groups and around campfires, and from pulpits and Sunday school basements to boardroom podiums. These nonfiction stories are not dusty antiquities or boring academics; they've been commissioned to find an enduring place among your favorite reading memories.

I made two encouraging observations in the process of committing my stories to writing for incorporation into a book. The first was when I noted that stories and storytelling in general appear to be on the edge of revival. I can't say with certainty that presently more stories are being written and read, but I have definitely noticed that, as a genre, stories are receiving more attention, as many people in the media are stressing their value. The following quote from Donald Miller's *How to Tell a Story* is a typical example of my observation: "Story is no longer a tool only for artists. The rest of the world is beginning to understand that entire cultures are being shaped by the story tellers; and business leaders, pastors and parents are starting to wonder how they can incorporate more stories into their communication methodology. And they will all be benefited for doing so." I didn't know about this trend or intend to be part of it; but if I am now, that's fine, because I believe in the pleasures, benefits, and purposes of the story genre.

I read several good books on writing as preparation for *Uncommon Character.* One of the best was *On Writing Well* by William Zinsser, the thirtieth-anniversary edition of a recognized classic with sales of well over a million copies. Within its pages I found the second observation in his statement: "Writing is related to character. If your values are sound, your writing will be sound." The reader will easily observe that my values are closely interwoven within the character stories now emphatically recorded in print. Saul Bellows famously said, "You never have to change anything you got up in the middle of the night to write." I hope he is correct, as these stories represent a fair amount of scribbling in the dark on notepads stored next to my bed. I've observed that what comes to a mind awakened from sleep in the quiet of the night has unique clarity. I intended for my stories to contain sufficient truth to inoculate them against fading.

The Bible contains over five hundred true stories, as well as a handful of fictional illustrations. Overall, by percentages, it's reported to be a mix of 75 percent stories, 15 percent poetry, and only 10 percent unadorned teaching principles. It's not so much the story of God, as is so frequently stated; it's much more the story of man. In the preface to his book *The Gates of the Forest*, Holocaust survivor Elie Wiesel tells a story that ends with the statement: "God made man because He loves stories." There's a movement growing in popularity, especially among missionaries, to teach and preach the Bible evangelistically in the form of stories. This is variously called *Bible telling* and *chronological Bible storying.*

Gary Alan Taylor of Red Letter Christians defines stories as the "currency of human contact." He reasons that:

> We tell stories about ourselves that reveal a great deal of what we
> as a people believe and value. If you want to understand a culture's
> values, listen to her stories. The prevailing American narrative [for

example] consists of Godly Puritans at Plymouth Rock, Captain John Smith at Jamestown, George Washington on the Delaware and brave white settlers heading west into the sunset to claim the land God set aside for them.

Just as Taylor has generally noted above, the stories within *Uncommon Character* also seek to reveal and stress beliefs and values. Boris Johnson expressed a complementary sentiment to Taylor's when he wrote that the life of Winston Churchill proves "history is a tale of singular individuals and shining deeds."

My approach to examining the biblical principles, lifestyles, and people that are offered within the stories is fairly secular – not what the world labels *churchy* or *preachy*. Referring to the foundational Bible narratives in the book of Genesis, Jewish filmmaker Darren Aronofsky said, "If you can realize the mythological power of these stories and these characters, you can learn from them in a lot of ways, and it also makes them [into] living texts." I concur with his statement in its original context referring to the book of Genesis, as well as in a broader sense as applied to any good story dealing with human nature, when it's immersed in a noble challenge and faced with a moral choice. My primary mission in writing *Uncommon Character* was to create a special collection of living stories of this type, so their inherent instructional and inspirational value would be easily accessible to readers – especially knowing that my children and grandchildren will be counted among them.

Near the conclusion of the film *Saving Mr. Banks*, a fictionalized Walt Disney gains the confidence of reluctant author P. L. Travers by convincing her that she can trust him to portray her characters respectfully and as she intended. He does so with the following words, which are a fitting summary of the film's theme: "That's what we storytellers do. We restore order with imagination. We instill hope, again and again and again." Such is my intended approach when crafting stories from the themes, events, and individuals under my care.

Occupying an antiquated position in the digital age, the employment of straight-up oral storytelling is fairly rare today, but when offered in the right setting, it is still appreciated. In the not-too-distant past, it was the most prevalent method of values education and of communicating history, traditions, and beliefs. In her collection of essays and lectures, *Mystery and Manners: Occasional Prose,* short-story virtuoso Flannery O'Connor accurately stated storytelling's subsequently diminished circumstances: "There is a certain embarrassment about being a storyteller in these times when stories are considered not quite as satisfying as statements and statements not quite as satisfying as statistics; but in the long run, a people is known, not by its statements or its statistics, but by the stories it tells."

In her book *The Story Keeper,* Lisa Wingate writes, "Our stories are powerful. They teach, they speak, they inspire. They bring about change. But they are also fragile. Their threads are so easily broken by time, by lack of interest, by failure to understand the value that comes of knowing where we have been and who we have been. In this speed-of-light culture, our histories are fading more quickly than ever. Yet when we lose our stories, we lose ourselves."

I heartily endorse the sentiments expressed about stories (and storytelling) in these quotes, as I hold that there are attributes to be highly valued in stories – especially true ones. During the creation or selection of a story intended for narration, I adhere to six volitional criteria: character, nonfiction, age, oral presentation, sticky-points, and heroes. These criteria have generally survived after being committed to written format. The following outline on these criteria begins with character and concludes with heroes, while the other four criteria are presented in random sequence. I didn't find it necessary to assign further priority because the middle four have roughly uniform weight. Character and heroes are addressed at the greatest length, have some overlapping relationship, and serve as sturdy, balanced bookends. Choice and character have often been noted as continuously close companions in life; throughout this book, I consistently draw parallels to their relationship, but I have not treated choice as a separate story criterion.

Character

The first story criterion is character, as in demonstrating unselfish virtue and moral integrity in difficult circumstances. (Additional definitions of, and supplemental information on, character are available in the next two Appendices.) When the word *character* is used in *Uncommon Character,* it's always used with the intent of referencing a positive attribute unless specifically noted otherwise by a negative adjective preceding it. To describe a protagonist or antagonist as a character – as in meaning either a participant/ actor or a person possessing an odd nature – is never the intended use of the word anywhere in *Uncommon Character*. As already suggested, there are numerous parallels between the first story criterion of character and the sixth story criterion of heroism. While I venture to stand behind the generalization that all heroes have character, I would be uncomfortable in insisting that everyone who has character is a hero, but the essential qualities are there to potentially become a hero when circumstances are amenable.

People who possess character accept personal responsibility for situations and circumstances beyond how these affect their individual lives. Then, they actively extend their concern to the victims of a society that's gone harmfully wrong. That sentiment is supported by Dietrich Bonhoeffer's position that one of the three principle duties of the Christian church is to care for the victims of a reprobate government. The importance of applying his principle is seen in the degree to which civil governments tasked with protecting their citizens not only fail to do so, but also become the primary source of their abuse and demise.

The protagonists in *Uncommon Character* are never heard to utter the cop-out adjective *unfair* as applied to their personal circumstances. The conceit behind this word is so popular and so overused that one study indicates it's uttered in current society an average of 8.5 times per person/ per day, as in "That's not fair." Life really is never fair. This is true even if a majority refuse to accept it. It's never fair in the sense that we are individually equipped with vastly differing capabilities and we are born into and live under widely varying circumstances. Faith in God, obedience to His Word, and fervent petitioning prayer are what God offers us to level the playing field.

There is no such spiritual condition as *fair*; it's not a biblical word or concept. There's justice, as in receiving what retribution we deserve; and there's mercy, as in receiving what grace we don't deserve. In the parable in the Bible of the daily wage, the workers who toiled all day received the just wage offered and agreed upon; the workers who toiled only an hour for the same wage received mercy; fair was not a legitimate petition for anyone to raise. Fair is some gray, fallacious, murky rationale that was conceived to compromise and cover those unpleasantries in our lives that we refuse to accept or refuse to rectify. If we approach this with honesty and impartiality, we would not really want the justice we deserve and we would be grateful for receiving the mercy we do not deserve. The protagonists have found that some of life's disagreeable elements are changeable and have chosen to strive at improving them. They have also found that some are unchangeable and have chosen to strive at accepting them. The alternatives are always whether to get better or to get bitter.

The antagonists in *Uncommon Character* illustrate the absence of good character in ways that are true to their actions in life. The book, by its nonfiction nature, accurately depicts real-world villains. Antagonists with insufficient character are frequently those who spend too much time with a fringe faction that reinforces their aberrant thinking, until finally they see the strange lifestyle or mindset as normal and, thus, fully acceptable as witnessed within their deviant support group or surrogate family. To offer an analogy, it's as though they crawled into a tunnel and began living all of their lives inside it until the tunnel eventually came to be seen as the whole world (statement paraphrased from Malcolm Gladwell in *What the Dog Saw*). This resulting aberration has also become known as *drinking the Kool-Aid*, as occurred literally at Jonestown, Guyana, South America, or figuratively within the Charles Manson family in California. This may sound like it affects only small communities, but there's no upward limit. During the buildup to World War II, both the Germans and the Japanese, as whole populations, exemplified anomalous mindsets in favor of their countries, cultures, and peoples, and against most other countries, cultures, and peoples. When in possession of this mindset, others are viewed as having diminished human value or as a means to an end. A current example is the Islamic fundamentalists who hail from multiple ethnic groups, races, countries, and nationalities. (Several of these situations are represented by stories within this book.) Consider the following major historical examples of deviant – but acceptable – group-think: the Spanish and Portuguese populations during the three hundred years of the Catholic Inquisition; the widespread ill treatment of native American Indians leading to the Trail of Tears, broken treaties, and forced enclosure on reservation land; and the majority of citizens in the American South prior to their being forced to disengage first from slavery by a massive civil war, and thereafter from the reactionary persuasions of the Ku Klux Klan and Jim Crow segregationists.

The antagonists may be actively aggressive or just submissively passive.

Those who are aggressive are often few in number and don't account, by themselves, for the resulting widespread damage. Those on the scene who are passive are usually far greater in number. Their inaction may not be the catalyst, but it does give tacit support and a steady green light to the aggressors, due to their continuous failure to act in opposition.

Within my social circle, there's ongoing discussion as to whether simple, dissuasive actions by an individual are effective deterrents. In other words, can they influence another individual to stop or improve their antisocial behavior? I'm a longtime proponent that small alerts can be effective wake-up calls for others to realize they're engaging in harmful or rude practices, and perhaps even be a catalyst for subsequent correction of their former blind spots. Those holding opposing views often interpret these attempts at preventive action as useless vigilantism. If their negative label is accurate, and I hold it is not, then the protagonists in these stories should be labeled vigilantes. One protagonist, Stetson Kennedy, began a national campaign he called *frown power*. It admonished the general public to respond individually to bigoted speech by simply frowning (it was part of his effort to discourage the re-emergence of KKK-like hate groups by discrediting them individually through displays of immediate, open disapproval). At its heart was the belief that the world around him could be changed one person at a time. This remains the only reliable way to do so, as is demonstrated within these stories and universally by the manner that the gospel message, when received, changes individuals, one heart at a time. One-on-one is the proven effective method for transmitting and receiving life-changing truth.

The longer opposing action is delayed, the more inertia builds toward the good, and momentum increases toward the bad. Electing to take counteraction, as opposed to just accepting the status quo, is vital in preventing inevitable degeneration from the small and controllable to the widespread and out-of-control. On a larger scale, for example, New York City officials found that simply repairing graffiti and broken windows in public places had the more profound consequence of reducing crime and general lawlessness; while conversely, ignoring and accepting it sustained or even hastened the progression of a downward spiral. In my community, running stop signs began with a few drivers doing so with impunity. It rapidly accelerated to the point where, within a few years, only an occasional driver stopped, and even when not in pursuit, the police officers were guilty of widely demonstrating the same poor behavior. The authorities tasked with enforcement have, instead, passively accepted this form of lawlessness and no longer act to prevent its spread. Thereafter, break-ins, vandalism, dope dealing, and arsons were "unexplainably" on the rise.

One study concluded that for prevention and/or cure of lawlessness or rudeness, it must be demonstrated to the public that someone notices the small antisocial acts and finds this behavior unacceptable. In our massive, anonymous society, it is often assumed that no one cares about or is keeping track of what we're doing, with the result that bad behavior grows unchecked. Associated experiments show, however, that most of us are more likely to travel the straight-and-narrow route when we find, or think, we're being observed. This is part of the strategy behind the ubiquitous placement of cameras – real and fake. Rarely does anyone review the images; just knowing that someone is potentially watching, or could watch the video later, is an effective deterrent against anti-social activity.

The concept is well summarized by a quote widely attributed to Edmund Burke, and represented as, "The only thing necessary for the triumph of evil is for good men to do nothing." This isn't just referring to a historical circumstance from which the world has already evolved. It's easily observed all around us today. For example, in the face of suffering ever-restricted freedoms and even exacerbating open abuses, many Christians in America are divorcing themselves from politics, are folding into the opposition's camp as ancient doctrines are watered down, are accepting compromised beliefs while allowing themselves to be like the frog in a boiling pot of water, or are refusing to vote while offering weak rationalizations for their dilatory inaction. Theodore Roosevelt held similar sympathies to Burke's, but said that neutrality in the face of good and evil is serving evil.

As a current worldwide example of complacent agreement and complicit approval, Muslims in America, Europe, and Australia are enjoying generous Western lifestyles and permissive religious-societal-political securities, while simultaneously declining to voice any condemnation of those violent, hate-filled practitioners of their religion who loudly proclaim their opposition to these same liberties. These are the ones individually undermining Western-Christian culture in their own neighborhoods as well as doing so internationally on a collective basis. Ancient and modern histories have repeatedly taught us that peace-loving Germans, Japanese, Chinese,

Russians, Rwandans, Serbs, Afghans, Kurds, Jews, Somalis, Nigerians, and Armenians have been slaughtered by the tens of millions because, in part, the quiet, uninvolved majority did not speak up before it was too late. The concept of the silent majority was briefly, and erroneously, promoted during the Nixon and Ford presidency years as a powerful and complimentary concept. It is not so. It represents wasted potential to do, or to endorse, what is right and good, and to oppose evil on a timely basis. For a population to be imputed as having great potential is only complimentary if it is applied at some reasonable point; if not applied in a timely manner, being characterized as having potential eventually becomes a negative attribute – or even a sin or crime – as in having the unutilized ability to do good or prevent evil.

Silence represents compromise, endorsement, or acquiescence, but rarely, opposition. Martin Niemöller is perhaps best remembered for the following quotation that unforgettably delivers this point: "When the Nazis came for the communists, I remained silent; I was not a communist. When they locked up the social democrats, I remained silent; I was not a social democrat. When they came for the trade unionists, I did not speak out; I was not a trade unionist. When they came for the Jews, I remained silent; I wasn't a Jew. When they came for me, there was no one left to speak out."

Encouragingly and instructively, history has recorded a few, small, righteous examples in which the general population has taken an early and enduring stand against violent national/ethnic prejudices and movements. Such was the case in WWII in the French Huguenot village of Le Chambon-sur-Lignon, where a population of twenty-six hundred people sheltered an estimated four thousand Jews; or in the small Dutch village of Nieuwlande, where every household sheltered one Jewish family. These brave actions – though implemented by a small number of supporters – were sufficient to dissuade the mighty German majority from enacting its desired atrocities.

Assimilating a clear vision of the big picture (not getting lost in the immediate, or in a fad, or in the details), while remaining engaged in fighting evil, are two aspects of the underlying character theme woven throughout *Uncommon Character*. The primary purpose herein is not to draw further attention to evil men and evil deeds, but to let our attention linger on those protagonists who, while caught up in those situations, still refused to comply with popular and profitable evil. Instead, they retained a hold on truth and goodness, thereby acting as a light in the darkness that continues to illuminate the right choices for generations to come.

Sometimes otherwise decent people will actively adopt the wrong side due to a misconception or misapplied loyalty. Such circumstances are especially problematic if the commonplace, modest passivity is abandoned. In becoming active, they contribute substantially to the damage or evil already unfolding. As an example, during our Civil War (aka the War against Secession and Slavery), being sincerely wrong was tragically exemplified by both Robert E. Lee and Thomas "Stonewall" Jackson. These two men had substantial capabilities and otherwise admirable personal qualities; but these were misapplied to the further detriment and wasted lives of countless more Americans, causing the war to be painfully extended by years. This should engender a "good Southerner" debate not unlike the "good German" post-Nazi debate. How can one be good when supporting, or deliberately ignoring, a wicked regime simply because it's incorporated into the state or country one was born in and purportedly loves? Lee supported the Southern cause because his home state of Virginia demonstrably did so by seceding and taking up arms against the Union; yet he was a Virginian by less than one mile, the distance from the Potomac River to his Arlington estate, while just another mile in the opposite direction took him to the capital of the United States to which he had once sworn allegiance. It would have been far better if Lee and Jackson had opted to work for the end of slavery and the defeat of secession, or at the least had opted to do nothing active for either side. The paths they selected are all the more grievous when considering the oft-reported knowledge that Lee and Jackson were Christian men who didn't personally favor the nefarious causes promoted by the side they both served all too well. *Woe to those who call evil good, and good evil; Who put darkness for light, and light for darkness; Who put bitter for sweet, and sweet for bitter!* (Isaiah 5:20).

The choices made by an individual have great personal and sometimes unintended universal consequences. Again, the Civil War offers a uniquely American example of such an outcome. After the defeat of the South, its viciously effective lead cavalry officer, Lieutenant General Nathan Bedford Forrest, chose not to wholly accept the established new order and in doing so, his resistance helped to establish and promulgate the Ku Klux Klan. This was the beginning of its long and ugly tenure. (See the Stetson Kennedy story.) That's why when choices are inevitably before us, we are admonished to make a choice and not to straddle the line as a lukewarm compromiser. In choosing, we are further advised to be certain to choose wisely, not leaning on our own understanding. Not deciding is a default decision; and being sincere when making the wrong choice is just being sincerely wrong. Choice is another aspect of the underlying character theme in *Uncommon Character*, and it is well illustrated by the real-life actors presented herein. Their character is revealed by the choices they made. Writer Robert McKee puts it this way: "True character is revealed in the choices a human being makes under pressure – the greater the pressure, the deeper the revelation, the truer the choice to the character's essential nature."

Believing in the goodness of man's nature has been consistently shown, since the garden of Eden, to be a seriously fallacious and misleading conviction. Man needs watchful eyes upon him from both heaven and earth. Being a loner is not a good policy, because man's nature is essentially depraved and our surroundings are in a fallen state. We all need to look to someone bigger than ourselves for inspiration and goals. We do this by finding proven authorities, counselors, and role models who have left an enduring legacy of goodness and virtue. To paraphrase and reapply Newton's second law of thermodynamics: things and men left to their own do not improve with time, but rather degenerate. Summarizing his observations of a twentieth-century United States after an extended visit, Rudyard Kipling said that we had "unlimited and meticulous legality, but of law abidingness, not a trace." This remains true regardless of the level of sophistication or civilization attained.

To give this concept the attention it deserves, I offer the following: If we have our eyes on the wrong role models (this is discussed further in criterion six on heroes), or if we see ourselves as victims, or if we are expecting more out of life than we are willing to invest in it, or if we think we can enjoy a life free of responsibilities, then we are guilty of having chosen foolishly and of acquiring tunnel vision, of drinking the Kool-Aid. We have lost sight of what is virtuous and vital for both our personal good and the greater good. We are guilty of seeing nothing on the horizon bigger than ourselves. As Paul said in his letter to the Romans: *Professing to be wise, they became fools* (1:22).

We need to progress to the business of building our character around the absolute truths of self-responsibility and everyday common virtue (statement paraphrased from *A Nation of Victims* by Charles J. Sykes). The positive societal contributions of good character, and the negative consequences of its alarming decline in America today – especially as it relates to the public education system and to public/government service – are two sides of a single critical issue. These contributions and consequences may generate a cause-and-effect nature that continues beyond and outside of our own singular life. This is comparable to the familiar ripples-in-the-pond analogy. The continuing influence of our actions is yet another aspect of the underlying character theme in *Uncommon Character*. In other words, each one of us does make a difference in the world around us.

An unforgettable story illustrating this aspect was researched and presented by Bill Gothard of the Institute in Basic Life Principles. He speaks of two specific Englishmen who founded families in the eighteenth century. One man led a selfless life, and generation after generation of his posterity was documented as being heavily populated by doctors, lawyers, and ministers. The other led a life of depravity and crime, and generation after generation of his posterity was documented as being heavily populated by rapists, murderers, and thieves.

These aspects of character reveal some of the reasons I was motivated to select it as the dominant theme of this story anthology (as well as emphasizing the related concept of heroes below). Just as I have frequently shared this theme in the classroom, I'm now anxious to share it wherever I'm able to place *Uncommon Character*. It's my hope that a fuller, more accurate understanding of character will result from a complete and careful reading of the heroic stories contained herein. (Supplemental exposition on the nature of character, especially as it relates to America today, is available in Appendix Two.)

Nonfiction

The second story criterion is nonfiction, as in being essentially true. Incidental factual accuracy may have been lost due to the original oral nature of the stories. (This is discussed further under the fourth criterion, oral presentation.) Whereas data may occasionally be either partial or subjugated, principles never suffer these fates. Presentation of timeless, unchanging truth is the overarching goal.

While I sparingly use exact quotes or even paraphrases, I prefer them to what I call *pseudodialogue*, which I completely avoid using. Pseudodialogue is a nonfiction writing technique of fairly modern origin that is most acceptable when employed in historical fiction, although it's now used to a lesser degree in nonfiction as well. It works like this: Dialogue or thoughts are contrived by the author when the exact words or thoughts of the actors are unknown, but the general situation or motivations are known. It effects a feeling of being there because the conversations are inferred. Its use without prior disclosure is unjustified in nonfiction, because the subjective nature may mislead the reader or misrepresent the actors. Such a contrivance will not work well in the classroom with oral presentation. Thus, I've chosen instead to let the protagonists' deeds speak, rather than assume to know their actual thoughts or words. I'm satisfied their actions reveal for us the essence of their lives wrapped within a larger story of redeeming truth. The great thing about truth is that not only is it unchanging and not relative, but it also applies to everyone without regard to place, time, or culture. When a truth applies to one protagonist, it applies to me, to all the others in *Uncommon Character*, and to every reader/hearer.

The non-parable stories are based on a combination of real people and historic events. I want the hearer, or reader, to be able to trust that anything positive derived from the story is solid, proven, and dearly worth retaining (this is discussed further under the fifth criterion, sticky-points). If the protagonist succeeded in any way, so can we. Positive personal vision and values, the degree to which we strive to peacefully and productively fit into society, and the quality of what we hide in our heads and hearts, are three of the foundational stones of virtuous living that are consistently demonstrated by protagonists within *Uncommon Character* (even the parable stories are built upon these three foundations). The lives of the protagonists have taught me and refined me, and my affinity for them has only deepened with the repeated sharing of their stories.

As briefly indicated, some of the stories have been labeled as parables in order to act as a clear indicator that the story may have one or more of the following special conditions: It may be in part an exception to my bias for nonfiction; any aspects of this nature will be obvious to the reader as fiction. Or, the story is not constructed around a single, unifying protagonist; that is, it is not centered on someone's life, but it is centered on the specific principles or lessons that it is intended to illustrate. Thus, it is more parable-like, differing from most of the other stories in *Uncommon Character*, which are closer to mini-biographies. Or, finally, where lessons are woven within the parable stories, they often reflect personal lessons that I learned slowly over the years the hard way. If anything confessional that I share directly or indirectly helps reveal a shorter, better, or clearer path for the reader, then another objective of the book has been met.

While writing *Uncommon Character*, I occasionally heard, "So, you are writing a book of short stories." While the word *story* is often accepted to mean it is a created work, this is generally not so with *Uncommon Character*. Further, a short story is frequently thought of as fiction; again, this is not so with *Uncommon Character*, even though the stories are of relatively short duration with each able to stand on its own. When recited, their time ranged between ten and forty-five minutes. The reason short stories bring fiction to mind is that in the timeline of American literature, the short story began as fiction, and it remained as fiction until after the middle of the twentieth century. Every famous writer strove to create a great fictional short story, even after firmly establishing a reputation as a novelist. After WWII, the fictional short story lost popularity to full-length novels. It is only in recent years that the short-story format has been revived, but now as nonfiction, not as previously in a fictional format. As a reader, you are, therefore, near the cutting edge with *Uncommon Character*.

Reading fictional short stories was a preoccupation of mine after graduating from college – likely a reaction to so many years spent reading thick, factual textbooks. I strove to transfer what value was gleaned from those reading experiences into my current stories. I've subsequently observed that when nonfiction is presented in the format of a short story, especially an oral one, it may unintentionally acquire the feel of fiction. When this occurs, it captures the most intriguing qualities of both genres, thus proving to be an uncommonly absorbable and integrated communication style. I've purposed to select stories incorporating truth that reads better than good fiction.

Age

My third story criterion is acceptance by an audience widely disparate in age, roughly from fourth grade forward without limit. It may seem a bit incredulous to include ten-year-olds in the target audience, but my class-room experience indicates their interest, and reasonable comprehension, are solidly present during an oral presentation. I do acknowledge that when formalized in a book, it will be a challenging read at that level.

Often when the word *story* is encountered, it is assumed to connote material – whether fiction or nonfiction – that is presented primarily at a child's level and with children as the intended audience. While I have attempted to write at a level that will appeal to the broadest possible read-ership, *Uncommon Character* is definitely not a children's book. In fact, I suggest that parents exercise discretion regarding some of the stories, such as those presenting subject matter relating to crime, the Holocaust, war, prejudice, martyrdom, and terrorism. To adequately present acts of heroism, choice, and character, it is necessary to contrast them with the unwholesome backgrounds in which they transpired. Evil and good are frequently found in juxtaposition. Times of great evil produce men and women of great renown.

Because I have shared these stories frequently in oral presentations to multiple age groups, I had confidence they could be converted to written format with reasonable readability and reliability, even when targeted at a broad audience; that is, I used a shotgun, not a rifle. I hold this belief despite acquiring two handicaps in the conversion process. The first handicap was losing the option for customizing the stories to my specific audience because now I no longer know my specific audience, which is partially the reason for the parental advisory given immediately above. Placing the previously oral stories in writing seems like freezing them in time. It feels a little unnatural to me, because the constant modifications I formerly practiced have been exchanged for a fixed selection of words.

The second handicap is my unwitting propensity to default to a formal writing style and vocabulary. This is the unintended outcome of many years of business writing. As a corporate planner, I regularly engaged in produc-ing hi-tech white papers, research studies, and marketing plans that were succinct, bullet pointed, logical, easily summarized, and intended to be read and evaluated by individuals possessing high education levels. These were obviously nonfiction in nature. I am still writing nonfiction, not for busi-ness, but for leisure. Fortunately, nonfiction in either form is more accepting of formality than is fiction. Further to my benefit, the stories gained some relaxed carryover in the process of the many informal, verbal repetitions. The style found in the stories is, I promise, more congenial than that used in the ancillary sections of the book. The prologue, epilogue, and appendices reflect more formality than do the stories.

I've incorporated three stylistic elements into the composition of *Uncommon Character.* They're all loosely related to age-appropriate considerations: honest labeling, presenting broad scopes with universal themes, and wrapping the stories in their historical context.

Regarding the first stylistic element, the reader will not find herein any of the all-too-common compromises in favor of using politically correct speech. The protagonists in *Uncommon Character* are plainspoken truth-tellers known for refusing to conform to the shifting winds and moods of their societies. In adhering to their convictions, neither have I watered down my language and concepts in order to favor current fads, demographics, pressures, favoritism, demands, or overly sensitive feelings. Politically correct language pretends an empathy with freedom of speech while really denying it, thus practicing censorship equating to totalitarianism or deliberate obfuscation through the use of double-speak or Orwellian "newspeak" euphemisms. The primary intentions and outcomes of such speech are indoctrination and subjugation.

Political correctness should be relabeled *cultural Marxism*, because many of its adherents deliberately erode fundamental American and Christian values in favor of the communist values like those of the Frankfurt School of ideology. Politically correct speech is not practiced by, nor characteristic of, those holding traditional or conservative views, since they are known to continue endorsing what's already proven by time and experience. Rather, it is widely and frequently employed by those advocating ultra-liberal, deconstructionist, elite progressive, and communist-leaning views. Proponents of politically correct speech use it to facilitate change, and subsequently intend to permanently secure the resulting change by acting as though it were, indeed, always the superior and natural order of life. Hypotheses and untruths are promoted as facts until they erroneously become accepted as facts. Existing and alternative ideas and speech are labeled with mean-spirited expressions such as *ignorant, regressive, uneducated, curmudgeonly,* and *provincial* in order to dismiss them as without credibility and thus deny them any further opportunity for expression or consideration. Freethinking and open dialog, continued interpretation and observation, dissent, and discussion are thereafter repressed and eliminated. Two sure signs of a weak concept or program are: first, if its existence or acceptance cannot withstand any competition; and second, if it's dependent on the protection mustered by a rigid politically correct code encircling it like a thick fortress wall guaranteeing the restrictive presence of safe zones and trigger warnings to insure freedom from any vague micro-aggressions.

Politically correct concepts are aggressively enforced dogmatically on university campuses, and from the classrooms they filter into books, texts, journalism, newspapers, theses, literature, and K-12 education, and even into our laws, regulations, and courts. In his essay "The Sin of Nice," Allan Erickson writes, "And the Left marches forward, insisting we [conservative Christians] be 'nice.' Today, they call it 'political correctness,' the embrace of multiculturalism, the demand we conform to their new world order, that we do this willingly, with a cooperative smile. Object and you are immediately convicted of 'hate' speech, proving your unworthiness." This politically correct methodology is frequently leveraged against proponents of, and topics pertaining to, creationism, pro-life, school vouchers, welfare alternatives, freedom of religious expression, traditional marriage, sexual morality, educational choice, natural gender differentiation, strict Constitutional construction, support for the State of Israel, absolute values, environmental issues, abstinence education, the First and Second Amendments, and anything relating to a Supreme Being. *Uncommon Character* intentionally upholds these falsely maligned concepts as a prescription for the damage done by the liberal biases inherent in political correctness.

Politically correct concepts are riddled with dogmatic contradictions, the only consistency being their unrelenting lack of logic. Examples of their contradictions are: the rejection of Christianity as too religious, while embracing neo-paganism, atheism, humanism, Satanism, magic, and witchcraft – all of which are religious in nature and practice; rejection of the obvious proofs offered by a wondrous and complex universe or biological cell while embracing far-fetched and just-plain-silly alternative hypotheses as fact; and rejection of innocent, unborn human life while attempting to prolong the lives of convicted serial killers and protect endangered insects. (See the story on Gregory Jessner.) Consequently, there can be no tactical justification for employing such a literary ruse as politically correct speech in *Uncommon Character*. These stories and the protagonists within them stand firmly on their own innate and durable merits and virtue. Everything in God's economy is based on truth; so it should be with the nonfiction writer's production as well.

The second stylistic element is presenting broad scopes with universal themes. Stories that are designed with this in mind innately have higher multi-generational appeal, and because they are more enduring, they have greater cross-generational appeal as well. I appreciate stories, films, songs, and books that are epic or saga-like in nature. By this, I mean they present a large canvas and their themes are not limited to a single time period or people group. I believe the reader will find this description applies to many selections within *Uncommon Character*. There's also significant content with underlying political and spiritual orientations; these find their personal underpinnings in a BS degree in political science and a master's in Christian education. I've been told, on the positive side, that I have Renaissance-like eclectic tastes and interests, and more toward the negative side, that I have serious attention deficit disorder. Be forewarned: I am interested in nearly everything, but deeply knowledgeable in nothing.

The third stylistic element is history. My enduring interest in history is on obvious display throughout the book. There's a sizable amount of history presented within the stories, but it's offered for both context and clarity. History is always the stage on which character acts. Several of the stories have the Jewish Holocaust as a backdrop or present heroes who acted on that stage. This seems unavoidable, as it was an exceptionally unique period (as was the Civil War in America), one that exposed both great horrors and great heroes. Survivors, victims, and rescuers, including or especially those from the Holocaust, are some of our best history teachers; but, as the eyewitness generation diminishes due to increasing age, it's up to us to tell their stories. Holocaust survivor Henry Greenbaum (known in his native Poland as Chuna Grynbaum) documented his story for the United States Holocaust Memorial Museum. In doing so, he said, "On the death march [from Auschwitz to Dachau] we promised each other that we would tell our story, and I have kept my promise."

This book, as denoted above, is not strictly speaking a history text; however, if the contents of education textbooks were written more in the style of *Uncommon Character*, I believe the subject's popularity would soar with

K-12 students and as a college elective. I offer the story of young Colonel George Washington as a compelling example; it was previously found in history texts, but was removed sometime just prior to 1960. History is the continuing tale of our lives; that is, who we are. History is more than just factual times, movements, and locations. Most of my generation had history introduced to us as *His Story* – alluding to its overarching scale and infinite purpose. Today, history is taught in a relative, touchy-feely way that subjectively promotes ever-changing, politically correct, popular pet issues rather than an eternal narrative of truth supported by a bedrock of proven facts.

Oral Presentation

The fourth story criterion is twofold in nature. One is that the stories were created for oral sharing; the second is that in doing so, I adhere to and become part of the time-honored and long-lived storytelling tradition that knows no ethnic, historic, or generational limitations. Over the years of teaching, many of my stories were committed to rough drafts for purposes of general reference, research-based notes, and updating, but the level of written substantiation varied widely. A few were nearly complete, in that they read reasonably well on their own, whereas most were outlines at best. A few were held completely in my head and not worth the paper they weren't written on. It didn't matter greatly to me and generally depended on the amount of time I was able to commit to them at their inception. It didn't matter because the stories were intended to be extemporaneously shared verbally, not to be read to, or by, the audience from a written text or listened to from a recorded format. Because most of the stories were created ad hoc for oral presentation, and were thereafter shared multiple times verbally over a period of years, some of their exact origins/sources have been forgotten or lost; they were not documented at the time and now depend on my best recollections. Most stories have three general roots: an initial primary catalyst like a book or documentary or story, my own experiences and imagination, and some specific supporting or fact-checking data researched from multiple Internet sites and library resources. At the conclusion of many of the stories, I've included an author's note providing the attributions for known source material.

Oral presentation permitted me to vary the stories to my current audience, to fit them within the available time frame, and to tailor them to a specific purpose. Any fixed, written form did not suit these objectives, as it would be static as opposed to dynamic, or at best, it may have occasionally served as a reference aid for a failing memory. Having now committed the stories to written form, I've come to belatedly realize I have lost at least three other useful tools I readily had available when in the classroom. I can no longer display photos at timely intervals; I can no longer go to the whiteboard at will and sketch an illustration whenever helpful; and I can no longer utilize hand gestures and body language to emphasize and to act out. An additional observation worthy of note is that the process of converting the stories from informal oral form to formal written form was not as easy as I once anticipated it would be. In other words, it proved to be challenging beyond my expectations.

Perhaps the best analogy to represent the oral stories that eventually culminated, and have now matured in written form, is the phrase *based on a true story* (sometime stated as *inspired by true events*). I've often noticed this phrase introducing a film or following somewhere in the rolling end credits. It so struck me as an accurate label for *Uncommon Character* that I seriously considered it for the book's title. What should carry forward is the admonition that while the stories are nonfiction unless otherwise noted, not all of the evolved details may hold fast if subjected to close scrutiny. Again, this is unavoidably and unapologetically so for a number of reasons, the most influential being the retelling of the stories. With numerous retellings, a story would become mildly customized to better fit the setting, the sticky-point I wanted to emphasize, or the listening audience. Of those three customization incentives, the sticky-point has survived; consequently, I continue to be highly motivated to promote the sticky-points.

Most of my stories are composites. Their final form resulted from a number of sources. The most common sources were news reports, book reviews, nonfiction books, Internet websites, and lectures. Frequently, the sources were not in agreement as to facts and circumstances. Some were primary research sources; most were secondary. Therefore, subjectivity is incorporated and objectivity is not guaranteed. Even with sincere intentions by my sources, memories are still unreliable and the Rashomon effect may be in play: contradictory interpretations of the same activity or event by different people.

It's worth noting that occasionally a fact presented will be seen as true or false as a matter of the writer's, or the reader's, perspective. The story of Haym Salomon, for example, illustrates this potential in that the iconography of the dollar bill has been ostensibly proven to be both wholly Masonic on the one hand, and wholly Christian on the other, regarding its origin and intent. More correctly, as explained within the related story, there was an alliance at that time in history between the two, which is now largely antithetical to our modern, bifurcated, and fixed viewpoints. George Washington's personality, for example, was clearly an amalgamation of Christian and Masonic influences and activities.

I encourage the reader to utilize solid fact-checking before relying wholly on a story for any purpose beyond which the story was intended. My stories are primarily intended as vehicles for demonstrating heroic character and the related sticky-points. In the process, I may overstate or understate a subject matter. As a writer and thinker, I'm not without my preferences and prejudices. I further encourage the reader to find complementary readings and supplemental research beyond my simple story outlines. There is so much more to uncover about the lives, times, and contributions of these interesting people. Motivating the reader to undertake further educational pursuit is an intentional objective of *Uncommon Character*. If you go beyond my work, then I further encourage you to also share your findings with audiences of your own. Good stories based on virtuous people will hold up to extended development. Many well-known Founding Fathers like George Washington and Thomas Jefferson, for example, have had hundreds of books written about each of them, with new ones containing fresh information released annually.

In the oral storytelling tradition, the original sources fade quickly from memory as the good stories are passed on person to person and generation to generation. Borrowing and/or elaborating and/or merging related material is acceptable in storytelling. It's also long been acceptable with folk songs. In one story, the reader will meet a man (Stetson Kennedy) who collected southern folk stories professionally during the Depression era; then he became the recipient of a folk song about his life written by Woody Guthrie. The story-and-song oral traditions shared common roots and purposes prior to mass-media entertainment and formalized education.

In oral storytelling, time and effort are not given to documenting sources and references, or to providing accurate verbatim quotes. Storytelling was my initial, and only, purpose for years – especially the decade immediately prior to writing this book – and it is still regularly my primary purpose; the written output came secondarily and far later. In the act of committing these stories to writing, I purposed to preserve the inherent spontaneity emerging from the ever-evolving oral versions. It was, perhaps, too much of a challenge. Some was retained; much was likely lost. In hindsight, this creation process seems not unlike the game called *telephone*, where a message is passed from individual to individual until the concluding message bears little resemblance to the original. Some of the stories, or portions thereof, had probably already gone through the telephone process with other parties prior to my receipt and adaptation. Additionally, with some stories, I was creating my own telephone-like iterations with each subsequent retelling.

While I never deliberately contemplated plagiarizing – and did all I could to avoid the same – it remains possible, when following tradition, to have modestly crossed the line at some unknown points. This seems nearly inevitable to me, because I readily sought and generously used many good written and oral sources during my research for the verbal presentation stage. All of the stories are the outcome of multiple source material; thus, facts were freely borrowed. Facts are the building materials for story structure for anyone's work, as they are rarely proprietary. Distinguishing which of the details are mine from those planted over time from any number of sources – including the public domain – is now highly indeterminate. Having so clarified the general creative environment, all of my known sources are accurately cited and I've made every effort to provide generous attributions for my influences.

Also worth noting in *Uncommon Character* is an expansion of tradition beyond anything related specifically or solely to storytelling. I strove to treat our historical Judeo-Christian and Western cultural traditions with a dignity that is currently too often lacking in the arts, politics, and publishing. Mass-media info-entertainment and public educational institutions in particular promulgate a destructive pretense that old and conservative are bad, and new and liberal are good. This is closely aligned with their out-of-perspective and almost aggressive promotion of youth culture, feel-good leisure activities, radical progressivism, multiculturalism, victimhood celebrations, diversity extremism, decadent morals, anti-police/anti-military viewpoints, exaggerated coverage of violent and rude demonstrations, insistent and unbalanced politics of blame and outrage, lifestyles of conspicuous consumerism, ethical relativism, and bigotry toward nearly any form of constitutional republicanism, capitalism, conservatism, and Christianity.

An alternate mindset is sprinkled throughout the Old Testament like hidden treasures. This more lucid point of view is represented by wise biblical admonitions such as: *Do not remove the ancient landmark*; *let its foundations be retained*; *the foundations were laid by the Lord, the boundaries are your inheritance*; *if the foundations are destroyed, what can the righteous do?*; and *these stones shall be for a memorial ... forever.* These venerable instructions continue to well serve our generation and our posterity when adhered to diligently. Within themselves, they are an interesting dualistic blend of concrete, mean-exactly-what-they-say declarations and less-specific analogies having broad, universal, and eternal meaning. In simple translation, they counsel us to be respectful of those things established in past ages that have been carefully preserved and thoughtfully handed down to us for our present appreciation and future application. Christianity is based on a longstanding covenant relationship, as is the origin and the purpose of America (and Israel). Blessings follow adherence, and curses follow abandonment of established covenants – especially those sealed by blood.

Sticky-Points

The fifth story criterion I call *sticky-points*. As noted earlier, I had the opportunity to orally present the stories in this book hundreds of times before thinking to give them formal representation. During the telling, I not only observed that the stories were particularly well received, but in later follow-ups – sometimes a year or two later – I also found certain elements seemed to stick in the listener's head or heart. During recitation, I am careful to distribute sticky-points in a nonintrusive, complementary manner throughout the story as it naturally unfolds. They are also offered in a more deliberate, concise manner during each story wrap-up. The sticky-points are readily useable as a teaching aid. I understand their inclusion violates some core concepts of proper nonfiction short-story writing. I accept the criticism and readily admit guilt; however, I've consciously included them to more strongly pursue my goals relating to heroic character recognition and application. I want my stories to entertain the reader, but I'm prepared, as well, to risk being a bit too didactic in the process, perhaps even covertly motivational/

self-help-ish in orientation. Education is the destination; entertainment is its path. I'm less interested in soaring prose than in helping shine a brighter light on truth, which is always on the highest plane. Perhaps, in retrospect, I could have relaxed some on this goal, because the truth does not need a lot of help. Truth has an inherent way of lasting and sustaining as nothing else can. It is ultimately truth that sticks in the listeners' and readers' heads and hearts, not my narrative.

All truth comes from God and is part of His being. In our lives most truth is not new to us. We've either applied it in whole or in part upon hearing, or we've consciously avoided it. If the latter, any further exposure – such as reading it – can be an uncomfortable experience. I hope so. Personal change is universally difficult; it's universally a fundamental part of life as well. (See the stories "Parable of the Flat Earth" and "Parable of the Four Farmers.") We are responsible for what we hear. When it's embraced, truth does make us free. So, when confronted with the truth, we first apply it and then we share it. When we share it, we become a teacher. We pay it forward, knowing it helped us and that it will likewise help others. One of my underlying objectives in committing two years to writing *Uncommon Character* was to leave a legacy for future generations – my family, friends, students, church, and beyond. I'm not just passively okay with readers electing to share these stories; I'm actively encouraging it. The stories have been a successful resource for me, and I know they will continue to be so for others.

The concept of sticky-points is a personal one, the experience and the value having been recognized in my own life. Years after an initial hearing, I can easily recall certain words of counsel offered to me throughout my life journey by influential men and women. The point usually seemed, at best, to be merely intriguing at the moment of delivery. Thinking it had no immediate value, it was set aside – often unconsciously – only to be resurrected years later from some deep, unused compartment in my memory. The sticky-point would then function as a wise admonition or timely guide pointing me in a favorable direction or helping to confirm a key decision. Sticky-points are not just for today's hearing occasion. They are, perhaps more critically, for recall many tomorrows from now when they are helpful in providing the insight necessary for resolving a life juncture or crisis. Subsequently, I deliberately determined to include sticky-points within the stories.

Several stories depart from the usual focus on a protagonist with heroic character and, rather, focus only on a practical life principle; that is, on a sticky-point. Such are the parables of the "Flat Earth," the "Four Farmers," and the "Overnight Success." Many of the sticky-points reflect personal failures and mistakes that I've made, and they are offered so the reader may benefit from my hard-earned lessons in wise living. It's often quoted that experience is the best teacher. Maybe so, but it's not the only teacher. We can learn from others' successes and failures as well. Therefore, in addition to what's been included from my life, many more sticky-points are presented from the lives of heroes (some unsung) who come to us as successful businessmen, brave soldiers, Christian martyrs, Founding Fathers, and ordinary lawyers, farmers, and physicians. A good book or instructor provides useful or interesting information, but a great book or instructor forever changes the lives of readers and students for the better.

Writer Donald Miller expresses similar thoughts about story sticky-points while applying a different phrase to the concept:

> Stories do more than entertain, though. If you want people to understand and identify with a complicated concept, tell a story about it. Telling a story often creates a "clicking experience" in a person's brain, allowing them to suddenly understand what someone else is trying to say. As such, those who can tell good stories will create faster, stronger connections with others…. A story is the most powerful tool you can use to connect with another human being. Whether we're recapping our day or telling our kids bedtime stories, our deepest selves reach out and connect through the recounting of events…. Story, in some ways, is still as mysterious to me as music. I can't pretend to understand it fully, but I feel its effect and I'm grateful.

A fundamental reason for the natural stickiness of the key points is that they nearly always reflect eternal biblical principles and/or passages, and the protagonists always illustrate Christ-like attributes. There's no way to say all of the protagonists are Christians per se, and there is no abiding reason to do so. Only one story is overtly Christian: "Who Do You Say That I Am?" No defense need be made for the fact that the Scriptures have endured since before the dawn of recorded history, or to further note or prove they have served humanity well.

When using biblical principles or scriptural quotations within the stories, I've frequently adopted a soft approach, simply offering paraphrases or applied circumstances, rather than direct quotes with chapter and verse references. This is not done out of disrespect or because of space constraints. I find it expedient not to provide them for seven reasons: one, so that I am able to share my stories in publicly funded environments; two, to help ensure the stories have the broadest appeal, not limiting them to specific groups; three, because it is a natural outcome of the story venues (they take place in everyday secular situations); four, the flow of a story is disrupted by providing references (I don't do so during oral presentation); five, it's generally unnecessary, as the scriptural concepts are often already well known; six, how a verse reads varies widely depending on preferred translation; and seven, the chapter and verse combinations are reference tools, not anointed Word. Only one story was taken directly from the Bible and features a Bible character. Scriptural principles are sometimes included in the story dialogue, and they are nearly always included in the sticky-points of a story's conclusion. If there is any lingering suspicion that I am ashamed of the gospel of Jesus Christ, it will be disavowed after a reading of the final story.

Heroes

The sixth and final criterion for story creation is seeking and presenting only real heroes or heroines whose lives exemplify the positive and selfless character traits and the inner integrity detailed earlier in the first story selection criterion, character. It is my express intent to ignore personalities within the entertainment-driven professions like sports, acting, and singing. Those are usually the fluff and stuff of inflated egos, enormous salaries, and pandering editors. These people are false and foolish idols, and are routinely found in *People* and *Us Weekly* magazines. They also compose the core of surface-cruising television/cable coverages such as MTV, ESPN, *The Tonight Show*, *E! News*, and *Dancing with the Stars*, as well as the plethora of reality shows and celebrity talk shows. I may not have listed the best current examples of human bling coverage, but since I haven't had a television since 1980, I'm unable to be more exacting.

As I write this section, the prosaic daily *USA Today* (December 24, 2014) named a singer as Person of the Year. The newspaper disclosed, in an article written by Andrea Mandell, that he released "one of the best-selling singles of all time, earned an Oscar nomination, and spawned joyful tribute videos around the world." Impressed? I hope not. Their featherweight Entertainer of the Year and TV Person of the Year awards went to other individuals, thus confirming that the Person of the Year award was intended to be their most solemn and meaningful appointment – you know, something equivalent to facilitating world peace or finding the cure for cancer. Readers may recall that actual awards relating to world peace were greatly curtailed when Barack H. Obama was handed the Nobel Peace Prize for no apparent reason in 2009, thus seriously diminishing the value of anything bearing the name *Nobel* as well. The adjective *silly* is all too often the most appropriate adjective to describe those whom the world honors.

I'm not opposed to promoting the lives and deeds of businesspeople. While that statement may surprise some readers, given my stand above, it is fully defensible. I know many businesspeople who have made substantial positive contributions to greater society in terms of the world's standard of living, employment, products and services, charitable assistance, community support, philanthropic giving, promotion of education, personal volunteerism, and much more. My own career encompasses much of this, and was a rewarding and creative outlet for me, one that I thoroughly enjoyed. I worked twenty-five years for the owner of a large corporation whose life was both exemplary and inspirational. My time in business yielded contributions in the form of products that met previously unfulfilled needs, created employment opportunities, and improved the economy and standard of living for the general population. Several of my story protagonists are businesspeople; I simply chose not to focus their stories on the business aspect of their lives, since there are already multitudes of good books available on business. There's no shame in advocating capitalism with its adherence to market forces and profit motives; that is, the promotion of free enterprise. Proof of its positive nature is overwhelming, historically sound, easily observed, and – many believe – substantiated by the Bible.

A significant majority of both my student and adult audiences appear to have only a vague concept of what qualifies as a true hero, one whose life is worthy of study or emulation. Instead, they invest their personal and financial resources into admiring – often even attempting to emulate

– pseudosuperstars who are often fallen in addition to false. Therefore, to follow with more of the same would be promoting misplaced values. I'm averse to contributing further to shallow lifestyles and rudderless thinking. We all desperately need to be prepared for discerning between positive role models and the overwhelming storm of cheaply manufactured idols thrust upon us by an unrelenting immoral and worldly media.

Man looks on the outside, but God looks inside at the heart. The men and women selected by God to become His heroes are often the small, the weak, the underequipped, or the less prepared. That's why so very many real heroes are the martyrs of the faith: men and women who refuse to deny Jesus, who smuggle in Bibles, who facilitate underground congregations, who stay and endure persecution (torture, imprisonment, denial, discrimination, and death) in order to evangelize and sustain their neighbors. God may grant the task to us, but He likes to be part of the action so that we don't forget to give the credit due Him when we're celebrating and enjoying the outcome. In one exceptionally unique and enduring story, God looked approvingly at a young, small, inexperienced shepherd boy with a sling, while without exception, armies of men extended their approval or deference to a giant, armor-clad warrior of renown and reputation.

Above, I've noted categories in the real world of people who are too often mistakenly regarded as worthy of receiving our attention. I've noticed another misplaced focus, one that frequently occurs related to fiction writing, and, in particular, is observed in the reading habits of K-12 students. Reading has of late received increased emphasis in the schools, as driven by presidential commissions, national regulations, and test standards. This is admirable in itself, but I've seen a dark side. As I regularly inspect the books being stocked, checked out, read, and reported on, they are nearly all fiction, which is not a problem per se. In my own family, while I prefer nonfiction, my wife is a voracious reader of historical fiction. The problem is that the fictional themes chosen by and/or available to the students are largely about vampires, magic, witchcraft, sorcery, rebellion, and zombies. This is not an exaggeration; it's more closely an understatement. I have no abiding compunction against the comic-book superheroes currently so popular in the media, for at least they mostly exhibit altruistic virtues. In general, students would benefit by adhering to an admonition from author Edwin Paxton Hood: "Be as careful of the books you read, as of the company you keep; for your habits and character will be as much influenced by the former as the latter."

Even the few nonfiction books that are found in school book fairs, classrooms, student backpacks, and libraries frequently have subjects which fall into the previously referenced false-idol category. They are embarrassingly shallow and void of substantive content because they generally celebrate contemporary entertainment and sports figures. They contain as many or more illustrations and photos as text pages, and often they are presented in comic-book fashion, euphemistically now renamed *graphic* or *illustrated novels*. These, at best, should be deemed personal elective (non-classroom and non-credited) reading rather than endorsed and provided by the formal educational system. The material sold at school-sponsored book fairs is unabashed pandering to the students at the basest level; I cannot recall having found a classic fiction book offered in the past decade. In order to raise funds, the schools permit the selling of carnival-style junk only loosely affiliated with education. The book fairs could be an opportunity to encourage good reading choice, to examine laudable heroes, and to instruct in high morality, but they are not. Please note that my specific public school reading and book selection-related experiences are largely gleaned from three well-run, financially viable education corporations located in a traditional-minded, small city within a Midwestern conservative state; how much potentially more misguided and needy are those schools in big/inner cities located within liberal coastal states. What may be concluded is that small components – like my local school systems – are influenced, if not dominated, by trends manufactured in the larger whole of the federal regulatory and teachers' union levels.

Finding any book in the possession of a student that does not deal with these sinister or hollow themes and people is so rare, that whenever I do, I never fail to offer a compliment and give an award as encouragement. Sadly, I find very few opportunities to give out either. In the addendum on character, several esteemed professionals are referenced for their conclusions that educational reading programs would be far better served by the promotion of stories and classics with themes about truth, character, and heroes. Again, as noted, this is one of my motivations for *Uncommon Character*. In his book *Story: Style, Structure, Substance, and the Principles of Screenwriting*, Robert McKee states it this way: "A culture cannot evolve without honest, powerful storytelling. When a society repeatedly experiences glossy, hollowed-out, pseudo-stories, it degenerates.... Stories are the creative conversion of life itself into a more powerful, clearer, more meaningful experience. They are the currency of human contact." That closing sentence deserves restatement to give it additional emphasis: Good stories are the ways and means of positive human social and societal contact.

The concept of what constitutes a hero, as well as the parallel concept of having personal heroes, is regarded by many as out of fashion today (comic-book superheroes notwithstanding). Its origins are indeed ancient. Attempts by modern society to replace *hero* with hollow-sounding nouns like *star* and *superstar, celebrity, diva, legend, champion, demigod, icon, master, ace,* or *idol* are often phony and frequently devoid of meaningful substance. There are, of course, some misunderstandings and misuses associated with the noun *hero*. For some unknown and presumably good reasons, the word is mostly still used sparingly and respectfully; it seems to have been saved from the extreme overuse and under-meaning common to the pretender labels. The term *hero* is often still, rightfully, applied to military personnel (as well as to those working in law enforcement and fire prevention) who risk their lives for us in remote and lonely locations around the globe. Thankfully, the unique aura associated with *hero* remains difficult to apply to an actor, politician, singer, or athlete, no matter how well they may execute their performances.

Having mentioned athletes, I have a further observation to make about America's near and often actual worship of them. All immoral and imprudent behavior is accepted, overlooked, or forgiven simply because they can handle a ball of some shape in a remarkable fashion. Think about the truth of that fact; then consider its incongruity. Should they really be admired, much less given a free pass to do nearly anything? One well-known football player was acquitted of jealously murdering his ex-wife and was, in a separate incident, convicted of armed robbery. A well-known basketball star was infected with AIDS as a result of decades of promiscuous sex – and his popularity increased as a result. There are many more such examples of popular athletes who are placed on pedestals where they are never held responsible for the bad public example they shamelessly model, especially to our youth. They don't come close to meeting the definition of hero; these people are not heroes.

Success does not equal heroism. Affectionate and popular nicknames like *Juice* or *Magic* do not create a hero. Record-breaking paychecks do not create a hero. Being photogenic or constantly in front of the cameras does not make someone a hero. The true heroes are almost never celebrated, or even known and identified. The true heroes faithfully operate outside of the spotlight in realms of denial and persecution for the benefit of others, often dying as a result of their contributions. The true heroes are not necessarily hard to find, but we must look in non-mainstream media sources such as the *Voice of the Martyrs*' monthly publication, or visit them behind the scenes as they volunteer to minister in prisons, recovery centers, pregnancy care centers, refugee camps, city missions, summer camps, retirement homes, and hospice centers. As a motivational side note, nearly every protagonist herein was confirmed to have contributed a substantial amount of lifetime volunteer service. We will never view these heroes on *American Idol* or in the pages of *People* magazine.

This is not to say that some athletes are not good or even outspoken Christians. But by comparison, the greater heroic figure is the one willingly undergoing consistent persecution in Iran, Colombia, or North Korea as he evangelizes, delivers Bibles, and holds illegal prayer meetings for miniscule earthly remuneration, as opposed to the athlete who praises God for his ten-million-dollar annual employment contract and recent playoff victory. It's worth remembering that sports are games and/or personal careers, not life-and-death ministry for the advancement of God's eternal kingdom, or even for the betterment of temporal society. We should all live our lives in a manner glorifying to God, no matter our occupation; this is called lifestyle evangelism. The Rotary Club Hall of Fame quotes a 1939 letter from Sir Nicholas Winton (a wartime rescuer of 669 children known as the *British Schindler*) as follows: "There is a difference between passive goodness and active goodness, which is, in my opinion, the giving of one's time and energy in the alleviation of pain and suffering. It entails going out, finding and helping those in suffering and danger, and not merely in leading an exemplary life, in a purely passive way of doing no wrong." A ball game that was won or lost today cannot compare with someone who was saved, set free, healed, or released from bondage.

That we do not see and hear much about the real heroes is a great loss, because their lives are truly inspirational and worthy of emulation. In paraphrasing Richard Wurmbrand, not everyone may be called to become a martyr, but everyone is called to be a co-martyr: we should all feel a bond with them, weep with them, help bear their burdens, and support and comfort them. This is where personal and media attention should rightly be focused. There is a misconception about martyrdom that's dominating media attention and world politics today that grossly distorts its actual nature. True martyrdom can come in two manners: either externally inflicted death or a life of coerced deep suffering – both the result of hatred directed at a person for his beliefs by a despotic person or society. Islam promotes so-called suicide martyrdom, which is both false and an oxymoron. It is false because it is an act of pre-meditated murder, which causes the martyrdom of others, and it is an oxymoron because suicide is deliberate and self-inflicted, thus it cannot be martyrdom.

In *The Hinges of History*, I appreciate Thomas Cahill's following description:

> History is also the narratives of grace, the recountings of those blessed and explicable moments when someone did something for someone else, saved a life, bestowed a gift, gave something beyond what was required by circumstance…. But the great gift-givers, arriving in the moment of crisis, provided for transition, for transformation, and even for transfiguration, leaving us a world more varied and complex, more awesome and delightful, more beautiful and strong than the one they had found.

Cahill didn't specify *heroes*, but what he offered is a fitting and poetic description of them. Beyond that, it's also a strong statement about the influence heroes have on the world and why we need them.

I use the masculine form *hero*, but without any intent of indicating that women are not capable of attaining the status. Several of the protagonists in *Uncommon Character* are of the feminine gender. I've simply found the masculine form more commonly accepted and utilized, and the feminine form *heroine* sounds distractingly identical to the drug *heroin* when spoken.

Over one hundred years ago, the value and nature of heroes came to the attention of Andrew Carnegie following a mining disaster in one of his facilities north of Pittsburgh. Thus motivated, he initiated the Carnegie Hero Fund Commission in 1904 to recognize and reward heroes in America. Since its inception, almost ten thousand heroes have received attention, totaling a payout of thirty-five million dollars in attendant grants, tuition, and awards. A few of these heroes were involved in significant, well-publicized disasters, like the San Francisco earthquake of 1906 or the World Trade Center bombing on September 11, 2001. The vast majority have, by design, been small, local heroes. In commenting on the 100th anniversary of the fund, the *Wall Street Journal* picked up the theme and reiterated why it also believes that America needs heroes now more than ever, especially local, ordinary ones.

Heroes serve an important function in our lives. Whom we pick displays, and determines, what we value and who (the type of person) we'd like to become. Here again, choice has a vital role. We should choose wisely, for as Magda Arnold first stated, and Austrian neurologist and psychiatrist Dr. Viktor E. Frankl (a bona fide hero) re-emphasized, "All choices are caused, but they are caused by the chooser." In his classic study *Man's Search for Meaning*, Dr. Frankl has much wisdom of his own to share with us about personal choice, mostly learned as a Holocaust survivor of the ghettos and death camps.

> The one thing you can't take away from me is the way I choose to respond to what you do to me. The last of one's freedoms is to choose one's attitude in any given circumstance…. Forces beyond your control can take away everything you possess except one thing, your freedom to choose how you will respond to the situation…. Between stimulus and response, there is a space. In that space is our power to choose our response. In our response lies our growth and our freedom…. When we are no longer able to change a situation – we are challenged to change ourselves. I do not forget any good deed done to me and I do not carry a grudge for a bad one…. It is not freedom from conditions, but it is freedom to take a stand toward the conditions…. Life is never made unbearable by circumstances, but only by lack of meaning and purpose…. Life ultimately means taking the responsibility to find the right answer to its problems and to fulfill the tasks which it constantly sets for each individual.

Like Dr. Frankl, many of the heroes in *Uncommon Character* are real victims in the sense that they were oppressed, threatened, denied, persecuted, and tortured. Real heroes often die during their unselfish acts – frequently killed by men of low character to whom they were in opposition. Not every protagonist hero has an antagonist villain. Sometimes they are simply pitted against circumstances or nature; many are faced with more than a single challenge. A majority of the heroes in this book experienced opposition from surprising sources, in addition to the expected opposition of their enemies. These include family members, friends, neighbors, and country-men who either disliked the person and his actions or misunderstood the circumstances and motivations. Oftentimes, a hero's chosen course of action sets great responsibility upon their family and associates. When opposing maleficent authority, a hero's family may come under the same risk of pun-ishment or death. Even when a hero is able to act with family impunity, the loss of his presence – due to incarceration, incapacity, or death – places a major burden on the surviving members, making them victims due to the irreplaceable loss of a parent, a sibling, or a spouse. (This was the case for the Arland D. Williams Jr. family as outlined in his story "Lost in the Water").

Heroes are not victims in the sense that they've resorted to blaming and shaming others for their circumstances while refusing to extend any personal effort to facilitate their own redemption. The all-too-common current mentality of "Society owes me; I deserve to be served" runs con-trary to a hero's selfless motivation and inherent character. Because they have maintained a servant's heart while often rising above difficult circum-stances, their contributions are doubly worth remembering, retelling, and assimilating. President Kennedy's inaugural "Ask not" statement famously articulated this mindset.

Most of the heroes I've chosen are, by design, relatively obscure, thereby providing a deep source of untapped resources related to their rich lives. When a chosen hero is familiar, such as George Washington or Ronald Reagan, I've selected a little-known incident to develop. Presently in my personal library, I have six anthologies purporting to tell the lives of heroic people worthy of our attention. I disagree with the inclusion of some of the selections, but beyond that, all of the heroes have one thing in common other than their supposed contributions to mankind: They, and their activities, are already well known by the educated public in Western countries. In contrast, I've endeavored to avoid well-known people of character or heroic deed, instead pursuing those who are much more like the majority of us – plain men and women to whom we can readily relate. I developed this preference when participating in national men's organizations. I recognized that they promote only a few famous people, as opposed to promoting testimonies of the many quietly effective ordinary men like those offered for decades on Pacific Garden Mission's *Unshackled* radio program. *Uncommon Character* was written, with a few exceptions, with its hero stories written from the bottom-up rather than from the usual top-down approach.

The Bible says we are surrounded by a great cloud of witnesses. It is referencing the pervasive and potential influence of saints and martyrs, but I believe that same imagery can be accurately applied to heroes. To illuminate this, in perusing the current events reported in my focused (that is, non-traditional news reporting) email subscriptions yesterday, I read of the following heroes: A forty-year-old man in South Haven, Michigan, was told of two teenage girls caught in a rip current and five-foot swells. He swam out an incredible nine hundred feet from the Lake Michigan shore to successfully pull both unconscious victims from twenty-foot depths. A nine-year-old girl in Jacksonville Beach who had just been bitten in her thigh by a shark (requiring ninety stitches to close) walked herself to shore, then realized her six-year-old companion was still in the water, so she returned, bleeding, and led the panicked friend to safety. Three off-duty unarmed American servicemen waiting on a train platform in France brought down a terrorist who was wielding and employing multiple weapons. And a commercial fishing boat licensed to a small Eastern European country rescued a large group of Christian refugees fleeing from pursuing murderous Muslim radicals. Heroism is not dead, just frivolously misapplied or shamefully under-represented by a commercial media that feeds its readers a steady diet of negativity – some self-manufactured to serve their own purposes in a constant search to create victims and perpetrators (for example, inflating race issues). In a Memorial Day ceremonial speech, President Reagan stated, "Those who say we live in a time when there are no heroes, they just don't know where to look."

A few of the heroes presented in *Uncommon Character* I know personally; a few others are presented because their work and/or lives inspired me. Most of these, and a few others within the stories, are still alive; thus, their full stories are not yet written. On occasion, I've chosen a publicly unknown figure only to have that person become exposed and well known. Such is the case with Irena Sendler and Rose Valland. This is simply an observation and not a problem, because I delight in these previously obscure heroes finally receiving the overdue attention they deserve. Such will hopefully be the case with many more of my protagonists, perhaps in part due to exposure in *Uncommon Character*. The memorial to Chiune Sugihara (a Holocaust rescuer) in his hometown of Yaotsu, Japan, is centered in a pond with ever-larger, permanent, concentric rings emanating outward. This is intended to symbolize the widening ripple effect of a single life or act of kindness. Its imagery is perfect for all the heroes in *Uncommon Character* because the good that they set in motion has never stopped flowing forward.

I believe *Uncommon Character* is unlike any other book in respect to its focus on unfamiliar heroes and little-known situations. I don't intend that statement to be immodest. Many of the other books focusing on heroes only offer a couple of pages on each protagonist (in addition to them being already well-known personalities). For my own enjoyment, I searched for several decades for a nonfiction book with a similar theme and treatment to mine, and I didn't find it. If one or more do exist, it's unlikely they are based on a conservative Christian point of view and unlikely that they offer much background insight. Thereby, I'm convinced there's a need and opportunity for *Uncommon Character*.

Samuel Oliner was saved from a Holocaust-related death by a rescuer. Reflecting on his experience years later, he wrote, "Acts of heroic altruism are not the exclusive province of larger-than-life figures such as Mahatma Gandhi and Albert Schweitzer. Rather, they are manifestations of ordinary people whose moral courage is born out of the routine ways in which they live their lives – their characteristic ways of feeling, their perceptions of authority, the rules and examples of conduct they have learned from family, friends, religion, political leaders, their schools, workplaces, and all their associates." To Oliner's list, I'd add two additional influencing factors in the development of our moral courage: the heroes we pick and the choices we make en route. He describes the majority of heroes as ordinary people, those like Arland D. Williams, Gregory Jessner, and Kimberly Munley (their stories are included) and most of the other protagonists in *Uncommon Character*. When heroes are asked by the public at large, as well as by those who benefited directly from their actions, why they did what they did, their almost-universal response is, "I did nothing special, only what any decent person would have done in the situation. I should have done more." These are the almost-verbatim words stated by several of my protagonists and later confirmed in my research.

I've long been especially impressed by three men (two of whose stories are included in this book) whose heroic and selfless lives are worthy of emulation, and who are, not coincidentally, also known for their ability to tell a purposeful story of lasting value. These men are, in the chronological order of their time on earth, Jesus Christ, Abraham Lincoln, and Ronald Reagan. They're men whose legacies of character have long tenures, remain worthy of our study, and have resisted fading with the passing of time (more likely, have grown in stature). Each represents both a storyteller and a story. Their lives are the stories most deeply inspiring to me. I'm humbled to be participating in the same tradition as these great and worthy predecessors – my heroes.

Conclusion

These six criteria form the framework for every story shared herein. Within their outlines, I've detailed the book's goals and illustrated the nature of the protagonists, having already mentioned several as advance examples of what is to come. Familiarity with this six-point model will increase understanding and appreciation of the stories I offer.

Within any skillfully crafted, well-presented story, a substantial amount of teaching can be infused – and offered in a manner more certain to be solidly embraced and remembered. A good story is an open door to opportunities. Sometimes the story does not just encapsulate or deliver the message; at times, the story is the message, by which I mean it is deliberately left open to multiple personal interpretations and practical take-aways.

How does information become easy to remember? Move it out of the realm of pure facts such as names, events, and dates. Those are the kinds of things we encounter – and don't like – in a final exam. Transform the information into a song, a poem, a story.

Appendix Two

An Anatomy of the American Character

The Old Testament prophet Micah outlined the requirements for attaining and practicing godly (Christ-like) character as follows: *He has shown you, O man, what is good; And what does the* LORD *require of you But to do justly, To love mercy, And to walk humbly with your God?* (Micah 6:8).

Everyone has character. If you have what Thomas Wolfe referred to in another realm as the *right stuff,* then – in simple terms – you have good character. If you have the wrong stuff, then you have bad character. Generally, when we say that someone has character, we imply the good. The word usually carries positive attribution. The words *integrity-filled* or *virtuous* are interchangeable with *character* because they have approximately the same connotations. What follows is an open advocacy on the nature of, and the need for, good character – personally, politically, and corporately; it's purposefully infused with an essentially American orientation.

When conducting the first module in my Character Building course, I ask the students to formulate in writing their personal understanding of what defines character. Among the better responses, I have recorded the following:

- Displaying a consistent Christ-like nature

- Acting unselfishly during a crisis

- Not compromising commonly held ethics

- Accepting being unpopular, even disliked, for living your beliefs and values

- Being respected by your like-minded peers, and sometimes even by your enemies

- Demonstrating personal responsibility in all matters

- Living life in accord with biblical principles

- Having a servant's heart in your relationships

- Matching your words and actions

- Never viewing yourself as a victim, and never engaging in finger-pointing behavior

- Putting the good stuff inside while rejecting the bad

- Doing what you know to be right

- Making the best choice in all situations

- Being less concerned with your rights and more with your responsibilities

- Working to improve your personal faults while admitting your mistakes

- Paying your debts, and readily asking for forgiveness

- Striving to stay in right relationship with God and man

- Selecting wisely between moral options

- Serving others before yourself

- Holding convictions higher than practical circumstances

- Following the Golden Rule as originally founded in Matthew 7:12

I endorse these insights and acknowledge that, individually and collectively, they refine our practical understanding of the nature of good character. My personal favorite, which I share with the class to continue to seed their thinking, is that character is exercising personal responsibility when no one is watching, when it costs or hurts us to do so, when we may have to act entirely alone, and when it benefits others – even our enemies – more than self.

David Brooks, in chapter 10, "The Big Me," of his book *The Road To Character*, proposes: "The meaning of the word 'character' changes. It is used less to describe traits like selflessness, generosity, self-sacrifice, and other qualities that sometimes make worldly success less likely [the giving traits]. It is instead used to describe traits like self-control, grit, resilience, and tenacity, qualities that make worldly success more likely [the taking traits]." I believe what he is indicating is that when we center everything on ourselves, we distort the better traits associated with truly good character. It becomes all about us, not about others.

Prior to Brooks' observations, John Steinbeck noted a different – somewhat more severe – dichotomy that often surrounds the nature of character in our society. In his mini-novel *Cannery Row*, his protagonist, Doc (based on his real-life friend Ed Ricketts), states, "It has always seemed strange to me, ... The things we admire in men, kindness and generosity, openness, honesty, understanding and feeling, are the concomitants of failure in our system. And those traits we detest, sharpness, greed, acquisitiveness, meanness, egotism and self-interest are the traits of success. And while men admire the quality of the first they love the produce of the second." Applying this on a personal level illustrates the battle in everyone's heart as we make the many character-defining decisions and choices that cumulatively create the essence and legacy of our lives.

In the realm of socioeconomic studies, I've found little research (including both theory and field experiments) that can be attributed directly to the study of character. There is, however, a workable amount dealing with altruism. Altruism has substantial overlap with character, so it's worth brief development here. It is defined as "the principle or practice of unselfish concern for or devotion to the welfare of others." Certainly this is yet another pertinent explanation of good character. If you exhibit altruism, you are displaying positive character, as in the classic example within the Good Samaritan parable. Altruism is consistently witnessed in the activities of the protagonists in *Uncommon Character*.

Within this appendix, the intended focus is a study of character that's specific to the people of the United States of America. I believe that the character qualities introduced above are generally to universally shared across the globe; however, the stage set hereafter is post-modern America. Even after limiting the scope to my own country, I acknowledge that the coverage is not intended to be comprehensive. I have modestly targeted education, politics, history, religion, and several bellwether social trends while barely mentioning many other significant elements such as civility, the military, ethnicity, business, the arts, marriage and the family, popular culture, and the legal system.

In the 1980s, a number of notable American economists believed they had substantiated that citizens of the United States were considerably more altruistic than most other nations. One proof-result supposed that we give more money or time when circumstances required it. More recently, their conclusions were disproved, as better experiments demonstrated otherwise, and after serious errors were uncovered in their research methods. The bottom line, coming at no surprise to most of us, was that people are people. People will respond to incentives, and people can thus be both motivated and/or manipulated in either direction by pushing the right buttons. There are some who are wonderfully generous, caring, and heroic, as well as others who are brutal, self-serving, and evil. Within the group of appropriate traits, many can be interpreted as being altruistic in nature, even though their underlying motivations may not be. True altruism, that is, exercising quality of character, is displayed in the absence of any direct personal gain and/or when we act even though we risk personally losing, rather than gaining, that which is precious to us. The latter motivation served well as my qualifier for the protagonists selected for inclusion in *Uncommon Character*.

In his groundbreaking 1992 book *A Nation of Victims: The Decay of the American Character*, Charles J. Sykes offered observations and recommendations on the subject of the declining character in our society that were well ahead of most of his contemporaries. Sykes pointedly describes in clear terms the developing famine of character in America, as well as draws our attention to the accelerating downward spiral of character that we have since witnessed. To summarize this trend for decline, I offer several of Sykes's key concepts, primarily selected from chapter 18 of his book. Verbatim statements are in quotation marks; the others are close paraphrases. All express exceptional and timeless wisdom (they preceded, and perhaps anticipated, the extreme breakdown America has since suffered with its safe-places, micro-aggressions, trigger warnings, extreme societal diversifications, rude demonstrations, promotion of self-absorption, and violent demands for special rights and privileges or exemptions from responsibility and obligation).

- "We must start with the concept of character. At the bottom of every plan for change, every design for improvement, every educational or political reform lays the question of the personal conduct of individuals."

- Private virtue must come before public policy. We must all recognize that public problems arise out of defects in character formation; that is, the lack of private morality. We must begin any positive action with the politics of personal responsibility. We must be citizens in community, not clients and victims. We must stop replacing private sin with the concept of collective guilt. We must be givers and doers, not takers and fakers.

- "There must be a moratorium on blaming our problems on others and on expecting others to take care of our needs. We must rise above thinking that we are nothing more than the victim of our circumstances. All of us experience unfairness and injustice in our lives, but that does not mean we need to turn them into all-purpose alibis. Don't confuse being different with inequity and oppression."

- "What are the prospects for a society that has emphasized rights over responsibilities, refused to hold individuals accountable for their own behavior, and made manufacturing grievances into a national industry?"

- "Instinctively and rationally, we know our responsibilities; we know that we are not sick when we are merely weak; we know that others are not to blame when we have messed up; and we know that the world does not exist to make us happy."

- "Students are steeped in an environment of self-esteem regardless of their actual behavior or of the quality and quantity of their performance. They are taught to see themselves as the center of the universe which, unfortunately, they already believe all too well. The currently popular 'politically correct' thinking prevents real dialogue and distorts our moral orientation. If we really desire to see a return to a positive and productive society, changes are required by the schools in regard to how our children are taught."

- An emphasis on character will help deposit the damaging concept of ethical relativity into the dustbin of history where it belongs and help reestablish the absolutes of right and wrong which served us so well for centuries.

Readers are encouraged to review more of Mr. Sykes' insightful writings on their own, because delineating them further here is somewhat beyond this book's primary focus.

Chiune Sugihara was a Japanese diplomat to Lithuania during WWII, and he is credited with saving the lives of three thousand Jewish people. The philosophy he was taught, and by which he lived, is perhaps the most succinct instruction set for a principled life that I've uncovered since Mark 12:31. I found it in *A Special Fate: Chiune Sugihara – Hero of the Holocaust* by Alison Leslie Gold: "(a) Do not be a burden to others, (b) Take care of others, and (c) Do not expect rewards for your goodness." Chiune was also known to place his faith in a Japanese proverb: Shimbo shiite seiko suru, which translated means: "Success [in acquiring good character and in assisting others] comes through overcoming adversity."

Mr. Sykes' and Mr. Sugihara's positive character philosophies and recommendations are complementary to those expressly promoted in *Uncommon Character*, but further evidence of a contrary epidemic is conspicuous throughout the overly misapplied *Diagnostic and Statistical Manual of Mental Disorders, Third Edition - Revised* (known as the DSM-III-R). It is presently 886 pages long, and it lists 297 mental disorders. The first DSM documentation effort was in 1917, and it listed only twenty-two disorders. Since then, the overall result has been that any bad behavior can be defined as a disease, with the perpetrator thought of as a helpless or blameless victim devoid of any personal moral responsibility. These bad behaviors have been given impressive-sounding names and have been added to the DSM – with a growing number being added annually (often, unsurprisingly, bearing the "discoverer's" name). What is initially recognized as a singular behavior anomaly is all too soon, and all too often, declared a disease that quickly grows into a popular mania, with many suddenly being afflicted by it, and with anyone holding an opposing outlook disparaged as unfeeling, unknowing, intentionally hurtful, or prejudiced. There's been a concurrent staggering growth in the number of supplicants for handicapped vehicle license plates, and the over-indulgent use of related set-aside parking spaces – the qualification for handicapped is not limited in nature to physical maladies. The use of the word *handicapped* is so compromised, easy to attain, and over applied that it has nearly restored the need to return to the use of supposedly politically incorrect, but more specific, descriptors like *retarded* and *crippled*.

Every lax and easy attribution of victimhood status cheapens the genuineness of those who are truly society's deserving and suffering members, such as terror victims, Holocaust survivors, quadriplegics, refugees seeking asylum, disabled veterans, abused and raped women, the deaf/dumb/blind, sexually assaulted children, crack babies, and those afflicted with Down syndrome and other serious congenital or acute diseases and physical malformations. There's no shortage of truly afflicted people who desperately need and are deserving of our attention. Inviting pretenders into their numbers is not doing them any favors, and it diminishes the available resources, awareness, funding/donations, and compassion. Many assumed and presumed victims are simply victims of their own bad choices or are plainly defrauding society, such as the lifetime and multi-generational welfare abusers. Other pretenders claim victimhood by playing the race card, gender card, religion card, sexual orientation preference card, and so forth, on into an eternity of minority/diversity statuses, quotas, and causes, each with their own claims of incumbent special privileges and supposedly violated or denied civil and legal rights. Identity politics, with its superfluous creation of hyphenated minorities and special-interest groups, has done nothing for our sorely needed national integration and harmony, and it has, in reality, brought about overall cultural annihilation through the promotion and pursuit of multiculturalism and diversity objectives.

The massive increase in the welfare lifestyle/victimhood mindset may also be gauged by a third of the adult population who consistently binge in government-provided economic benefits while paying little to nothing into the source funds via income and real estate taxes, or offering alternative contributions through volunteer work. This increase in government-sponsored indulgence continues to occur even though the standard of living has dramatically improved at all levels of society. There's no way to fully address the nature of character in America while bypassing a discussion of government entitlement programs and their recipients. Former Senator Jim DeMint, subsequently a Heritage Foundation president, observed that in our nation's past, there were only two ways to proceed in life: the legitimate way (work hard, play by the rules, and live within your means), which led to earned success; and the illegitimate (criminal) way, which – hopefully – led to prison. Now he adds that there's a third way: living off the largesse of big government. It is not right, but it is legal, and it has become acceptable beyond reasonability and morality. Most welfare programs no longer place much responsibility on their recipients and thus exacerbate the receivers' moral and civic laxities.

Lifestyle choices are, unfortunately, not factored into the welfare qualification and management equations. Treating all applicants as though they are blameless victims caught in circumstances beyond their control is deliberately turning a blind eye to or inattentively failing to apply minimum qualifications and monitoring. It is common practice for agencies to aggressively solicit new recipients in order to deplete, increase, and renew their annual budgets and to insure personal job security – at times even fraudulently adding friends and family to the rolls (sometimes for kickback).

The authentic American Dream is not one of intentionally growing into, and remaining, a government dependent. Governor Scott Walker points out that our opportunities for improvement and advancement may be equal, but the outcome is still up to us. Character and success are built on the dignity of work. I saw a poster that made a lasting impression upon me: "Will work for work." That phrase connotes plenty of wisdom, not the least of which is an advocacy for performing volunteer work as a prelude to obtaining an associated paying job. (See the related story on Rose Valland.)

Those living off the government aren't all citizens in the lower tiers of the population. The municipal, state, and national so-called leaders who occupy the highest tiers are also entrenched and enriching themselves at public expense. These are the numerous chummy politicians who won't honor volitional limited terms. They stay for life, enjoying immunity from most laws; accepting questionable large donations with strings attached; peddling their names, speeches, and influence for cash and favors while reaping the legitimate and the questionable special perks associated with their offices. Without good examples at the top, the challenge to live right is made all the more difficult and unattractive for everyone beneath. Proverbs 29:2 confirms this: *When the righteous are in authority, the people rejoice; but when a wicked man rules, the people groan.* The negative trickle-down influence of our poor leadership is obvious in survey results wherein more than two-thirds of Americans respond as follows: We have no living heroes to emulate, elected politicians cannot be trusted to do right, and our children have no meaningful public role models.

Based on a combination of these factors, and their quantified statistics, potentially more than one out of every three people we randomly meet consider themselves a victim. They're prepared to blame anyone or anything other than themselves whenever they perceive they've been treated unfairly or they occasion some slight denial or resistance. Their auto-response and fallback position is akin to *I'm a victim; somebody better make things right for me so that I get the share of the pie I deserve.* This *taker* mentality weakens civil society as a whole, while simultaneously placing ever-heavier fiscal and moral burdens on only a few individuals whose rights and wills are progressively diminished. It's so prevalent today, and it's growing so exponentially, that this mentality must be recognized as a significant factor in the decline of American character. Again, Proverbs 30:12 recognized the problem: *There is a generation that is pure in its own eyes, yet is not washed from its filthiness.*

This sad, something-for-nothing outlook is unbiblical, but it is, unfortunately, promoted at the highest level of our government, as personified by Barak Obama's attitude. In his second inaugural address, for example, Obama irrationally claimed that acts of broad indulgence in entitlements "do not sap our initiative; they strengthen us." He followed up shortly thereafter on the flipside with his infamous "You didn't build it" statement. By this, he attempted to disprove that individuals create wealth and to discredit those who do. His position is that the government facilitates the success of entrepreneurs, who then falsely claim the credit. Nothing could be further from the truth. Government produces no wealth; it only takes wealth from its constructive citizens. Everyone has equal access to whatever outcomes result from government facilitation, such as roads, services, military protection, college loans, state-sponsored research, and public education; therefore, everyone has equal opportunity to convert those resources into something productive. Obama's words were calculatedly borrowed from his atheistic and anarchistic mentors: Saul Alinsky, Bill Ayers, Frank Marshall Davis, Frances Fox Piven, and Richard Cloward.

The growing government dependency malaise has also been labeled a *grievance-entitlement mindset* (*grievance* substituted for *victim*, and *entitlement* substituted for *welfare*); this mindset and the lack of good character are often found joined in the same soul. *Entitlements* are formally defined as "budget transfers of government receipts as benefits to individuals from whom no current service has been received, but who hold a right based on a law." That sums it up surprisingly accurately. Congress and the White House have not likely considered the implications of that definition since President Reagan left office. According to him, "We should measure welfare's success by how many people leave welfare, not by how many are added." As of this writing, government welfare expenditures are just under ten thousand dollars per American (our population was 320 million in 2014); many individuals receive far in excess of that amount while the remaining receive less. It's incongruous but true, that the more you contribute the less you receive. It's dressed up as *income or wealth redistribution*, a euphemistic term for government-mandated theft. The concept was massively tried, and unambiguously failed, throughout the last century under various forms of communism. In the 1960s, liberal political activists and Columbia University professors Frances Fox Piven and Richard Cloward called for deliberately overloading America's welfare system in order to precipitate a financial crisis that would usher in full socialism with the general population greatly dependent thereafter on the government. That strategy was accepted and promoted by many liberals, and it remained in play with readily observable and accelerated results throughout the Obama Administration.

In 1973, Senator Daniel Patrick Moynihan, a Democrat from New York, outlined similar circumstances from an accurate, clear-eyed perspective when he said the "issue of welfare is the issue of dependency." He went on to say that poverty is not dependency; that people who are poor can, and generally do, have character; while people who are dependent are like children who never grew up, never learned to stand on their own feet, and continuously live in an abnormal condition. He said the mark of a *completed* man or woman is that they are standing on their own feet. Poverty is a condition; dependency is a choice. Moynihan's position emphasized assisting people rather than just using them for political and party gain – a rare political avowal. At the time he made his related statements, entitlements were far less than a third of the federal budget, as opposed to today when more than two-thirds of the budget is distributed to nearly half the population. One can only wonder at his response if he were alive to witness our nation's present dismal position. As a measure of his own strong character, Moynihan declined a fourth term in the Senate despite his popularity, a move more aligned with patriarch President Washington before him, and thus helping retain the Founders' intent for citizen-politicians.

Handouts, set-asides, restitution payments, and reverse discrimination practices have done nothing substantive to lift minorities, those living in poverty, or immigrants, save making them more dependent. Star Parker recaps this situation as continuing to be enslaved on *Uncle Sam's Plantation*. The end result is more needs, more generations, more expectations, and more demands (all are the intended goals of the political party promoting the underpinning dependency policies). Heather MacDonald, the author of *The Burden of Bad Ideas*, wisely advocates the overwhelming need to once again "praise virtue and blame vice." In his book *The Tragedy of American Compassion*, Marvin Olasky states that welfare programs have never been proven successful without the application of deterrence, and that there are no shortcuts – such as the Great Society – to fighting poverty; that is, enduring, consistent obligations and expectations must be placed on the recipients and the providers must become and stay closely engaged throughout the process.

From many factions of society, I keep hearing something like, "I'm going to vote my pocketbook – whatever's in it for me." Really?! That is selling your vote, and it is a sin, especially for Christians. That's evidence of a lack of character. Biblically, it's the equivalent of selling your birthright for a bowl of stew. *Therefore, to him who knows to do good and does not do it, to him it is sin* (James 4:17). Voting godly long-term principles is the honest way. There is no righteous argument for separating politics from spiritual and eternal matters; they're interconnected. A man's politics reflect his faith, or said another way, faith determines political position, not the reverse.

In his classic *The History of the Decline and Fall of the Roman Empire*, Edward Gibbon wrote of citizens who had become insensitive to their civic duties, and who were more concerned with their self than with their society. He stated, "When the Athenians finally wanted not to give to society but for society to give to them, when the freedom they wished for most was the freedom from responsibility then Athens ceased to be free and was never free again." An American contemporary of Gibbon's, Benjamin Franklin, said, "When people find that they can vote themselves money, that will herald the end of the republic."

In 1887, Alexander Tytler of the University of Edinburgh wrote:

> A democracy is always temporary in nature; it simply cannot exist as a permanent form of government. A democracy will continue to exist up until the time that voters discover that they can vote themselves generous gifts from the public treasury. From that moment on, the majority always votes for the candidates who promise the most benefits from the public treasury, with the result that every democracy will finally collapse over loose fiscal policy, which is always followed by a dictatorship.

He observed that the average age of all great civilizations is roughly two hundred years, during which they progress through the following sequence, now called the *Tytler Cycle*:

> From bondage to spiritual faith, from spiritual faith to great courage, from courage to liberty, from liberty to abundance, from abundance to complacency, from complacency to apathy, from apathy to dependence, and from dependence back into bondage.

In the twentieth century, as a precaution against these astute historical observations, President Kennedy wisely advised, "Ask not what your country can do for you, ask what you can do for your country."

Jesus said that the poor will always be with us, by which He meant that being poor is part of the human condition, just like being wealthy is part. Being dependent is not a condition; it is a choice. They are not the same thing. Greed often arrives disguised as need. A noble alternative example of choosing not to be dependent was provided by Dave Roever (see his related story). He called the Social Security office to request that no more monthly government checks be sent to him even though he easily qualified for 100 percent lifetime disability. Over half of Dave's body was severely damaged while serving our county, but he didn't want to be a victim and a ward of the state; instead, he chose to live by faith. For a season thereafter, he was poor, but he worked his way out of that state, and millions of others have since been better off because of his efforts. Being poor doesn't have to be one's permanent condition. The idea of a minimum wage is not to sustain you for life; it's to sustain you during a starting, entry-level pay-scale position until you gain some minimal work skills and prove yourself deserving of a promotion or a wage increase, followed by another, and then another. Employers seek and reward capable employees because they are difficult to find and they want to retain them. We step out of the crowd and away from poverty by demonstrating that we are the sought-after good workers deserving of increased responsibility and compensation. (See the Rose Valland story.)

Misdirected bureaucratic provisioning and unearned individual gratification have together served to collectively mask God as our Savior and provider. Worldly government largesse is substituted for His proper place and our proper role. Wanting what is not ours is envy; taking what is not ours is theft. Personal charitable giving – the conscientious giving and receiving of gifts by and to individuals – is the appropriate alternative. In the realm of government-sponsored charity, want is often confused with need. At its rare best, welfare is a short-term patch; its continuous application is a poor substitute for the necessary moral changes, lifestyle adjustments, and personal growth that collectively nearly guarantee lasting, positive results. This approach requires planning and application that are long-term in scope, not just patching previous quick fixes.

"Today's socialists and progressives support not only more governmental redistribution but every aspect of the sexual revolution from no-fault divorce to pornography, abortion, the ever-widening LGBTQ agenda, and the legal assault on marriage. All of it leaves women and children at the mercy of the state. When families fail, the state grows to pick up the pieces" (quoted from "The Realty of a Pipe Dream," an article by Robert Knight). Ultraliberalism always has rationalistic and relativistic God-is-dead-and-we-didn't-need-Him-anyway elements associated with it. As a tried-and-true test, look for this perception; it's always found underneath the facade of any pretentiously compassionate social proposal, policy, or program; and just beneath the skin of any aggressive proponent of a liberalistic lifestyle, education, or philosophy. We should not accept as the real thing what is only a veneer; the truth is always available, but like the pearl of great price, it must be industriously sought and then held securely.

Generosity is a virtue, but being generous with other people's money is not a virtue; it's simply false and pharisaically overblown. Liberals like to use compassion as another weapon in their continued bullying of conservative Christians by trumpeting how freely they validate every indiscriminate entitlement cause while demonizing our discernment and long-term fixes with their non-stop libeling, name-calling, and disparaging labeling like *stingy*, *selfish*, *greedy*, *racist*, and *uncaring*. Author Lynne Truss writes that engaging in such uncivil "abuse is the weapon of the weak." The truth is – regarding true humanitarian causes, not their political coverings – conservatives have a strong record of out-giving liberals from their personal resources, and evangelical Christians give exponentially more from them than do both liberals and non-Christian conservatives. What liberals don't mention is that their generosity only extends to foundation spending (for example, the Ford, Annie E. Casey, John and Catherine MacArthur, and Robert Wood Johnson foundations) and confiscatory tax revenue spending; that is, other people's money and not their own money (with the exception of the small-tax portion which a minority of liberals are forced by law to pay). They speak of *fair share*, but in reality about a third of adults contribute almost nothing because they pay little to no taxes; thus, *fair* is applied only to getting, not to giving. For *fair share* to be truly fair, taxes should be levied on all citizens based proportionately on income from all sources, including the freebies. Everyone should have skin in the game, as it helps assure their active participation and interest in – as well as appreciation of – the outcomes related to our common good. Indiscriminate and institutionalized giving is far more harmful than helpful. Replacing God with government does not change His role in our lives, despite the growing faulty acceptance that God and government are interchangeable providences. When something becomes too popular, that's a certain indication that a sanity check is overdue, and that swinging the pendulum back toward the center is necessary. To be a success, the society must be essentially Christian in its practices.

Conservatives rightfully ponder whether there's any upward limit to the growth of the welfare state or government intrusion, regulation, and expansion; that is, whether there is any point where the liberal mindset would be satisfied and willing to rest from further agitation against traditional values and fundamental processes; that is, to disassociate from an ill-advised mindset that Marvin Olasky has variously labeled *promiscuous material distribution*, the *subsidizing of disaffiliation*, *universalizing depersonalizers*, *a culture of delegated compassion*, and *false comfort*. Each of his descriptors peels away and exposes additional layers of liberal falsehood, obfuscation, and deceit as associated with their politically correct labeled programs. I don't believe there is a point where leftists will say, "Entitlements and/or government are too big" or, "They are not working."

I hold the following five reasons as support for my position. First, welfare spending is a simple-sounding solution. It sits right at the top of the stack of quickie fixes and is easy to grab and run with, especially since that would be safely traveling incognito and in the same direction as the rest of the pack. Conservative solutions require thorough thinking, research, and implementation planning with post-execution monitoring and accountability; doing so causes one to stand out, perhaps alone. Because these contrary solutions are opposed and ridiculed by the pack – with recriminations often exceeding personal slander – advocates must be exceptionally brave and are therefore few in number. Second, it's a practical and proven Machiavellian method to secure the support of the masses for purposes of gaining and retaining political power. Fabian George Bernard Shaw says, "A government that robs Peter to pay Paul can always depend on the support of Paul." Third, liberals believe problems like poverty or education are solved just by throwing money at them; they don't know that solutions require depth and time (see the first reason above). Liberal thinking is: see the problem, throw money at it; still see the problem, throw more money at it. If the problem remains, it must be because conservatives are preventing them from throwing enough money at it. Factually, the money often becomes a major part of the problem. Fourth, they haven't dealt with the three underlying issues. One is personal sin, such as resentment, rebellion, and envy; sin on the part of those allocating the supporting funds and on those receiving them. The second is their genuine guilt (rooted in personal sin and overriding rebellion toward God); they falsely assume that this guilt can be avoided or alleviated by mindless funding of issues related to the poor. Until these two factors are recognized and addressed, they remain surreptitiously negative influences. Effective remedying of sin and guilt requires responses that promote the healing of their relationships with God and man. The last of the three underlying issues is their erroneous belief in the essential goodness of mankind. A brief review of just the twentieth century should be convincing proof to the contrary. Fifth, giving tax money to the poor is an outlet for liberals to feel self-righteous. Leftists live outside of a truly righteous relationship with God and they are not motivated by biblical principles. Therefore, tax-based giving is desirable as an inoculation against having to deal with the underlying truths they prefer to ignore. After all, big government is their god, so let their god give; that's what gods are for.

Olasky writes, "Cultures build systems of charity in the image of the god they worship," and "It seems that our ideas about poverty always reflect our ideas about the nature of man, which in turn are tied to ideas about the nature of God." He goes on to say that in early America, when a theistic God of mercy and justice was the center of our policymaking, our compassion could have been described as "hard-headed but warm-hearted." Tax-and-spend big government believers hold that the Christian God has the same nature as the conservative citizen: supposedly stingy or unconcerned. Recipients and proponents of everything-for-nothing politics, regulations, beliefs, and lifestyles often wrap themselves in a deceptive cloak they call *social justice*. It would be more difficult to sell their true objectives if they nakedly called them what they are: communism or one of its many insidious configurations or euphemisms such as socialism, Fabianism, ultra-liberalism, economic democracy, Marxism (including neo-Marxism and cultural Marxism), Frankfort School philosophy, corporate fascism, financial redistribution, and progressivism. All these social change theories and *-isms* have the same underlying motivations: envy and resentment, as well as rebellion against traditional biblical standards. Claiming to promote an ambiguous and ethereal fairness, the leaders are purveyors of class and race division. Their violent reactions to fabricated hate crimes are the true, overt acts of hatred, thus removing their benign outer sheep coverings to display the ravenous wolves within. Their varying belief systems are slightly different paths to the same destination: a life filled with an abiding attitude of ingratitude. Many advocates infiltrated the church, education, and legal professions during and after the 1960s, some disguising themselves as Christians and preferring to appropriate and misuse spiritual and pastoral titles such as *Reverend* to gain credibility – applying them far more extensively for political purpose and personal gain than for spiritual practice.

Those "religious leaders" endorsed by the liberal media should go unheeded by true adherents to Christianity – if not outrightly opposed. Genuine spiritual leadership is sourced in a personal, covenantal relationship with our Creator, and its societal expression is pastoral in nature; it's not a radical political position, a program to solely benefit a factional group, a personal fund-raising platform, or a fleece-the-rich economic practice. The pseudospiritual leaders are proponents of self-centered, contrived faith, to which they bestow coded labels like the *social gospel* and *libertarian theology*, and which they primarily apply to tangential community issues like race or class relations and welfare programs. These are perverted forms of Christianity fashioned into their own worldly image for personal gains in income, popularity, and power. They grossly distort Jesus' purpose by claiming, in essence, that He was a Robin Hood-like historical figure who advocated that His disciples take from, and subdue, the rich while giving to those in need, thus making Him an income redistributor just like them. It ameliorates the commandment referencing not to covet a neighbor's goods. Jeane Kirkpatrick states, "I conclude that it is a fundamental mistake to think that salvation, justice, or virtue come through merely human institutions." The social gospel is a precursor to communism, and communism is always intimately linked to atheism; it is a world system that not only ignores God, but also actively hates God and opposes the body of Christ on earth. Psalm 83:2-3 warns, *For behold, Your enemies make a tumult; and those who hate You have lifted up their head. They have taken crafty counsel against Your people, and consulted together against Your sheltered ones.*

The practice of true Christianity is the best expression of, and most effective means of, relevant charity. It requires caring for the needy, both spiritually and physically, by letting God work His purposes through us as we agree with Him and yield to Him – including our purses and wallets. To accomplish these ends, Jesus promoted charitable giving out of our own blessings, time, and production; not forcibly taking from our neighbor and then giving or keeping what is not ours. That isn't godly no matter what label it's been accorded, and it certainly isn't noble or wise. Such methods are neither self-sustaining nor effective, and they are more akin to theft than to charity. These are *cleptoparasitic* in nature; that is, parasitism by theft, as when one animal takes food away from another animal whose efforts derived it through catching, collecting, or preparing (definition paraphrased from Wikipedia). Robert Knight of the American Civil Rights Union says, "There's something about deploying the government as a mugger to obtain the fruits of someone else's labor that appeals to the worst in us. But it invariable leads to poverty, dishonesty and even tyranny." John Timmer's Dutch parents hid Jews in their house during the Holocaust. He wondered what motivated his parents to take such risks with six of their biological children in the home. John concluded that God shows compassion (aka charity, care, or welfare) to us, so we are expected to show the same to others. In taking such actions, he says, "rescuers make themselves the equal of the rescued because both are equally dependent on the compassion of God."

Olasky asserts that making contributions because they're tax deductible is not nearly as involved, direct, or effective as offering a room in your house to a homeless person or to a pregnant, abandoned woman. Gilt-edged liberals remotely operate their charitable practices hands-off from a safe distance, assuring that they suffer no personal cost or inconvenience while smugly basking in the reflection cast by their very public humanitarian gestures. Someone must, however, pay the real costs caused by their fallacious generosity, and it's usually the working/ giving/caring middle class and the Christian outreach ministries. A hands-off approach is in contrast to: *Let brotherly love continue. Do not forget to entertain strangers, for by so doing some have unwittingly entertained angels. Remember the prisoners* **as if chained with them**—*those who are mistreated—since you yourselves are in the body also* (Hebrews 13:1-3, emphasis added).

Peggy Noonan writes in "How Global Elites Forsake Their Countrymen" that those in power positions who enact these programs and policies see others not as countrymen but as aliens who must be anticipated and managed so that those non-elite others remain responsible for getting their hands dirty with the post-implementation repercussions and costs. She says, "Affluence detaches, power adds distance to experience.... this division between the leaders and the led." Her most prominent example in the article relates to Muslim immigration. She quotes from State Department data indicating that all but 9 of 121 Syrian refugees resettled in Virginia during a ten month period were placed in communities with low incomes and high poverty rates that are located far from the homes of any lawmakers. (For clarification, the elitists to whom Peggy and I refer are those at the pinnacle of influence in their fields who directly form public policy and opinion from places and positions like Washington, D.C., Hollywood, the mainstream news media, Wall Street, the courts, and the universities – clearly not those in the middle classes who suffer the burdens or those in the lower classes who obtain the benefits.)

Capitalism – like Christianity – is also a better approach than any of those with socialistic overtones, but capitalism is not Christianity; it is, however, built upon the biblical principles of labor, production, investment, research, initiative, and creativity. These are God's ways, as He demonstrated throughout Genesis, where we see the dignity and value of work. Capitalism does best in a nation adhering to Christian principles. It's why America is the greatest land of opportunity and affluence in all of history, why peoples the world over are still coming here and have been for century after century, and why they rarely go back with their earnings after succeeding here. Capitalism also does best when the means of production are fully in private hands. When government controls and/or owns the means, it is not true capitalism. It's been labeled *corporate fascism* because inefficient, greedy, regulation-prone, controlling, prejudiced, and unseasoned bureaucrats operate the economy from myopic fair-share and personal-share agendas. Ayn Rand exposes this concept effectively in her classic novel *Atlas Shrugged*.

In my home state of Wisconsin during 2013-2014, unionized teachers and other unionized state employees selfishly indulged themselves for months in and around the capital building in Madison. They practiced uncouth, lawless, obscene, and destructive *mobocracy* during their excessively prolonged – albeit unsuccessful – attempt to take down the legitimately elected government and discredit its majority-passed legislation. Their bullying was thought justified because they felt entitled to a continuation of ever-increasing benefits without any associated productivity measurements, personal contributions, or merit-based performance standards. They entered into acts of violent resistance and attitudes of mindless insistence, despite the fact that the state government had been drowning in red ink because of their history of receiving special privileges. Many of the paid thugs were shipped in from all around the country and were not even direct stakeholders; they represented the larger global agenda of the moldy, old dictatorship of the proletariat. The private sector had already peacefully accepted and successfully adapted to fiscal responsibility, belt tightening, productivity demands, performance-based incentives, and spending cuts two decades earlier. Greater detail about the related, shameful circumstances are in Governor Scott Walker's book *Unintimidated: A Governor's Story and a Nation's Challenge*, as referenced in the recommended readings listed below. Twenty years earlier, former New York City Mayor Rudy Giuliani suffered an unjustified fate similar to Governor Walker's as he also undertook effective measures to reduce out-of-control entitlement spending and bloated debt in the nation's largest city.

Employment is a negotiated, contractual bond – some would even say covenantal – between the employer and the employee, with each party having its own set of responsibilities under the agreement and within their relationship. If a problem ensues, Jesus clearly counseled us in the proper means and attitude for addressing a true grievance when He said to go directly and personally to the other party, potentially taking along one or two others as witnesses. He never advised collective, impersonal, third-party representation such as a union, and He certainly never advocated lawless mob action. Jesus' first and best preference is for us to always let Him be our advocate. Unions are inherently subject to corruption, as history has dramatically shown to be true. Their leadership regularly pillages and pockets funds, promotes violence, forces both workers and employers against their will, and finances unsavory causes and candidates. The time of unions promoting any good is demonstrably in the distant past.

Because I'm concerned with the increasing malaise of a grievance mentality wed to an entitlements lifestyle, much of my propriety curriculum and personal instructional focus has been on providing an antidote. While details are beyond the scope of this addendum, my endeavoring can be outlined with several four-letter words. No, not that kind; we don't need any more angry, violent, hateful, rap-like dialog. Presented here in application sequence are my best practices for individuals to acquire character-driven personality and its incumbent success: pray, work, read (study), give, save, love, live (be active and enjoy life), and rest (Sabbath). Without my saying another word in their defense, these eight words quietly speak volumes for themselves. They remain universally effective, just as they've been for millennia. Truth does not change with the times, situation, or crowd. These practices are the building blocks for a return to individual character building. Booker T. Washington offered similar wisdom a hundred years ago when he admonished: "Nor should we permit our grievances to overshadow our opportunities." Ten simple but powerful words of counsel – that when adopted by a sufficient number of citizens – have the potential to reset our nation on its former constructive course.

For America to recover her corporate character, I suggest a reemphasis on the four fundamental Cs that successfully underpinned the country since its inception: Christianity, Capitalism, Constitutionalism, and Conservatism. An express combination of these four elements combined in an earlier century to form America's greatness of character. As the preeminence of these elements declines in the post-modernity setting, so does America's character, as measured by our faltering exceptionalism. It would be wise for us to cease being defensive about these four elements, and instead offer assertive, well-articulated supporting narratives, and even better still to go on the offensive. In his wonderfully provocative essay "The Sin of Nice," Allan Erickson says, "We have failed to confront evil aggressively and so evil confronts us relentlessly.... Leftists and their jihadist allies look upon 'nice' as weaknesses, and exploit it."

Too often evil is labeled as good, and good as evil. Compared to our past, are we as influential now? As excellent? As unique? If the tree doesn't bear good fruit, prune it; if it still doesn't, remove it by its roots. America is due for some pruning if there is any hope of saving its roots. We have strayed too far into public policies and agendas that are openly anti-Christian, anti-free-enterprise, full of cronyism, judicially active, politically correct, regulation-prone (an executive branch dictatorial method that reached over eighty-one thousand pages at the close of 2015), and pro-socialist/progressive. If my recommendations sound too naïve or simplistic, I respond that life really is an interplay of good versus evil, light versus dark, truth versus error. It is that simple. Black and white are readily discernible. Gray happens when we start confusing them and mixing them together in some complicated, handmade, compromised solution that reflects a myopic, all-is-relative, rationalistic, and humanistic viewpoint; that is, an anti-biblical mindset. The enemies who are out to destroy our values are not confused. They clearly understand that they are purveyors of black (if traditional American values are white), but they perpetrate and utilize the grey as their most effective tool – a fog covering – to accomplish their insidious goals. This technique dates back to its earliest application in the garden where the Tree of the Knowledge of Good and Evil stood planted. America's antagonists are those *who exchanged the truth of God for the lie, and worshiped and served the creature rather than the Creator* (Romans 1:25), *And even as they did not like to retain God in their knowledge, God gave them over to a debased mind, to do those things which are not fitting* (Romans 1:28).

A country cannot have national character if a majority of its citizens – and nearly all of its leadership – lack personal, individual character while retaining a compromised spiritual outlook that cannot discern, or is afraid to label, evil for what it is. We are once again Lincoln's house divided against itself with some willing, and some unwilling, to call evil and good (black and white) for what they are by their very nature.

America and democracy (we really don't have or want democracy as a form of government; we have and want a constitutional republic with some democratic processes) are not elements of Christianity; Christianity is always able to stand on its own. It has frequently stood on its own elsewhere around the globe and in other historical times, but America and our form of government have benefited – like none before us – from embracing it. America was never fully a Christian nation, but it was undeniably and verifiably a nation founded on the Bible and Christian principles. It was fathered by men who soundly endorsed both, and the related tenets were practiced or respected by an overwhelming majority of the population. Just as undeniably, God had (still has?) special purposes for America. The unique form of government forged in America in the eighteenth century was successful here only because of our biblical foundations and practices. That's why it hasn't been successful when we quixotically attempted to transplant it into Islamic-fascist cultures such as Iraq, Afghanistan, and the rest of the Middle East, except Israel. That's also why it would subsequently fail in America if our biblical foundations and practices are destroyed.

In addressing our educational system (a subject thoroughly covered by Mr. Sykes), secular author and former Clark University Associate Professor of Philosophy Dr. Christina Hoff Sommers has written in her astute and oft-quoted essay "Teaching the Virtues": "There is an overemphasis on social policy questions, with little or no attention being paid to private morality. I noted that students taking college ethics are debating abortion, euthanasia, capital punishment, DNA research, and the ethics of transplant surgery while they learn almost nothing about private decency, honesty, personal responsibility, or honor. Topics such as hypocrisy, self-deception, cruelty, or selfishness rarely come up."

To Dr. Sommers' list of specific topics that are studied, over-emphasized, or surreptitiously endorsed, I would add that there's overt and pervasive general subject bias toward gender, race, sexual orientation, political party, culture, and economic class preferences; and conversely a bias against others. These favoritisms are the deadly sins of liberalism that permeate and distort every aspect and level of education – especially in the teacher colleges and educational degree programs. To Dr. Sommers' list of rarely-to-never promoted topics, many more could be added, including virtue, morality, guilt, standards of behavior, principles, values, sin, manners, abstinence, traditional family and marriage, merit, self-control, school choice and vouchers, community, society, character building, integrity, cheating, altruism, the Bible, ministry, ethics, patriotism, missions, conservatism, volunteerism, attitude, home education, gender differences, civic duty, the Constitution, charity, vocation, the military, workfare, and – from positive perspectives – capitalism and Israel. Most certainly Christianity and Judeo-Christian history, beliefs, and their related contributions are ignored. This is evidenced, in part, by the wholly secular attributions leveled against the accomplishments, intentions, and personalities of America's Founding Fathers, as well the accusations of mean-spirited behavior laid on the Pilgrims and Puritans by the postmodern, progressive revisionist cartels. The subjects on Dr. Sommers' and my lists have been pushed to the sidelines by harsh, close-minded, self-righteous political correctness; anyone promoting or endorsing them from a Christian/biblical perspective will be immediately discredited and subjected to personal attack and professional criticism.

It should not be any wonder that a small island of sanity has prospered via tuition-based private, parochial, and Christian schools. These have been established – along with non-tuition alternatives like home education and charter schools – in the presence of free education and have succeeded well despite them, with many politicians and public school professionals preferring to place their own children in these as superior alternatives to the ubiquitous government-union schools that have become fully premised on situational ethics and relativistic verisimilitudes. (The latter should qualify as an oxymoron, but it describes the real circumstances where truth has been twisted into contradictory whatever-you-want-it-to-be pretzel-like amalgamations.) Regardless of the added burdens on the parents associated with these alternatives, as well as their having to pay twice (taxes and tuition) for their children's private education, many have responsibly found it well worth the extra effort and expense to avoid the public school system entirely.

In her landmark 1993 contribution titled "Teaching the Virtues" (a follow-up to her 1991 "Ethics without Virtue"), Dr. Sommers offered three wonderfully simple, perceptive, and prescient recommendations for repairing the tragic and permissive educational circumstances outlined above.

> "Schools should have behavior codes that emphasize civility, kindness, self-discipline, and honesty."

> "Teachers should not be accused of brainwashing children when they insist on basic decency, honesty, and fairness."

> And my personal favorite: "Children should be told stories that reinforce goodness. In high school and college, students should be reading, studying, and discussing the moral classics."

Summarizing, Dr. Sommers states, "I am suggesting that teachers must help children become acquainted with their moral heritage in literature, in religion, and in philosophy. I am suggesting that virtue can be taught, and that effective moral education appeals to the emotions as well as to the mind. The best moral teaching inspires students by making them keenly aware that their own character is at stake."

I heartily endorse all of her recommendations, and I propose a complementary fourth one: Teachers, administrators, school boards, and parents should be role models demonstrating positive lifestyles. I've adhered most intently to her third recommendation of which I am particularly fond: "[telling] stories that reinforce goodness." These four recommendations are the antidote to values-free education with its saturation of relativism and revisionism. However, they are anathema to elite progressive educators who for nearly a century have specifically targeted traditional stories – filled with their supposedly backward morals and values – for elimination in favor of replacement by a preponderance of politically correct nonsense taught in a classroom rife with "modern" methods like student-centered environments, collaborative (team) learning, whole-language reading, and metacognition (knowing without knowing). Isaiah 28:10, 13 is the antithesis of progressive education: *For precept must be upon precept, precept upon precept, Line upon line, line upon line, Here a little, there a little.*

In *The Road to Character,* David Brooks advises, "You can't build rich … lives simply by reading sermons or following abstract rules. Example is the best teacher. Moral improvement occurs most reliably when the heart is warmed, when we come into contact with people we admire and love and we consciously and unconsciously bend our lives to mimic theirs … And when we think of them, it is not primarily what they accomplished that we remember – great though that may have been – it is who they were. I'm hoping their examples will fire this fearful longing we all have to be better, to follow their course."

I am far from attaining the goal of acquiring good character, but I know its value and am pursuing it, in part through self-examinations in the quiet of the night, in part by reading about the lives of good role models and then absorbing the related sticky-points, and in part by striving to pass the related concomitant trials, temptations, and tests. Through regular sharing of their stories, the people in this book have become my heroes; and though my life does not begin to compare to theirs, the planned route is to make good choices, follow their lead, and finish well.

Appendix Three

Recommended Reading and Bibliography

The following list represents many of the tutorial resources that profited me while researching the nature of positive character and the men and women whose lives exemplify it. Thus equipped, it's anticipated that readers are better prepared to continue their grand exploration of heroic, uncommon character.

A Century of Heroes ~ Douglas R. Chambers

A Man Called Norman: The Unforgettable Story of an Uncommon Friendship ~ Mike Adkins

A Million Miles in a Thousand Years: What I Learned While Editing My Life and *Scary Close: Dropping the Act and Finding True Intimacy* ~ Donald Miller

A Nation of Takers: America's Entitlement Epidemic ~ Nicholas Eberstadt

A Nation of Victims: The Decay of the American Character ~ Charles J. Sykes

A Special Fate, Chiune Sugihara: Hero of the Holocaust ~ Alison Leslie Gold

And the Sea Is Never Full ~ Elie Wiesel

Bill & Dave ~ Michael S. Malone

Caged Heroes: American POW Experiences from the Revolutionary War to the Present ~ Jon Couch

Captivating ~ Stasi and John Eldredge

Character Building ~ Booker T. Washington

Character Sketches Volumes 1–3 ~ Bill Gothard, IBLP (Institute in Basic Life Principles)

Come On, People: On the Path from Victims to Victors ~ Bill Cosby

Conscience & Courage ~ Eva Fogelman

Coping with Criticism ~ Jamie Buckingham

Crisis of Character: Building Corporate Reputation in the Age of Skepticism ~ Peter Firestein

Don't Give Up, Don't Give In: Lessons from an Extraordinary Life ~ Louis Zamperini and David Rensin

Don't Waste Your Life ~ John Piper

Experiencing God ~Henry and Richard Blackaby

Foundations of Character Homeschool Curriculum Kit ~ David Barton and Nita Thomason

Foxe's Book of Martyrs ~ John Foxe

Give and Take: Why Helping Others Drives Our Success ~ Adam Grant

Healing Where You Hurt on the Inside ~ John Eargle

How to Win Friends and Influence People ~ Dale Carnegie

I'm No Hero ~ Charlie Plumb

Incorrect Thoughts: Notes on Our Wayward Culture ~ John Leo

In the Company of Giants ~ Rama Dev Jager and Rafael Ortiz

Legends & Lies: The Real West ~ Bill O'Reilly

Lincoln the Unknown ~ Dale Carnegie

Lincoln's Own Stories ~ Anthony Gross

Love & Respect ~ Dr. Emerson Eggerichs

Man's Search for Meaning ~ Viktor Frankl

Men in Black: How the Supreme Court is Destroying America ~ Mark R. Levin

Mobocracy ~ Dr. Jake Jacobs

More Than Conquerors ~ John D. Woodbridge

Please Stop Helping Us ~ Jason L. Riley

Profiles in Courage ~ John F. Kennedy

Quest for Character ~ Charles Swindoll

Righteous Gentile: The Story of Raoul Wallenberg ~ John Bierman

Ronald Regan: Fate, Freedom and the Making of History ~ John Patrick Diggins

Stories in His Own Hand: The Everyday Wisdom of Ronald Reagan ~ Kiron Skinner

Talk to the Hand: The Utter Bloody Rudeness of the World Today ~ Lynne Truss

Teaching the Virtues ~ Dr. Christina Sommers

The 100 Greatest Heroes ~ H. Paul Jeffers

The Book of Virtues and *The Moral Compass* ~ William J. Bennett

The Burden of Bad Ideas: How Modern Intellectuals Misshape Our Society ~ Heather MacDonald

The End of Racism and *What's So Great About Christianity* ~ Dinesh D'Souza

The Greatest Generation ~ Tom Brokaw

The Light and the Glory ~ Peter Marshall and David Manuel

The Overcomers ~ Richard Wurmbrand

The Practice of Nouthetic Counseling ~ Jay E. Adams

The Righteous: The Unsung Heroes of the Holocaust ~ Martin Gilbert

The Road to Character ~ David Brooks

The Snapping of the American Mind: Healing a Nation Broken by a Lawless Government and Godless Culture ~ David Kupelian

The Tragedy of American Compassion ~ Marvin Olasky

The Truth Project ~ Dr. Del Tackett

The Upside of Inequality: How Good Intentions Undermine the Middle Class ~ Edward Conard

The Words & Works of Jesus Christ ~ J. Dwight Pentecost

Three Felonies a Day: How the Feds Target the Innocent ~ Harvey Silverglate

Tortured for Christ ~ Richard Wurmbrand

Uncle Sam's Plantation: How Big Government Enslaves America's Poor and What We Can Do About It ~ Star Parker

Unintimidated: A Governor's Story and a Nation's Challenge ~ Scott Walker

Unoffendable ~ Brant Hansen

What Should I Do with My Life?: The True Story of People Who Answered the Ultimate Question ~ Po Bronson

When Character Was King: The Story of Ronald Reagan and *What I Saw at the Revolution* ~ Peggy Noonan

Wild at Heart ~ John Eldredge

Readers, regardless of age, are further encouraged to pursue additional biographies, autobiographies, and memoirs on the heroes studied in this book, as well as those of their own choosing; just please select your personal heroes carefully, perhaps utilizing the criteria outlined in *Uncommon Character*. My list is offered only as suggested reading. The best literary resource to begin with, and to continue returning to, remains the Bible. I underscore that for thousands of years, the Bible has been the premier authority for numerous expositions on the attributes of virtuous character. Here are a few universally favorite selections:

- Daniel's three friends under threat of King Nebuchadnezzar's fiery furnace ~ Daniel 3

- Jesus in His role of servant ~ Luke 22:26-27

- Parable of the good Samaritan ~ Luke 10:30-37

- Psalm 1 ~ King David

- Beatitudes from the Sermon on the Mount ~ Matthew 5:3-11

- Profile of a Spirit-filled and Spirit-led man ~ Isaiah 61:1-3

- Paul's recap of responsibilities toward society ~ Romans 12:9-14:1

Indisputably, the Bible also contains numerous examples of individuals who display faulty character. These offer comparison and reveal the deadly yield of a life void of positive character practices. The passages referenced above and detailed below, however, provide a cross-sample of our predecessors whose enduring teachings and inspiring lives help to define and supplement our current understanding of what constitutes uncommonly righteous and heroic character. Inspiration that begets inspiration.

Who through faith subdued kingdoms, worked righteousness, obtained promises, stopped the mouths of lions, quenched the violence of fire, escaped the edge of the sword, out of weakness were made strong, became valiant in battle, turned to flight the armies of the aliens.... Others were tortured, not accepting deliverance, that they might obtain a better resurrection. Still others had trial of mockings and scourgings, yes, and of chains and imprisonment. They were stoned, they were sawn in two, were tempted, were slain with the sword. They wandered about in sheepskins and goatskins, being destitute, afflicted, tormented – of whom the world was not worthy. They wandered in deserts and mountains, in dens and caves of the earth. Therefore we also, since we are surrounded by so great a cloud of witnesses, let us lay aside every weight, and the sin which so easily ensnares us, and let us run with endurance the race that is set before us, looking unto Jesus, the author and finisher of our faith, who for the joy that was set before Him endured the cross, despising the shame, and has sat down at the right hand of the throne of God. (Hebrews 11:33-38 and 12:1-2)

About the Author

Douglas Feavel retired after thirty-seven years in technology marketing and management positions. He obtained a bachelor's degree in political science from the University of Wisconsin-Oshkosh and a master's degree in Christian education from Bethany Divinity College. He and his wife, Barbara, have been married for nearly fifty years. Appleton, Wisconsin is their hometown, but Vincennes, Indiana is their current base. They volunteer at non-profits in teaching, outreach, and ministry roles domestically and abroad when not with their children and grandchildren. Speaking engagements may be arranged through contact@dougfeavel.com and additional information is available at www.dougfeavel.com. Bulk purchase and other discounts are available through the publisher at www.anekopress.com.

Related Titles by

ANEKO
PRESS

Often disguised as something that would help him, evil accompanies Christian on his journey to the Celestial City. As you walk with him, you'll begin to identify today's many religious pitfalls. These are presented by men such as Pliable, who turns back at the Slough of Despond; and Ignorance, who believes he's a true follower of Christ when he's really only trusting in himself. Each character represented in this allegory is intentionally and profoundly accurate in its depiction of what we see all around us, and unfortunately, what we too often see in ourselves. But while Christian is injured and nearly killed, he eventually prevails to the end. So can you.

The best part of this book is the Bible verses added to the text. The original *Pilgrim's Progress* listed the Bible verse references, but the verses themselves are so impactful when tied to the scenes in this allegory, that they are now included within the text of this book. The text is tweaked just enough to make it readable today, for the young and the old. Youngsters in particular will be drawn to the original illustrations included in this wonderful classic.

Pilgrim's Progress, by John Bunyan
Available where books are sold.

Is humility a Christlike attribute that should be pursued? And even if it should be, can genuine humility actually be attained? Often so practical in application that it is overlooked, the answer is found by studying the life and words of Christ (*whosoever will be chief among you, let him be your slave*). This little book is a loud call to all committed Christians to prove that meekness and lowliness of heart is the evidence by which those who follow the meek and lowly Lamb of God are to be known. Never mind that your initial efforts will be misunderstood, taken advantage of, or even resisted. Instead, learn from the One who *came not to be ministered unto, but to serve*. For a Christian to be alive, for the life of Christ to reign in and through us, we must be empty of ourselves, exchanging our life for His life, our pride for true, Christlike humility.

Humility, by Andrew Murray
Available where books are sold.

American bush pilot Russell Stendal, on routine business, landed his plane in a remote Colombian village. Gunfire exploded throughout the town, and within minutes Russell's 142-day ordeal had begun. The Colombian cartel explained that this was a kidnapping for ransom and that he would be held until payment was made.

Held at gunpoint deep in the jungle and with little else to occupy his time, Russell asked for some paper and began to write. He told the story of his life and kept a record of his experience in the guerrilla camp. His "book" became a bridge to the men who held him hostage and now serves as the basis for this incredible true story of how God's love penetrated a physical and ideological jungle.

How did this incredible true story affect Russell? "At first my mind went wild with thoughts of revenge and violence. Then, after a while, I was able to see through their attempt to break me down and brainwash me. I started making a determined effort to throw all their stories and dramas out of my mind and not to let my thoughts dwell on them at all. I would trust God that He would take care of my wife and I would close my mind to my captors' input. I decided to think about positive values instead."

"I told them that they had two choices, either kill me, or let me go for whatever small amount my family could afford. One of the guerrillas turned and asked me if I was afraid to die. I replied that dying is obviously uncomfortable, but yes, I was prepared to die."

Rescue the Captors, by Russell M. Stendal
Available where books are sold.